Law, Power and Justice in England and Wales

Law, Power and Justice in England and Wales

EDITED BY

Ian K. McKenzie

Foreword by John Hoddinott

Law, Power, and Justice in Comparative Perspective
CHRISTINA JACQUELINE JOHNS, Series Adviser

PRAEGER

Westport, Connecticut
London

Library of Congress Cataloging-in-Publication Data

Law, power and justice in England and Wales / edited by Ian K.
McKenzie ; foreword by John Hoddinott.
p. cm.—(Law, power, and justice in comparative
perspective, ISSN 1096–2891)
Includes bibliographical references and index.
ISBN 0–275–95881–7 (alk. paper)
1. Criminal justice, Administration of—Great Britain. 2. Crime—
Great Britain. I. McKenzie, Ian K. II. Series.
HV9960.G7L387 1998
364.941—DC21 97–38546

British Library Cataloguing in Publication Data is available.

Library of Congress Catalog Card Number: 97–38546
ISBN: 0–275–95881–7
ISSN: 1096–2891

First published in 1998

Praeger Publishers, 88 Post Road West, Westport, CT 06881
An imprint of Greenwood Publishing Group, Inc.

Printed in the United States of America

The paper used in this book complies with the
Permanent Paper Standard issued by the National
Information Standards Organization (Z39.48–1984).

10 9 8 7 6 5 4 3 2 1

For Sam, Amie and Lilly, the next generation.

Also, for the hundreds of practitioners and criminal justice students on both sides of the Atlantic Ocean, who, for more years than I care to remember, it has been my pleasure to teach, to advise and to assist, and from whom I have learned so much.

Finally, for Tricia, without whose love and support none of this would have any meaning.

Contents

Figures and Tables

FIGURES

TABLES

Series Foreword

Most of the texts currently available in the field of Comparative Criminology are texts which are descriptive in nature and which do not really compare criminological issues in different countries or cultures. What they compare is the formal structure of the criminal justice or legal system. These texts take crime and the law out of their social, economic and cultural contexts.

Criminologists now make a firm distinction between the formal law as written and what has been termed the "law in action." The formal structure of the legal system is a far cry from how that system really functions. Mexico, for example, has a beautifully written Constitution, filled with all sorts of democratic ideals, but when one really examines Mexican society, the way in which the justice system works, one finds that reality is in stark contrast with the ideals of the Constitution.

To describe the formal structure of the legal system and give some crime statistics from a particular country is simply not adequate to allow the reader to understand the problems which exist in different cultures and countries. For example, it is not easy to explain to students why the formal structure of any particular legal system is relevant. The tenure of judges in Nigeria is not relevant in and of itself. It becomes relevant only in connection with larger issues.

Crime rates are notoriously inaccurate within advanced western countries; they are even more inaccurate in developing countries, like those of Latin America and Africa. The presentation of these statistics, therefore, is virtually meaningless, and the comparison of official crime rates for different countries is misleading at best. In addition, many of the crimes that are crucial to a society, and therefore in need of discussion within criminology—political, environmental, white collar, and the growing incidence of transnational corporate crimes (BCCI)—are not reported in official crime rates and not even considered in these texts.

This series seeks to change this focus within Comparative Criminology. It takes a country or a region and has noted scholars in the field examine the most pertinent issues that characterize that culture in the following topical areas: street crime, complaintless crime, white collar crime, corporate crime, political crime, police, courts, corrections, juvenile crime, and future projections. The book does not attempt to give a comprehensive discussion of corporate crime in England and Wales, for example, but to analyze a particularly interesting case of corporate crime, or development in the corporate crime field. Professors using these books as texts can have students select from among a number of countries and have texts which not only provide interesting discussion material, but which are similar in structure.

For example, a professor might choose to have half the students use the text about Haiti and half about England and Wales. Then, when the discussion focuses on corporate crime, the students have examples of the differences between Haiti and England and Wales to examine. In this way, we hope to turn the discourse in Comparative Criminology away from the formal descriptions of legal systems to the cultural and social factors which determine how the system works and the nature of crime within its social context.

The understanding of crime as a transnational phenomenon is increasingly important. Students of criminology must familiarize themselves with the nature of crime and the functioning of legal systems worldwide, not just within the borders of the United States. We hope to contribute in some way to that education.

Law, Power and Justice in England and Wales is the first book in the series, and we are extremely proud to have had this distinguished collection of scholars contribute chapters to the book. We feel it is a strong start to a series which will include titles on Haiti, Puerto Rico, Nigeria, and other countries. The series will provide volumes which present the problems of crime, law, power and justice within a broader context than is ordinarily presented, and located within an historical and economic context.

These books are designed to be multidisciplinary and will include:

- a chapter on different Issues in Law, Power and Justice in the particular country or region
- a list of recommended films and suggested discussion points
- a list of recommended novels and suggested discussion points
- other recommended material (history, social science, etc.)

Christina Jacqueline Johns, Series Adviser

Foreword

There are no single or simple descriptions of the nature of law, power and justice. Each of those concepts seems to depend one upon the others. Their individuality does not really exist, and we need to understand each of them in the context of the others.

The book considers a variety of contemporary issues, with contributions from a wide range of authors with their own valuable insights.

The topics examined in this book are at the leading edge of contemporary debate, for there continues to be lively discussion around criminal justice issues, the courts and the trial process. The debate is unlikely to diminish. We also need to deepen our knowledge of issues as diverse as terrorism, organised crime and street policing. As Europe develops, comparative studies of its policing arrangements become more engaging than the common UK/USA analysis. Ethnicity and the criminal justice system is a topic that deserves more than casual attention if we are to maintain equity and fairness. The organisation, structure and politics of policing and the criminal justice system have been debated throughout the 1990s, and reflection on them is timely. Criminal justice statistics are perhaps the least understood and most widely abused element of all; most practitioners would benefit from some careful thought about the nature and interpretation of statistical data.

This book has the attraction of dealing with contemporary issues by bringing together the talents of several able writers. It should both advance and enhance our knowledge. Success in achieving those aims is the true test of the book's value. I am confident it will succeed.

John Hoddinott, CBE, QPM, MA
Chief Constable, Hampshire Constabulary

Introduction

Two types of comparative texts are commonly found in the study of criminology, criminal justice and policing. First, there are those texts that seek to lay issues side-by-side in such a manner that the text compares and contrasts any given dimension in the form, "In country A so-and-so is the case, but in country B, such-and-such is the case."

The second form of text is that which describes at length a particular criminal justice system or process in country A, and then after a full exposition of it, introduces a second section that distinguishes country B from country A. These two methodologies of comparison are sometimes called the vertical approach and the horizontal strategy.

This book is neither. This is a text, much in the same form as Hirschel and Wakefield's (1995) examination of the criminal justice system of England, which occasionally adopts either a horizontal or a vertical approach but, in practice, seeks both to rely upon the knowledge of the reader to make the comparisons and draw the contrasts *and* to encourage the reader, whose knowledge is fragmentary, to seek out relevant sources so proper similarities and differences may be identified, evaluated and discussed. Thus, in the main, the text is intended to be *used* as a comparative text but is not *written* as one.

To that extent, this text is uncompromisingly British in its content and style. There are a few points at which, for the sake of clarity, the distinctions between British and American culture, language and political process are spelled out, but they are few. The chapters are both descriptive and critical of the features and philosophies of the *English* criminal justice system. It is the phrase "*English* criminal justice system" that needs the only bit of comprehensive explanation to be given. The United Kingdom (UK) consists of the countries of England, Wales, Scotland and Northern Ireland. Although there are some *similarities* in the legal processes and police practices in all four geographical areas, *they are not identical.* The English law, both common and statute, does apply, without exemption, in both England *and* Wales. However, there may be variations in either Scotland or Northern Ireland or both. The organisation and structure of policing and the courts, of the laws of evidence and the rules of police procedure and propriety are different in what may be seen as three policing/criminal justice environments: Scotland, Northern Ireland, and England and Wales. The problem is that too much of the literature of these areas does not make sufficient distinction, and it is relatively common to find that writers use the expression UK to mean each, any and all those parts of the United Kingdom. Similarly some (rather lax) writers use England to include Scotland—much to the chagrin of the Scots!

This book runs the gamut of aspects of the criminal justice system of England and Wales. In Chapter 1, Andrew Sanders examines the distinction between "models" of the criminal justice process. In so doing he looks at the organisation of the courts and a number of issues of contention in court processes: for example, bail, the right of silence and the role of victims in court proceedings. He concludes that: "In the contest between justice and power the clear winner is power."

Chapter 2, by Les Johnston, examines four separate but related topics: first, the concept of "the street" and "street crime"; second, an assessment, based upon empirical research, of trends in street crime and patterns of victimization and fear; third, police responses to street crime; and finally, a critique of Zero Tolerance policing as a strategy for addressing street crime and fear of crime.

W. A. (Bill) Tupman, in Chapter 3, outlines the nature of terrorist activity (by many groups, both homegrown and international) on the mainland and pursues the notion that, in many cases, terrorism may be viewed through a lens that reveals it to be both organised crime and commercial activity.

The organisation and structure of policing in England and Wales is examined in Chapter 4. This is the most comparative chapter; it seeks to answer the question, "How would police from the USA fare in England and Wales and vice versa?"

Simon Holdaway, in Chapter 5, considers the effect of the ethnicity variable in the criminal justice system in England and Wales. He examines both the way in which ethnicity affects prosecutions and other kinds of involvement in the system *and* the way in which police officers from minority ethnic groups are affected by their reception in the police environment. The chapter makes disturbing reading.

Although it is still seen as an "island haven," the British Isles (another term that is sometimes—and inaccurately—used to describe the UK) has become, to the chagrin of some political groups, a part of Europe. Paul Norman, in Chapter 6, considers the nature and shape of European policing, particularly as it becomes more clear that the "open borders" philosophy of the European Union (EU) means an inevitable increase in international and transnational crime. The development of adequate crime-fighting and crime-investigating bodies is essential. He concludes that, although there are others, the principal concern in developing such international policing bodies is the provision of adequate mechanisms of accountability.

Chapter 7 considers the nature of prisons and alternatives to prison in England and Wales. Mike Nash, a former probation officer, is critical of the stance taken by the last Conservative government, particularly in regard to the claim made, in the face of much research to the contrary, that "prison works." Although there is a possibility of a more flexible approach with the recent change of government, Nash is sceptical that things will move much beyond a concern for the achievement of short-term managerial targets, in particular the management of offenders in the community, with a tendency to ignore the need for programmes that produce long-term change in offender behaviour.

Law, Power and Justice in England and Wales ends with three essentially theoretical chapters. In Chapter 8, Ken Pease examines the nature of criminal justice statistics; in Chapter 9, Nigel Brearley writes about the history and development of radical criminological thought in England and Wales; and in Chapter 10, Stephen P. Savage considers the political processes that shape and (sometimes) develop criminal justice policy. Each of these three chapters allows the reader to examine and consider the preceding chapters with a more critical eye, for it is here that the boiler house of any criminal justice system lies. It is easy to believe that the development of the law, the application of control (i.e., power) and the administration of justice are fairly *ad hoc* events. They are not. In a democratic society it is an essential requirement that the democratic process is nurtured, developed and sometimes constrained, through a proper combination of criminological thought, through the analysis and interpretation of statistics and through the conversion of both facets into acceptable policy. Once policy is established, then the application of criminological thought (research) and the analysis of the statistical outcomes of such research may be used to show whether the policy, put into practice, works (or not); and if necessary it may be modified. So the wheel of a democratic criminal justice system turns.

CHAPTER 1

Criminal Courts in England and Wales

ANDREW SANDERS

MODELS OF CRIMINAL JUSTICE

Western criminal justice systems are conventionally divided into ''inquisitorial'' and ''adversarial'' systems, although we shall see in this chapter that no system is pure. Common law systems—such as those in England and Wales, Australia, Canada and most of the states of the USA—are supposedly adversarial. ''Civil law'' systems—which prevail in most of Europe—are supposedly inquisitorial. Scotland combines features of both systems. The principles underlying the two systems are often differentiated by characterising adversarialism as the search for proof and inquisitorialism as the search for truth. At first sight it seems bizarre that the two do not always go together. After all, how can we know the truth without proof? How can anything other than what is true be proved to be so? The apparent paradox can be explained by examination of the ''due process'' and ''crime control'' models developed by Packer (1968). These models can be applied to the whole criminal justice system, but this chapter will confine itself to the criminal courts.

In Packer's scheme, ''due process'' values prioritize civil liberties to maximize acquittals of the innocent, thereby risking acquittals of some guilty people. ''Crime control'' values prioritize the conviction of the guilty, thereby risking the conviction of some innocent people. Due process systems tightly control the actions of crime control agencies, while giving great freedom to citizens who may be suspected or accused of criminal activity. Crime control systems avoid using the law to control crime control agencies and do not allow suspects and the accused great freedom. A pure crime control system would prioritize the search for truth by adversarial law enforcement agencies at literally all costs. Police officers who ''know'' that someone is guilty would have this knowledge accepted as proof by a court without corroboration, and courts would not be concerned about how the information was obtained. A pure due process system would prioritize proof and system controls at literally all costs. Guilty verdicts would be allowed only on proof beyond literally all doubt, and law enforcement officials would be accountable to the courts for the ways in which they obtained the information used to prove guilt.

This makes the criminal justice system dilemma clear and shows why proof and truth are different. Absolute proof, and completely innocuous methods of securing it, cannot be required. But to insist on uncontrolled discretion in the search for truth is equally unacceptable. The stricter the standard of proof required—that is, the closer a system is to the due process ideal—the fewer convictions there will be of guilty people. Guilty verdicts would therefore generally be true, but many acquittals would be of people who were, in truth, guilty. The looser the standard of proof required—that is, the more that police evidence is accepted as it is in the crime control model—the more convictions there will be of guilty people and of innocent people. In this system, most acquittals will be true, but some convictions will be of innocent people. Overall there may be more true verdicts but at the cost of truth and proof for those who are wrongly convicted. Packer said that anyone who espoused either model in its pure form would be a fanatic, and it is hard to conceive of a system that would embody either model in its entirety (just as no system is entirely adversarial or entirely inquisitorial). However, in most systems the values of one or the other model appear to predominate. Both systems actually seek the truth. But they do so in different ways and are prepared to sacrifice different things in that pursuit—the conviction of some guilty people in the case of due process, and the acquittal of some innocent people in the case of crime control.

Similarly, adversarial and inquisitorial systems both seek the truth, but in different ways and with different compromises. Under adversarialism the truth is sought by allowing each side to put its case forward and challenge the other side's case as best it can. This only works well, however, if both sides are powerful and well-matched. If the revelation of certain facts appears to be in the interest of neither side they are likely to remain completely hidden. Presentation of the full truth, in other words, is not the responsibility or duty of any person or institution. On the other hand, under inquisitorialism the truth is sought by impartial investigators. This only works well if the investigator is both powerful and impartial. In reality adversarial systems need institutions that have some duty to rise above the interests of each side (e.g., the judiciary), while inquisitorial systems need institutions that have some duty to the defendant (e.g., defence lawyers).

However, truth is not, and should not be, the only yardstick by which to evaluate a system. Justice and fairness are also crucial. Ashworth (1994, 1996) tries to give concrete expression to these slippery concepts by developing a framework of ethical principles derived from the European Convention on Human Rights. Although laudable, this approach creates as many problems as it solves. For example, Ashworth's principles include rights for victims, such as the right to respect and to compensation. This recognition of victims should be welcomed, as their rights and potential role in the criminal justice process play no part in Packer's models. However, Ashworth provides no guidance on how to reconcile victims' rights with those of suspects and defendants when conflicts occur. Many of Ashworth's other ethical principles are reformulations of key due process principles. Some are vague, such as the right of suspects to be treated fairly and without discrimination and the requirement that there be reasonable grounds for arrest and detention. What is reasonable, fair and non-discriminatory is a constant source of dispute. Those principles that are precise, such as the right of innocent persons not to be convicted, are not considered by Ashworth to be absolute, but may be undercut by crime control considerations. Although Ashworth does not explicitly acknowledge this, he says: "Maximum protection of the innocent may well have to be compromised . . . but this should be confined to the smallest extent" (Ashworth, 1996: 30). The rights of the accused therefore remain vague in Ashworth's model even where they appear to be precise. Clearly, the limitations of the Packer models are not solved by Ashworth's human rights approach. Its main value is to specify standards by which to evaluate the present system.

Sanders and Young (1994b) conducted a similar exercise, examining how far the law governing pre-trial decision making met the ethical standards imposed by the concept of the Rule of Law. They focussed on two elements of the Rule of Law: the extent of unjustifiable disparities in the treatment of people and the extent to which state agencies (namely the police) were controlled by, or accountable to, the law. Both of these elements form part of Ashworth's set of ethical principles (respectively, the principle of "equality of arms" and the principle of "legality"). Just as Ashworth found that in many respects criminal justice in England and Wales fails to adhere to his ethical principles, Sanders and Young found that suspects and defendants are not treated equally by state agencies, and that those agencies are not adequately controlled by independent legal authorities. This chapter's evaluation of the operation of the criminal courts in England and Wales will use all these three approaches to uncover the underlying values of the system and analyse the compatibility of justice and power.

POLICE BAIL

In England and Wales, for most offences, the decision about whether or not to prosecute may be taken by anyone. In practice, the decision is made by the enforcement agency, or occasionally the victim. Crimes such as pollution, tax evasion and breaches of health and safety laws are dealt with by specialised agencies. Their approach is very different than that of the police, and the contrast is instructive (Sanders, 1985; 1996b), but this chapter will be concerned solely with the police. If the police decide to prosecute, they will summons for minor offences but arrest and charge for anything of moderate seriousness. The arrest and charge process involves detention in a police station. Sometimes this is quite lengthy (up to 24 hours or more in very serious cases). Detained suspects are the responsibility of a custody officer (usually a police sergeant). After charge, the case becomes the responsibility of the Crown Prosecution Service (CPS), a nationally organised group of salaried lawyers who have the power to alter or drop charges if they wish. Before the CPS receives the case papers, however, the custody officer has to decide whether to release on bail or to hold the suspect in custody pending the next magistrates' court hearing (usually the next morning).

Suspects may be held in custody only if their real name and address cannot be ascertained, if they are unlikely to appear in court to answer the charge, if they are likely to interfere with witnesses or police investigations or if they are likely to commit further significant crimes. Most of these provisions require custody officers to predict what might happen if suspects were released. However, they have to rely on what investigating officers say, and on what little may be known about the suspect's previous record of such behaviour as appearing in court or offending on bail. Also, suspects cannot prove that they would not have committed another crime had they been given the opportunity to do so. Looked at from the viewpoint of Packer's models, due process appears to be subordinated to crime control: decisions are taken quickly on the basis of inadequate information. To protect suspects from the possible bias of the investigator, custody officer decisions are supposed to be made independently of the views expressed by investigating officers; however, most of the information they use comes from the very officers against whom this protection is provided; and assessment of the quality of decision making is almost impossible.

Therefore, the initial bail/custody decision is made entirely by the police, without real accountability. Although suspects are entitled to the services of a lawyer while in detention, a right asserted by around one-third of all suspects, it is rare for lawyers to stay in the station until the bail/custody decision is made, and few vigorously contest the issue (Sanders, 1996a). This is all difficult to reconcile with the two elements of the rule of law discussed by Sanders and Young, or indeed other ethical principles identified by Ashworth (e.g., the right to have reasonable grounds for arrest and detention). Adversarialism is only valid if each side is equally matched (Ashworth's "equality of arms" principle), and so the adversarial system is faulty in this regard. This has important implications for the relative bargaining positions of the police and suspects, which the police exploit in interrogation (Sanders and Young, 1994a: ch. 4). But for the purposes of this chapter it is the effect of these powers and relationships on what happens subsequently in court that is of concern.

COURT BAIL

Defendants who are granted police bail are not thereafter remanded to custody unless circumstances change. When defendants are not granted police bail, court bail may or may not be opposed by the police (through the CPS), and may or may not be requested by the defendant (usually through a solicitor). The CPS does not always comply with a police request to oppose bail. However, it almost invariably asks for conditions to be attached to bail (Morgan, 1996). Not surprisingly, magistrates usually reach the same conclusions as the police and the CPS. This is because they consider similar criteria and similar information (Simon and Weatheritt, 1984; Hucklesby, 1996). However, magistrates, like custody officers, have to make predictive decisions. The discretion this inevitably gives them leads to considerable disparity between different courts (Hucklesby, 1996; Paterson and Whitaker, 1994, 1995). Overall, bail is denied in about 11 to 13% of magistrates' cases each year. Of the cases committed to the Crown Court (generally, the most serious cases), 19 to 22% are denied bail (Morgan and Jones, 1992). Most hearings seem to take less than ten minutes (Doherty and East, 1985), which reflects the limited information that is usually provided (Hucklesby, 1996).

When information from more diverse sources is presented to the courts by the CPS, bail is less frequently opposed by the CPS and is more frequently granted. Bail information schemes, organized by local probation services, lead to the release of more defendants than normal, demonstrating the partiality (i.e., adversarial approach) of the police and the overcautious approach of many courts. Mair and Lloyd (1996), in an appraisal of bail information schemes, estimate that by 1996 these schemes covered over 190 magistrates' courts and 38 prison establishments. These schemes show that there is potential in the CPS for independence if independent information is provided to it. As it stands, though, the CPS appears to carry more weight with magistrates than do defence lawyers. Information from the CPS is seen as factual, but information from the defence is seen as partial. Magistrates even sometimes refer to prosecutors as "our solicitor" (Hucklesby, 1996: 218–19, 224). None of this comes into play, however, unless the suspect is first kept in custody by the custody officer. Given the minimal input of non-police information and perspective on this decision, this is clearly far from the due process model.

A suspect's being remanded in custody can obstruct defence work (including preparation of bail applications). Thus defendants remanded to custody are, all other things being equal, more likely to be convicted and, if convicted, to be given custodial sentences, than those given bail. But since not all defendants remanded to custody are convicted and given custodial sentences, some defendants who are legally innocent are held in custody, and some whose offence or circumstances do not warrant custodial sentences are also held in custody before sentence. In 1992, 39% of defendants in custody in the magistrates' courts received non-custodial penalties, and a further 21% were acquitted (Morgan, 1996). On the other hand, 10 to 17% of all persons released on bail commit further offences while at liberty (Morgan and Jones, 1992). Clearly magistrates have inadequate information on which to base confident decisions, yet the stakes are high. Offending on bail is undesirable; yet in a supposedly due proccss system, so is pre-trial imprisonment of some seven to ten weeks when so many remanded defendants are not subsequently jailed. The adversarial system clearly does not operate as it is supposed to when the balance is tilted so far towards crime control concerns and when this is corrected only by the provision of extra information to the magistrates from the prosecution (as distinct from defence lawyers).

GUILTY PLEAS

The overwhelming majority of defendants—around 70% in the Crown Court and 90% in the magistrates' courts—plead guilty (Ashworth, 1994). As McBarnet (1981) says, this is surprising in a system where one is presumed innocent until proved to be guilty. Why do so many defendants give up their right to put the prosecution to proof? The answer, put at its simplest, is that the legal profession—both its solicitor branch (McConville et al., 1994; Mulcahy, 1994) and the Bar (Baldwin and McConville, 1977; Morison and Leith, 1992)—persuade them to do this. There is little incentive for defence lawyers in most cases to act adversarially. This has been long recognised in the USA, where plea bargaining is even more entrenched than it is in Britain (Sudnow, 1965; Feeley, 1979). As discussed above, this is true in relation to police station advice, and it is equally true in relation to the courts. Research has found that legal firms are not geared up to contest cases; lawyers often lack the skills needed to contest cases; legal aid rates provide insufficient remuneration; and defence lawyers are often culturally more in sympathy with the prosecution than they are with their clients.

Defence lawyers often fail to attend interrogations, sending to suspects the due process message that it is the court, not police questioning, that is important (Sanders, 1996a). However, this facilitates the crime control practices at the police station that produce confessions—to take a particularly important example—leaving little for the defence lawyer to do in court other than to mitigate on a guilty plea and to bargain. By failing to be adversarial in the police station, defence lawyers often deny their clients the opportunity to be adversarial in court. Defence lawyers frequently make commitments on behalf of their clients, provide information to the prosecution that could remain confidential, agree not to press their case when it might succeed, and agree to "lean on" or "pressure" their clients or "beat them over the head" (Baldwin, 1985; McConville, Sanders and Leng, 1991; McConville and Mirsky, 1994). What is regarded by Baldwin (1985: 85) as "not standing on their rights" is in fact the defence failure to insist on due process.

Defendants are encouraged to plead guilty through bargaining. Explicit plea bargaining with the judge over the sentence is not permitted in Britain. However, courts are now urged by recent legislation to take into account guilty pleas, which they had done in practice for many years anyway. The sentence discount is around 25 to 30%, and the plea sometimes determines not just the length, but also the type, of sentence. However, since no offences other than murder have fixed sentences in Britain, the difference between reducing the sentence for a guilty plea or raising it for a not guilty plea is largely presentational. Bargaining also takes place over the seriousness of the charge and over venue (i.e., magistrates' court or Crown Court) because cases that remain in the lower courts are generally sentenced more lightly (Sanders and Young, 1994a: chs. 6–7). Many magistrates' courts have pre-trial reviews, which aim, among other things, to promote plea bargaining (Brownlee, Mulcahy and Walker, 1994).

Why do we *allow*, let alone encourage, this fundamental cornerstone of the due process value system to be eroded? There is a range of possible explanations. Some argue that it is because of bureaucratic pressures to process cases efficiently, while others argue that the guilty plea system provides a way for the police to impose their power on less powerful groups. Where there is a confession, for instance—as there is in very many cases—it is difficult to contest guilt. To do so would usually require an attack on how the police secured the confession, which many lawyers are reluctant to do, and which is difficult to do successfully. Confessions, then, guarantee guilty pleas in all cases except those in which the suspect can convince a court (note the shift in the onus of proof) that the confession was obtained unlawfully or is otherwise unreliable. The guilty plea system ensures that a high proportion of police arrests can be successfully disposed of through the courts without the processes of arrest, detention and questioning being embarrassingly illuminated. Not only is this crime control at its most deft, but the Rule of Law is violated as well: the pressures on defendants create inequality, and the police and prosecution evade accountability. Inevitably, some innocent people plead guilty: over 10% of those entering guilty pleas in the Crown Court claim to be innocent. In a similar proportion of cases the CPS believes there would have been a reasonable chance of acquittal. Although neither of these facts are, in themselves, evidence of innocence among guilty pleaders, around half of that group claim innocence and are believed by their barristers (Zander and Henderson, 1993). This is around 1,400 defendants in Crown Courts alone.

MAGISTRATES' COURTS

The role of magistrates is perhaps the most unusual aspect of the English court system. All cases begin in the magistrates' courts. Most of the approximately 28,000 magistrates are part-time, unpaid amateurs. They sit in panels of three and are guided by legally qualified clerks. There are fewer than 150 professionally qualified magistrates—stipendiaries—who sit alone in large cities. There is no jury in magistrates' courts. Some cases are triable ''summarily''—the term used for magistrates' court proceedings; others are triable in the Crown Court only; but most are triable either way. In such cases the venue—magistrates' court or Crown Court—is assumed to be the lower court unless either the magistrates or the defendant choose Crown Court. The choice of either side is decisive. This allows defendants a jury trial if they seek it but does not force it upon them.

Many defendants who contest their cases choose jury trials as they are perceived to be fairer than summary trials. However, many defendants change their plea to guilty at a later point. Government concern has centred on how to reduce the number of aborted trials, because they are costly in time and resources, rather than on how to alleviate the pressures on suspects to give up their right to contest their case, even after opting for a venue with more severe sentencing powers than magistrates' courts. Thus, following the recommendation of the Royal Commission on Criminal Justice in 1993, it is planned that magistrates alone should have the right to determine venue—reducing the scope for jury trial still further (McConville and Mirsky, 1994).

In all, about 95% of all cases—over 80% of either-way cases—stay in the magistrates' courts. The new rules on venue will lead to an even higher proportion of cases staying in the magistrates' courts. This is justified on the ground that the complex and time-consuming process of a judge and jury trial (which costs about seven times more than a magistrates' court trial) is unnecessary in trivial cases. Even if summary cases really are trivial this is hardly an argument that can be applied to either-way cases, such as assault, theft and deception. But if they are really so trivial, why prosecute? And if magistrates' procedures are so fair that the perceptions and preferences of suspects can be overridden, why preserve the Crown Court for any cases at all? In reality, magistrates make decisions of great importance—they send over 20,000 people per year to prison (albeit for sentences of no more than six months); they decide whether to hold defendants in custody; and they (and their clerks) decide whether to grant legal aid to defendants, to cite just three examples. Yet in the magistrates' courts defence lawyers are far less adversarial than in the Crown Court (McConville et al., 1994).

In the Crown Court the trier of law is the judge, while the trier of fact is the jury. When, for instance, the legal admissibility of evidence is disputed, this is heard by the judge in the absence of the jury. The jury is therefore unaware of evidence that is ruled inadmissible. In the magistrates' courts the magistrates decide if evidence is inadmissible. If they do so rule, they have to then try to forget this evidence when they later consider their verdict. These examples show that there are fewer due process protections in the magistrates' courts than in the Crown Court.

THE CROWN COURT: JUDGE AND JURY

There is a considerable literature on juries in both the UK and the USA. The impression is given that in most cases the jury is the central institution of criminal justice. This is true not just in the academic literature, but also in the world of the novel, film and television. Nothing could be further from the truth because:

- most cases are disposed of by guilty plea; therefore, usually there is no jury because there is no trial.
- most cases are heard in the magistrates' courts, where there is no jury even if there is a trial.
- jury decision making is guided by the judge, who sums up the facts and summarises the law.
- jury verdicts are based on the evidence presented in court rather than on the whole truth; this will be selected by each side in its own interest and further shaped by judicial decisions regarding such matters as admissibility.

Why, then, is the jury given such prominent attention? Leaving aside the romantic and dramatic side, more relevant to the non-fiction than the academic world, it may be because the jury embodies many of the central ideological features of criminal justice: the jury presides over the adversarial encounter, and due process is guaranteed because allegations of guilt have to satisfy a group of disinterested amateurs beyond a reasonable doubt. This chapter redresses the balance, looking instead at the institutions that replace or influence the jury. This is not just because of the irrelevance of the jury in most cases in the UK and the USA, but also because the issues of concern about the jury are the same in both countries and would not surprise an American reader. More information can be found in Sanders and Young (1994a: ch. 8).

In those few cases where there is a jury trial, jury verdicts can only be understood if the relationship between the judge and the jury is understood. In the adversarial ideal, the judge is a neutral umpire, not a participant in the trial. However, in the UK the judge can be, and frequently is, far more interventionist than is allowed in the USA. It is true that judges may not direct juries to convict; however, they may do the opposite—that is, direct acquittals—which in fact accounts for over half of all acquittals. This appears to be consistent with the due process model. However, judges often do make their views known and intervene accordingly. In some cases judges ask nearly as many questions as do counsel. In most, but not all, cases of gross bias the Court of Appeal quashes the conviction. However, the amount of intervention is not the real issue as far as due process is concerned. After all, adversarialism only works well if both sides are strong and well-matched. Arguably, in cases where this is not so, intervention from the judge can lead to a fairer and more efficient trial. The real issue is whether intervention compromises the substance or appearance of impartiality. In many cases it certainly seems to. In one case, the judge was grossly discourteous to the defendant's lawyer. In another he muttered, "Oh, God," and groaned and sighed throughout defence counsel's closing speech. In yet another, some defence witnesses were discredited by the judge. Yet in none of these cases were convictions quashed (Sanders and Young, 1944a: ch. 8).

In the UK, judges are allowed to make their views of the credibility of witnesses, and even defendants, clear as long as they leave it up to the jury to decide whether or not they agree with the judge. In reality, it is likely that juries are reluctant to disagree with a judge, and there is some evidence from research on the jury that much jury discussion revolves precisely around trying to ascertain what the judge wants them to decide (Mungham and Bankowski, 1976). Drawing on evidence from inquisitorial jurisdictions where judges and juries sometimes consider verdicts together, it seems that judges are more conviction-minded than are juries, and that juries are highly influenced by judges (Munday, 1993). The Royal Commission on Criminal Procedure (1981) recommended that judges be more, rather than less, interventionist, in the interests of both justice and economy. However, a survey by the commission found that defence barristers believe that judges intervene in trials and sum up against the weight of the evidence in favor of the prosecution in over 10% of trials (Zander and Henderson, 1993). The question for due process is not so much whether intervention is good or bad, but whether judges can be trained to change the way they intervene.

It is clear from the preceding discussion that jury decisions are not made on the basis of the whole truth but on what is put before them. While judges may unfairly shift the balance away from one side or the other through their interventions, they can also redress an unbalanced contest. This is also important from the victim's perspective. Judges clearly need to make decisions that determine much of what juries hear about the case, which is crucially important given that what juries hear virtually determines their verdicts. One important example of this concerns illegally or unfairly obtained evidence. In the UK only unreliable or oppressively obtained confession evidence is automatically excluded. Trial courts at their discretion may hear unfairly obtained confession evidence: for instance, from unlawful stops, police-car interrogations and after denial of access to legal advice for suspects in detention. The same is true of the admission of physical evidence—such as fingerprints, stolen goods and documents—however it is obtained. Such evidence obtained after even the most grossly unlawful actions by the police can still be used to convict. The courts exclude more evidence now than they used to, but no rigid exclusionary "fruit of the forbidden tree" doctrine—the hallmark of due process—is applied. Instead the emphasis is on the probative value of evidence, however it was obtained. This is the crime control doctrine at its most extreme and illustrates the problem of prioritising truth above legality (Sanders and Young, 1994a: ch. 9). The evidence on which juries make their decisions is not simply what really exists, but also what is allowed to be submitted to the jury.

Another example showing how what is evidence depends on what the rules are as much as what happened concerns the so-called right of silence—known in the USA as the privilege against self-incrimination. This is another cornerstone of due process and has long been the target of crime control advocates, who argue that only those with something to hide refuse to answer questions in police stations or courts. Whether this is so or not will be a matter of endless debate. In Britain, though, the crime control advocates won the argument in

1994 when government legislation significantly eroded the right of silence. Judges are now required to instruct juries that defendants who refused to answer questions or put forward explanations for, for instance, their presence at a crime scene, can have this silence taken into account at trial. That is, in lawyers' language, juries are allowed to draw adverse inferences from the silence of defendants if they had, but did not take, the chance to make their point when under questioning (Sanders, 1997a).

Both of these evidential rules are examples of the balance struck between due process and crime control values in the UK, and they are important for that reason. But they have a further importance too. When juries make decisions, they do so on the evidence before them. Judges in the UK exert considerable control over what that evidence is, and how it is viewed by the jury. In exercising this control they are guided by legislation (such as the law that eroded the right of silence), case law as set out by the Court of Appeal (as in the factors shaping the exclusionary discretion) and their own personal and professional values. Most cases bypass the jury, and the jury's preeminence even in trials is more apparent than real. The role of the jury is not so much to guarantee due process as to legitimate a hidden crime control reality. The jury thus has more of an ideological than an instrumental purpose.

VICTIMS

This chapter has been predominantly concerned with the position of defendants in criminal courts. This is because the due process-crime control spectrum is primarily about the treatment of defendants and the balancing of protections for them with rules and procedures that facilitate conviction. Similarly, the differences between adversarialism and inquisitorialism primarily concern the court procedures used to determine the guilt or innocence of defendants. But victims also have an interest in these matters: few crimes are victimless, and few victims are unconcerned about the verdict. This is something of a paradox, for in many jurisdictions, including the UK, victims have no status other than that of a witness. In Britain anyone may initiate a prosecution, and there is no obligation on the police (or anyone else) to do so. Whoever does prosecute has control of the case. In the early 19th century this was usually the victim, and so prosecution decisions were taken by victims. When the police took prosecutions over, victims became distanced from their cases. When the CPS was introduced in the mid-1980s, yet another intermediary body interposed itself between victims and their cases. It is not surprising that communication between victims and the prosecution is often strained, and that the interests of victims have become secondary. This is now being addressed in a limited way.

Some believe that it is in the interests of victims for criminal justice to be an inquisitorial system with crime control procedures. In this way, the truth (not legal proof) will be sought, and convictions will be maximized. This is not necessarily so, however. First, as argued earlier, the differences between the due process and the crime control models are not really between the search for proof or truth but concern different methods of reaching the truth. Crime control methods produce more guilty verdicts but not necessarily more *correct* verdicts. In the UK in the 1980s and 1990s, there have been a series of miscarriages of justice leading to the quashing of convictions (many for murder) of people who had served ten years or more in prison. This is a tragedy not just for the wrongly convicted defendants but also for the victims. Every wrongful conviction allows the real criminal to remain free. This cannot be good for victims. Furthermore, plea bargaining compromises put pressure on the innocent to plead guilty and also allow the guilty to be convicted of offences that understate their true crimes. In serious cases this is traumatic for victims.

Even if crime control and inquisitorialism did lead to more convictions of the guilty, human rights and the rule of law should not be forgotten. The idea that criminals are not worthy of such considerations because of the suffering of victims assumes that victims and defendants are from different sections of society. It is true that defendants are drawn disproportionately from the poorer sections of society (though that in itself should serve as a warning against the removal of due process protections by affluent middle class law makers and law enforcers). But it is also true that victims also tend to be poorer and more disadvantaged than the average person. Around one-third of adult males are convicted of at least one crime by early middle age. They are not a separate group from victims but, like victims, are part of society. We cannot protect victims by repressing defendants, for the same people occupy these different roles at different times. Fairness is, or should be, indivisible. The bureaucratic concerns that drive crime control processes have no more concerns for victims than they do for defendants. The interests served by crime control values are those of the law enforcement bureaucracy.

It seems that victims as a group find little comfort under either due process or crime control models. For particularly vulnerable groups of victims the problems are even greater. Rape victims, for instance, suffer greatly from having their lives dissected in trials where the defence argues that the victim consented. Due process allows the defence so much latitude that victims suffer secondary victimisation, and the attrition rate is alarming (Gregory and Lees, 1996). The crime control solution of plea bargaining a rape charge down to indecent assault is equally upsetting. Victims who are mentally handicapped or mentally ill suffer in the same way (Sanders et al., 1997b), as do children (Zedner, 1994). Adversarial trial procedures can be particularly unjust for mentally handicapped victims. In these cases, the Rule of Law, as applied to victims rather than defendants, is violated. The apparent equality of the defence and the prosecution is a fraud when the defence can, for instance, confuse or intimidate vulnerable victims through aggressive or convoluted questioning. In these circumstances research has found that more judicial intervention to redress the balance would be desirable. As it is, many such cases end in acquittal or are plea bargained drastically, when they are prosecuted at all. There are measures available to help vulnerable victims, such as allowing them to give evidence over closed-circuit television, but these have only a limited effect on the brutality of the adversarial system (Sanders et al., 1997b).

Ashworth's human rights model recognises these problems. It seeks to accord rights to victims to eliminate secondary victimisation. But in providing due process rights to both suspects and defendants, Ashworth fails to resolve the conflicts and confusions at the heart of the system. Only a victim-centred model of criminal justice can do this, but at the expense of both efficiency and protections for the defendant, except when these are permitted by the victim. Although a victim-centred model is not in the cards in the UK at present, some measures have been taken to recognise the legitimate interests that victims should have, despite their legal invisibility. First, victims now have the right to be informed of the progress of their cases when there is a prosecution (Home Office, 1996). Second, in some police force areas, victim impact statements are being used on an experimental basis. What impact they will have, and how far they will be used in making prosecution and sentencing decisions, remains to be seen.

CONCLUSION

To summarise, in England and Wales initial bail decisions are taken by the police with little input from defence lawyers or other agencies. Subsequent bail decisions by the courts are not determined by these initial police decisions, but they are often strongly influenced by them. Here there are usually considerable inputs from defence lawyers and, sometimes, other agencies. But magistrates' courts regard the prosecution perspective as less biassed than that of the defence. The pressures to plead guilty are particularly strong for defendants who are, or fear they will be, denied bail. There are pressures to confess for suspects who want the police to grant bail. Once a confession is made, the pressures to plead guilty are very strong indeed. Innocent defendants who confess to avoid being denied bail risk conviction and thus being jailed later. If they resist the pressures to confess, they are likely to be held in custody, which is a punishment in itself, and this will make further custody, and conviction as a result, more likely. The Royal Commission on Criminal Justice accepted that there is a risk of the innocent sometimes pleading guilty, although it underestimated the risks on scandalously thin grounds (McConville and Mirsky, 1994). It recommended plea bargaining because of "the benefits to the system . . . of encouraging those who are in fact guilty to plead guilty" (Royal Commission on Criminal Justice, 1993: 111).

The production of confessions and guilty pleas undermines due process in other ways too. For example, it hides the absence of legal grounds in many cases for arrest, detention and prosecution; this encourages "fishing expeditions" by the police, which impact not only on the legally guilty (whether factually so or not) but also on those held without charge (or prosecuted and acquitted) who should never have been deprived of their liberty without reasonable suspicion in the first place (McBarnet, 1981; McConville et al., 1991). The system also has discriminatory effects: for example, while black defendants contest their cases more often than white defendants, they also get heavier sentences (Hood, 1992).

For the person who enters a plea of not guilty, the chances of securing a jury trial are low and will be lower still in the future. It is believed, probably justifiably, that jury trial is more likely to lead to acquittal than trial by the magistrates. However, even a jury trial is shaped by the judges, who cannot be assumed to embody due process values to the exclusion of all others. At every stage, then, crime control values predominate over those of due process, adversarialism is undermined, and principles of justice and the Rule of Law are subordinated to maintain the power and interests of the police and other criminal justice agencies. Yet victims do not generally benefit from this. The interests of victims are not identical to those of the criminal justice system. Although undermined, adversarialism is not dead, and when it is suppressed by plea bargaining the results can be distressing. Prosecutors are no more attuned to contested trials than are defence lawyers. The reality of the criminal justice process is as far from the descriptions commonly found in the law books and on television as one can imagine. Criminal justice is a blunt instrument where all too often the wrong people are convicted, or the right people are convicted of the wrong things, or genuine victims suffer nearly as much from the attempt to redress the wrong done to them than they suffered from the wrong in the first place. In the contest between justice and power the clear winner is power. But it is not clear who or what benefits from this.

CHAPTER 2

Street Crime in England and Wales

LES JOHNSTON

INTRODUCTION

This chapter was written during a General Election campaign in which law and order, once again, became a central issue. However, the 1997 campaign differed from earlier ones. In the past, the Labour party tended to concede ground to the Conservatives on law and order, perceiving it to be an inherently right wing issue. That position has now changed with New Labour pledging itself to be "tough on crime and tough on the causes of crime." Much of this toughness arose from New Labour's realisation that rising rates of recorded crime rendered the Conservatives open to electoral attack. The result was a "Dutch auction," in which each party tried to outbid the other in the establishment of its law and order credentials. The resulting similarity between the policies ensures that, for the foreseeable future, law and order politics have become the politics of the hard centre.

One striking indication of this tendency was the degree to which both parties subscribed to the Americanization of criminal justice policy (Rutherford, 1996). Though growing American influence can be seen in various policy initiatives—for example in the Crime Bill, which sought to apply the principle of "three strikes and you're out" as a means of incapacitation and deterrence—it is most evident in approaches to the policing of street crime.

Nowadays, when the former Home Secretary, Michael Howard, and his successor, Jack Straw, seek advice about street policing, they look for inspiration to the streets of New York, rather than to the corridors of New Scotland Yard (Johnston, 1997). To that extent, the 1997 election campaign will be remembered for one image above all others: the spectacle of the major parties falling over themselves to declare their unequivocal support for American-style Zero Tolerance policing.

This chapter is divided into four sections. The first considers the concepts of "the street" and "street crime." Section two reviews recent evidence from the *British Crime Survey* (BCS)—a national survey of victims carried out periodically since 1982 by the Home Office—on trends in street crime and patterns of victimisation and fear. Section three examines police responses to the problem of street crime. The traditional enforcement-led response characteristic of the late 1970s and early 1980s is now supplemented by other policing strategies. These strategies involve the dispersal of responsibility for personal safety and crime control amongst those who are able and willing to bear it. This combination of enforcement for some, and dispersed responsibility for others, produces an inequitable and unstable system of policing. Furthermore, dispersal is predicated on a denial of social crime prevention at the very time when social exclusion, economic inequality and political marginality are increasing. This raises a problem: how to ensure police legitimacy and public order when the poor are marginalised and the rich increasingly disengaged from civil society and the public sphere. Section four considers Zero Tolerance policing as a strategy for addressing these problems. The essence of Zero Tolerance lies in its attempt to impose civility on the "dangerous classes." Though the "Broken Windows" (Wilson and Kelling, 1982) philosophy that informs this strategy recognises the pathological effects of a declining civic culture at street level, it outlines an impossible project. Civil society needs to be reconstructed, but it cannot be resuscitated through the civilising mission of Zero Tolerance policing.

THE STREET AND STREET CRIME

The identification of "street crime" as a problem presupposes a coherent concept of "the street." Yet, as Richman (1995) points out, sociological analysis of the street has been underdeveloped. Richman's point is not that the street is absent from sociological thinking, merely that it serves as an unarticulated background to the events that take place on it. To take a single relevant example, neither Northam (1988) nor Waddington (1992) index the term "street" in their studies of public order policing, despite being primarily concerned with the disorder and riots that occur there.

By contrast, the concept of "street crime" is overarticulated. Not only does the term relate to particular criminal acts occurring in particular locations, it also carries a complex symbolic and emotive content. Street crime embodies the threat of "the other"; the spectre of "the stranger": an age-specific, gender-specific and, more often than not, racialised figure capable of undermining personal safety, community order and social structure. This view of street crime is central to the imagery of British urban criminality during the last twenty-five years: mugging, football hooliganism, riots, vandalism, joy-riding, drug-induced criminality and aggressive begging by the homeless.

Although this idealised image of the aggressive stranger is the staple diet of electioneering politicians, it cannot be dismissed as mere "moral panic." Undoubtedly, politicians and the police have, in the past, made capital out of the politicisation of mugging and street crime (Hall et al., 1978; Blom-Cooper and Drabble, 1982) and continue to do so in the present.[1] Yet, as left-realist criminologists have insisted, crime remains a problem for beleaguered inner-city residents. And, as Waddington (1986) says, it would be unacceptable to dismiss incidents of racial attack and domestic violence as mere moral panics, so why do so for street crime? Neither is the reality of fear and victimisation restricted to the urban poor. Taylor (1995) comments on the high levels of fear of crime experienced by residents of Hale, an affluent suburb on the outskirts of Manchester. In this case, community newspapers reinforce local sensibilities about vandalism, noise and youthful occupation of municipal spaces at night. Residents make numerous phone calls to the police on weekends—far more, by size of population, than in other parts of Greater Manchester—many reporting the presence of strangers in the area. Yet, however unwarranted some of these fears, the level of recorded crime in Hale in the mid 1990s "is far in excess of anything reported in the three post war decades" (Taylor, 1995: 280). As Keith (1993a) suggests, street crime represents both a politicised moral panic and something that bears upon people's experiences of the realities of risk and victimisation.

The term "street crime" bears a resonance that impacts upon people's experiences of, and fears about, victimisation. Those experiences and fears will vary according to the particular social, economic and residential locations of individuals. The realities of victimisation are, in other words, the product of multiple interacting conditions. The street itself is also a locus of interaction, though of a rather more specific type. As White (1994) suggests, while the street refers both to specific features of the urban landscape (e.g., avenues, footpaths, roadways) and to more general open spaces (malls, shopping centres, parks), it also constitutes "the most frequent area within which police-youth contact takes place" (White, 1994: 103). It is also important to emphasise that the street upon which this interaction occurs is no longer synonymous with public space. Shopping malls and shopping centres constitute private legal spaces to which the public has limited access. Such limitation is defined by one's consumption potential. That is why malls and other forms of "mass private property" (Shearing and Stenning, 1983) are policed privately. The role of private security is to resolve the contradictions between public access and private ownership: maximising access to those who will purchase products and minimising access to those who might undermine the commercial imperative. This last category includes street musicians, beggars, vagrants, drunks, the homeless and, of course, young people. Paradoxically, shopping centres are the principal location in which youths spend time without necessarily spending money, a fact which brings them into conflict with those entrusted to police disorder (Spillius, 1995).

Initially, then, various observations can be made about street crime and street policing. First, merely being in certain places under certain conditions—the youthful non-consumer in the shopping centre—might constitute a reason for being policed, irrespective of the commission of some deviant or criminal act. Secondly, street policing is, by no means, the exclusive prerogative of the public police. In Britain, both commercial and municipal security forces police streets to an increasing extent, something which poses questions for the public police. Thirdly, street-level policing invariably throws up the issue of what Reiner (1995) calls "police property": those marginal social groups whom the police perceive as their essential constituency. White (1994) draws our attention to police harassment of young Aboriginal and homeless people in Australia, echoing similar accounts from Britain. He reminds us, however, that since the street is a place of social and territorial conflict, that process is an interactive one: "Young people . . . react to the police, just as the police in turn respond to the actions and behaviours of young people. . . . According to the police, officers are themselves often subject to harassment by young people" (White, 1994: 107).

The street then is a contested area in which routine, low-level incivility and disorder—along with crime—are handled in varying ways, according to the exigencies of police discretion. This leads to the fourth point: discretion is mediated by social conditions, not least those relating to social, political and economic exclusion. Bottoms and Wiles (1996), commenting on the erosion of cities as clearly defined geographical areas and their subjection to the "doughnut effect" ("dormitory towns around [a] city which is left with a hollow core" [Bottoms and Wiles, 1996: 18]), note three characteristic features of contemporary urban life. First, the lowest socio-economic groups, trapped in hollowed-out centres, may become ghettoised. Secondly, the most attractive future locations for property crime will be precisely those suburbs and rural hinterlands described by Taylor (1995). Thirdly, the most criminogenic groups—young males engaged in routine street crime and disorder—who in any case rarely travel great distances, will be associated with "impacted criminal areas with multiple victimisation and offending" (Bottoms and Wiles, 1996: 18). It is this third fact, in particular—that much street crime consists of low-level acts of male-on-male violence, where offenders and victims are more or less interchangeable—which is borne out by examination of survey data.

STREET CRIME: VICTIMISATION AND FEAR

As suggested earlier, the rhetoric and the reality of street crime are difficult to separate. Indeed, attempting to separate them may be counterproductive where—as in this case—one of the concerns is the social and political context of the police response to the problem. For this reason, the present section will focus on that category of criminality—contact crime—that most embodies the image of violent street crime. The BCS (see Mirrlees-Black et al., 1996) identifies four categories of contact crime. The largest number of incidents occurs where victims are acquainted, though not as domestic partners, with those who offend against them. The second largest category consists of acts of domestic violence. Third in frequency are violent acts committed by strangers. The fourth and smallest category consists of muggings (robberies and snatch thefts). According to the 1996 BCS (Mirrlees-Black et al. 1996, Table A4.2), in 1995, 12% of contact crime against men was domestic in nature, 9% was the result of mugging, 30% was the product of stranger violence and 49% arose from acts of violence committed by acquaintances. In the case of women, about 43% of violence was domestic in source, around 10% was the product of mugging, close to 14% was the result of stranger violence and about 32% arose from acts of violence committed by acquaintances. (*Note*: the figures here do not sum to 100% as, although rounded up, there are minor anomalies in the presentation of the original data.)

Both BCS figures and those recorded by the police indicate a rising trend in crimes of violence. Between 1993 and 1995, police figures showed a 6% increase in violence (3% for wounding, 18% for robbery), while the BCS indicated an overall rise in violent crime of 17% (13% for wounding, 32% for robbery). Trends in the four categories of contact crimes listed above also show a long-term increase. Since 1981 the largest increase in violence has occurred in the domestic category (a rise of 242%) and in acts of acquaintance violence (a rise of 123%). However, as the BCS reminds us, this could be because more victims are willing to report such incidents than hitherto because of improvements in victim services. That is unlikely to be the case, however, with muggings and acts of stranger violence where the victim and the offender are unacquainted. For that reason, it is assumed that trends in these two figures represent more or less accurate reflections of real tendencies.

Leaving aside cases of domestic violence, which are clearly outside the scope of the present discussion, the BCS provides the following analysis of the three remaining categories of contact crime.

Mugging

Mugging consists of "robberies, attempted robberies and snatch thefts, irrespective of any acquaintance between victim and offender" (Mirrlees-Black et al., 1996: 27). In practice, however, mugging is usually committed by strangers. The BCS indicates that incidents have increased by 54% since 1981, most of that increase occurring since 1991. Nevertheless, muggings are a relatively rare phenomenon, only 0.8% of respondents having been victimised in 1995. The highest rate of victimisation is amongst young (16 to 29-year-old) males (3%); young women have the next highest victimisation rate (1.3%). Men under 30 account for half of all incidents of victimisation. By contrast, amongst older age groups, risk is more evenly spread, with snatch thefts being mainly directed at women. Three-quarters of muggings are committed by strangers, virtually all of whom are male (95%) and young (70%). Half of all muggings take place on the street, and about one-third take place in or around transport facilities. By contrast, a quarter of muggings against women occur around their own homes. Only a minority of muggings take place after midnight (5%); most (about half) happen between 6:00 P.M. and midnight; and about one-third occur in the afternoon. Only a small minority of incidents involve weapons. In one-fifth of muggings the offender had a knife; in 4% of incidents, a gun. In 29% of cases victims were punched, slapped or kicked. Muggings were more likely than not (60%) to be reported to police. This compares with the reporting of less than one-third of incidents of domestic violence and about one-quarter of acts of stranger and acquaintance violence. Victims believed that drink was a factor in 17% of muggings and drugs a factor in 14%.

Stranger Violence

Stranger violence consists of "all violence, other than mugging, in which the victim knew none of the offenders" (Mirrlees-Black et al., 1996: 27). The BCS suggests that there has been a 12% increase in acts of stranger violence since 1981. Significantly, in light of the earlier discussion on the imagery of street crime, this was the smallest increase among all of the four categories of contact crime. As with muggings, young men are the main victims of stranger violence, 6.5% having been victimized in 1995. Overall, no less than 46% of all incidents of stranger violence had young men as victims. In most cases, groups of assailants were involved. (As with muggings, one-fifth of incidents involved groups of four or more perpetrators.) Male offenders were responsible for 90% of attacks against other men and for just under two-thirds of attacks against women. Victims believed that drink was a factor in 53% of incidents of stranger violence, an opinion supported by the fact that one-third of incidents took place in or around pubs, clubs and licensed premises. A further 30% of occurrences took place on or near transport facilities. Half of all incidents occurred in the evening, and one-fifth between midnight and 6:00 A.M.

Acquaintance Violence

Acquaintance violence consists of "all violence, other than mugging, in which the victim knew one or more of the offenders at least by sight, but excluding domestic violence" (Mirrlees-Black et al., 1996: 27). In 1995, 9% of young men and 3% of young women were victims of acquaintance violence. As for offenders, 30% were either friends or acquaintances of their victims, 23% were customers or clients, 12% were local children and 7% were neighbours. Half of the offenders were aged 25 or over, and 81% were male. However, nearly four in ten incidents against women involved other women as offenders. Over one-quarter of all incidents involved four or more offenders, and these were primarily against men. Three-quarters of incidents against women and 55% against men involved one person acting alone. Victims believed that alcohol was a factor in

45% of incidents, drugs in 22% and both alcohol and drugs combined in 13%. About one-fifth of incidents occurred, more or less equally, in streets, pubs or clubs, at work or on or near transport facilities. Half of incidents occurred during the evening, and one-third in the afternoon.

When considering figures such as these it is important to remember that high rates of criminal victimisation correlate with low levels of material well-being. As Matthews and Young (1992) point out, victimisation studies—particularly local ones (Kinsey, 1984; Jones et al., 1986; Crawford et al., 1990)—have shown that "the impact of crime is uneven. It falls disproportionately on the poorer and more vulnerable sections of the population and serves to compound . . . growing economic and social inequalities" (Matthews and Young, 1992: 2). This point is confirmed by Loveday (1996b), who notes that blacks in Britain can expect to experience longer periods of unemployment in greater numbers than any other ethnic group. This he suggests, should be kept in mind when considering matters of offending behaviour and victimisation. Commenting on Sir Paul Condon's pronouncement on black muggers,[1] Loveday notes:

> From this constituency are drawn [those] . . . identified . . . as 'street offenders.' . . . It would have been helpful if the Commissioner had . . . added that the incidence of victimisation was also highest amongst members of London's black community. (Loveday, 1996b: 6)

It is, therefore, illuminating to consider patterns of victimisation in respect of violent crime, broken down by ethnic group. These data are shown in Table 2.1.

Although dispute remains about whether black youths are the main perpetrators of muggings on London's streets or whether their high rate of offending is, at least in part, a product of racialised police practices (Blom-Cooper and Drabble, 1982), Table 2.1 clearly shows that Afro-Caribbeans experience the highest rates of victimisation for crimes against the person.

Finally, what about fear of street crime? Here, the BCS makes a number of observations:

- Unlike concern about other crimes, such as burglary, worry about mugging was not related to having been a victim of street crime, although those who knew other victims were more anxious.
- People most fearful of street crime—those who judged their risks to be highest—were in lower income groups, lived in disorderly neighbourhoods with lower levels of social support and were more vulnerable in terms of size, health and confidence in their own self-defence.
- Gender and age are important factors in determining levels of fear. There is a sharp difference between males and females and between the young and old in this regard. Accordingly, elderly women are, by far, the most fearful of street crime.
- Since 1994 there has been a small drop in fear of crime. In 1994, 54% of women felt very or a bit unsafe on the streets alone after dark. By 1996 that figure had fallen to

Table 2.1
Victims of Crime by Ethnic Group, 1993: England and Wales (percentages)

Personal Offences	White	Afro-Caribbean	Asian	All
Assaults	3.8	6.6	3.1	3.8
Threats	3.5	4.0	3.2	3.4
Robbery/theft from person	1.7	2.7	3.4	1.8
Other personal theft	3.7	5.2	3.2	3.7
All personal offences (excluding sexual offences)	8.5	13.2	9.3	8.6

Source: BCS 1993; adapted from Loveday 1996b: 7.

47% (15% for men). For women over 60 years of age, the figure stood at 60% (25% for men).

- Slightly more respondents took precautions against street crime in 1996 than in 1994. These precautions included avoiding particular places and people and not going out alone. More women than men engaged in these strategies.
- Overall, 3% of women (1% of men) never go out after dark for fear of crime. For women over 60 living in inner cities the figure stood at 17%. These figures have, in fact, changed little over the years and are similar to data from the 1984 BCS.
- Increased fear of crime for some categories of offences, such as car crime, corresponds to rising rates of victimisation. However, worry about mugging and street safety has not changed much since 1982, although robbery and theft from the person have, according to BCS and police figures alike, risen substantially since 1981.

Summary: BCS evidence suggests that much street crime is routine, drink-related male-on-male violence, about twice as much of it committed by acquaintances as by strangers. Muggings and stranger violence—the prominent image of street crime—are less common than crimes by acquaintances. Indeed, it is likely that the proportional difference is even greater than BCS figures suggest because of the disinclination of victims to report people they know to the police. However, both muggings and stranger violence are increasing: muggings by about half since 1981, stranger violence by 12% over the same period. Alcohol is a particular factor in the last case.

Several conclusions can be drawn about the social character of street crime. First, the most disadvantaged social groups are also the most highly victimised. Secondly, both victims and offenders are primarily young males. Thirdly, street crime is both an intra-class and an intra-neighbourhood phenomenon. On this last point Loveday (1996) notes that crime pattern analyses undertaken by the Metropolitan and South Yorkshire police forces indicate that offenders live in close proximity to victims. The more serious the offence, the more likely it is to be committed close to the offender's residence.

Finally, the relationship between risk of victimisation and fear of street crime is complicated. On the one hand, as with all categories of crime, "those who worry most generally have more grounds for doing so" (Mirrlees-Black et al., 1996: 55). On the other hand, though related to the likelihood of victimisation, levels of fear "are not particularly sensitive to changes in absolute levels of risk" (Mirrlees-Black et al., 1996: 57). Hough's (1995) analysis of data from the 1994 BCS makes three pertinent observations in this regard. First, he suggests that while the BCS does not draw any conclusions about the impact of lurid media campaigns on fear of crime, misrepresentations are hardly likely to soothe public anxieties. For that reason one could speculate that the media's obsession with street crime may be a factor in accounting for relatively constant levels of fear since 1981, irrespective of variations in rates of victimisation. Secondly, according to the BCS, direct experience of being mugged or attacked did not predict fearfulness, though indirect experience—knowing friends or neighbours who had been mugged—did increase worry. This would indicate that the "local crime climate" (Mirrlees-Black, 1996) is also a significant factor in determining levels of fear. Lastly, gender is a key factor in determining fear of crime, in general, and of street crime, in particular. As Hough suggests, "It is a useful over-simplification to say that men commit crime and women worry about it" (Hough, 1995: 44). Hough (1995) reminds us, however, that it is not merely crime that is at issue. Women's sense of safety derives from "their everyday experience of sub-criminal harassment rather than their beliefs about the risks of random stranger attacks" (Hough, 1995: 48). This issue of routine male incivilities will be reconsidered in section 4.

POLICE RESPONSES TO STREET CRIME: ENFORCEMENT, RISK AND DISPERSED RESPONSIBILITY

Neither street crime nor fears about its impact on the British social fabric are anything new (Pearson, 1983). Nevertheless, since the late 1970s, the problem of street crime has come to symbolize the ills of the British body politic. The key moment in this process was the importation of the term "muggng" from the United States. Mugging encapsulated respectable fears about two post-war developments: black immigration and youth cultures. The discovery of, and consequent panic about, mugging (Hall et al., 1978) was, moreover, connected to wider concerns about the apparent ungovernability of a British state faced by multiple intractable problems: recession, unemployment, strikes, the Ulster problem, inner-city decline and international terrorism, to name but a few. The Thatcher administration of 1979 was elected to resolve that governmental crisis, strong and effective policing being seen as a major element of Conservative domestic policy.

In that context, it was not surprising that robust government was accompanied by robust policing. Police use of stop and search tactics, particularly in the black areas of inner cities, was especially controversial. Research undertaken at the time (Willis, 1983; Smith and Gray, 1983) pointed to a disproportionately high rate of stop and search amongst blacks, compared to the population as a whole.[2] Added to that, the police's use of Section 4 of the Vagrancy Act of 1824—the notorious ''sus'' law—was, until its repeal in 1981,[3] a constant source of conflict between the police and black communities. In April 1981 the Metropolitan Police implemented an anti-street-crime operation—Swamp '81—in the Brixton area of London. Swamp involved the saturation policing of a black inner-city area, and during the course of the operation, no less than 943 people were stopped. It was during this operation that two plainclothes officers stopped and searched a minicab driver in Atlantic Road; this incident sparked off the Brixton Riot of April 10–12.

Lord Scarman's Report on the Brixton disorders (Scarman, 1981) noted that the police's use of saturation stop and search powers was manifestly incompatible with the very principles of reasonable suspicion that sanctioned the judicious deployment of those powers. More importantly, Scarman raised the matter of the relationship between the police's obligation to enforce the law and their duty to maintain the Queen's Peace, a point illustrated in an exchange between Scarman and one of the policemen involved in the Atlantic Road incident:

> If you are getting unfriendly reactions from a crowd is this not something that you might take into account in evaluating whether you are serving the cause of public peace better by continuing or not continuing the search?
>
> I think I would be failing in my duty if I was ever intimidated by a crowd in exercising my authority. (Greaves, 1986: 78)

Recognizing that, in reality, these two obligations—law enforcement and order maintenance—might come into conflict with each other, Scarman maintained that, where such conflict existed, priority should be given to the latter over the former. In maintaining this, his reasoning was clear. For not only might insensitive policies of enforcement undermine public order, they might also call into question the public's legitimation of the police.

Swamp '81, together with similar operations of the time, constituted an attempt to impose a police solution on the problem of street crime. This bullish solution has, of course, to be seen within the context of the time. Not only were the police involved in quelling riots between 1981 and 1986, they were also on the front line in the government's battle against trade union power, whose culmination was the Miner's Strike of 1984–1985. During this period the police, unlike other public services, were protected from the worst excesses of fiscal constraint. Yet, by the late 1980s this picture had begun to change, bullish (and costly) enforcement being supplemented by more diverse mechanisms. These supplementary methods for policing street crime are organized around two sets of principles: the dispersal of responsibility for personal and community safety, and the initiation of strategies for minimizing risk of victimisation.

Dispersed responsibility is partly the product of a growing awareness that high crime rates are normal, and the efficacy of criminal justice agencies in reducing them, limited. However, it is also linked to a wider issue: state sovereignty is itself undermined by the social, political and economic changes arising under late modernity. The product of these changes is a fragmentation of structures and a diversity of practices, which have major implications for the future of policing (Johnston, 1996). In particular, these changes explode "the myth that the sovereign state is capable of providing security, law and order, and crime control within its territorial boundaries" (Garland, 1996: 448). The result is a "distanciation" (Giddens, 1990), or dispersal of responsibility for the control of crime and the maintenance of public order to agencies outside the formal apparatus of state-policing. These alternative agencies—often organised into partnerships—may consist of municipal bodies, quangos (quasi-autonomous nongovernmental organisations), voluntary organisations, businesses, insurance companies, commercial security organisations and private citizens. They may engage in formalised multi-agency partnerships that are oriented towards community policing programmes, juvenile liaison initiatives and diversion schemes. Or they may be organized into ad hoc groupings for particular ends. A recent example of the latter involved public police, private security, and local authority bailiffs in pitched battles with groups protesting about a road building programme in the South of England.

Dispersed responsibility is increasingly influential in matters of personal safety and security on the streets. Individuals are encouraged to assess risks and to avoid potentially dangerous locations. Women, in particular, may seek to minimise their vulnerability by carrying alarms or by avoiding being on the streets alone. Others may participate in citizen street patrols, either under the auspices of Neighbourhood Watch, or through unofficial channels.[4] Individual consumers, groups of consumers or local councils may contract with commercial security companies for protective services.

An alternative response has involved local authorities in developing their own police forces as a way of meeting public demand for a uniformed presence on the streets.[5] These initiatives have taken two forms. Some local authorities—in particular a number of London boroughs—have set up or expanded existing constabularies, whose role is to police parks and open spaces. In these organisations, constables enjoy full police powers within a given territorial jurisdiction and deal, amongst other things, with low-level violence, drunkenness, traffic violations and indecency. Interestingly, in 1994, Wandsworth Borough Council tried to extend routine patrols by its security personnel to cover the open spaces of council housing estates. Metropolitan Police resistance to this proposal has, for the moment, put the matter on hold (Johnston, 1993; Jones and Newburn, forthcoming). An alternative approach has been for councils to set up security forces whose officers, though uniformed, do not possess police powers. The Sedgefield Community Force in County Durham was established in 1994 as the first local authority-run body to patrol the streets in a locality. The Community

Force bears some similarity to the Dutch City Guard schemes (Hauber et al., 1996), its role being to increase public safety and reassurance by providing 24-hour foot and mobile patrol and by consulting with the public and the police on matters of crime and antisocial behaviour. A comment from Sedgefield Council's community relations officer is especially relevant to our later discussion of Zero Tolerance policing, since it suggests that the task of such organisations is to police the very incivilities that the public police have abandoned: "The Police have to focus on priorities that move away from minor criminal activity and nuisance. We believe that we are filling the gap" (I'Anson and Wiles, 1995:4).

Dispersal of responsibility beyond the state has been accompanied by the initiation of risk-based models of policing and crime prevention. Though enforcement remains a fundamental part of the police's response to street crime, the last decade has also seen a growing emphasis on prevention through the minimisation of risk. This emphasis has, in turn, been connected to rational choice models of offending ("opportunity reduction"), to situational models of crime prevention ("designing out crime") and, more recently, to actuarial models of justice that focus on aggregates—rather than individuals—as the locus of risk and where the target of criminal justice is not so much the offender as "the community of potential victims" (Hudson, 1996: 154). The most striking application of this last principle may be seen in the widespread deployment of closed-circuit television (CCTV) cameras in British town centres, the development of which has been made possible by Home Office financial and political support. While CCTV cameras may assist in the identification of offenders, the investigation of offences, the gathering of information and the co-ordination of police responses, its fundamental purpose is to provide an "unremitting watch" over potential offenders and victims. CCTV is central to the fight against street crime, cameras being "most commonly used to tackle conspicuous anti-social and criminal behaviour" (Brown, 1995: v). Yet, evaluations suggest that, for crimes such as robbery and theft from the person, "care must be taken to ensure that these offences are not displaced to neighbouring areas . . . with partial or no camera coverage" (Brown, 1995: vi and vii). The problem for CCTV, as for all risk-based strategies, therefore, is to ensure equity between the different elements of the aggregate victim population.

The supplementation of enforcement-led policing with dispersed responsibility and risk management produces a potentially unstable and inequitable system of street policing. There are two aspects to this problem. First, as Scarman (1981) recognised, the potential for disorder arises when the public regard particular enforcement strategies as illegitimate. To that extent, legitimate enforcement—and, for that matter, police legitimacy—are predicated upon some communal expectation of fairness in police practice. However, this raises a second issue. The strategy of dispersed responsibility, which calls upon people to protect themselves and to contract with commercial companies for their own security, reflects a move to what has been called "the death of the social" (Rose,

1996): the development of privatised modes of policing and crime prevention, and with them, the relative contraction of social and public forms of provision. In these circumstances, the respectable community, far from being a residue of public legitimacy, becomes more and more an incoherent aggregation of subscribing consumers and active citizens. By contrast, the incoherence of less respectable communities—those areas now considered to be dangerous places—has its roots in structural inequality, economic redundancy, social exclusion and political marginality. This process of desocialisation—the poor disengaged from the social realm by exclusion, and the rich by consumption—begs a question. How is public legitimation (and public order) to be established in a system where the civil sphere is in a process of decline? In the long run, the answer to this question assumes the reconstitution of civic culture and the construction of a new (albeit diversified) mandate between the public and those diverse bodies engaged in the provision of safety and security. However, short-term alternative police solutions have been put forward. One of these, Zero Tolerance, which is particularly influential at present, is based on he premise that the control of street crime is, first and foremost, a problem of order maintenance.

Zero Tolerance Policing

Zero Tolerance policing came to public prominence in 1994 when William Bratton was appointed commissioner of the New York Police Department. Zero Tolerance was based upon the principles outlined in Wilson and Kelling's ''Broken Windows'' thesis of a decade earlier (Wilson and Kelling, 1982). Here, it was argued that community toleration of minor incivilities such as window-breaking, drunkenness, graffiti, public urination and begging gave rise to a spiral of community decline, an escalation of fear and the encouragement of more serious forms of criminal activity. Bratton's campaign combined two initiatives. First, police were ordered to arrest peddlers, drunks, vandals and others and then to run computer checks on them. Secondly, officers were required to police those ''quality of life'' offences that were allegedly the source of more serious crimes. As Bratton put it, ''Quality of life offences are like a melanoma. They indicate a more serious cancer underneath. You can't treat one without treating the other'' (Gibbons, 1996: 19).

The success claimed for Zero Tolerance over a two-year period in New York—serious crime falling by one-third, murders by almost one-half, motor crime by 40%, robberies by 32% and burglaries by 24% (Gibbons, 1996)—has led to its application elsewhere. For example, in Houston, Texas, during a ten-day period in December 1995, an estimated 10,000 people were stopped by the police, 1,015 of whom were arrested (*Boston Globe*, 1996). Its impact across the Atlantic has also been significant. In England, Zero Tolerance has been implemented throughout the Cleveland force area and in the King's Cross district of London. In the Republic of Ireland where, at the time of writing, an election is also imminent, a major public debate has arisen following Fianna

Fàil's expression of commitment to the philosophy (*Irish Times*, 1997). In Scotland, an initiative is under way in the Strathclyde force area (Potter, 1996a, 1996b) that aims to "reduce serious and in particular violent crime through identifying and tackling minor issues" (Orr, 1997: 115). Here, the 11 areas spotlighted as the focus of major public concern range from street robberies and carrying offensive weapons to truancy, drinking in public places and public nuisance offences such as dropping litter.

In Britain, as in the USA, the debate about Zero Tolerance has been highly politicised. The Labour Party's vocal support for the policy has been particularly controversial, critics seeing it as an unscrupulous form of populist politics. When, in the summer of 1995, Jack Straw pledged to "reclaim the streets from the aggressive begging of winos, addicts and squeegee merchants (cited in Travis, 1997:8), some felt that his comment amounted to a reversal of traditional Labour concern for the needs of the homeless. That suspicion was further fuelled in January 1997 when Party Leader Tony Blair, after suggesting that the homeless should be provided with "somewhere to go," added the culpably ambiguous addendum: "Yes, it is right to be intolerant of people homeless on the streets" (*The Big Issue*, 7 January 1997).

Liberal sensibilities have been further provoked by the fact that some leading proponents of Zero Tolerance seem to revel in the worst excesses of macho cop culture. A recent article ("*I Am the Law*") on Detective Chief Inspector (DCI) Ray Mallon, initiator of Zero Tolerance in Cleveland—shown in a recent TV documentary pumping iron in the police gymnasium—sets the tone by asking the question, "Is this man Britain's toughest cop?" (Bouquet, 1997). Mallon's claim to be the leading contender for that title was confirmed when, following his appointment as head of the Middlesbrough Criminal Investigation Department (CID), he stated that, if crime did not fall by 20% within 18 months, he and his two detective inspectors would ask to be relieved of their duties. In fact, within the first three months of the strategy being adopted in Middlesbrough, it was claimed that rates of recorded crime had fallen by 22% (Dean, 1997a).

As in the New York and Strathclyde examples, the Middlesbrough initiative focuses on a number of primary concerns: house burglary, antisocial behaviour by young people (particularly the intimidation of passers-by and the riding of motorcycles or bicycles on pavements) and quality of life offences such as dropping litter. However, Mallon's interpretation of the Wilson and Kelling thesis is a very particular one. His argument is not merely that broken windows create the preconditions for crime in general, but that they predispose individuals to engage in a criminal career:

> A burglar starts at ten or eleven years old but . . . not . . . as a burglar. He starts when he is hanging round on street corners . . . he does anti-social things, such as intimidating residents . . . smashing . . . window[s] and spraying graffiti . . . he allows himself to be carried [in a stolen car]. Next time he steals the car himself. Then he does his first break-in. (Mallon cited in Dean, 1997b: 17)

Mallon's conception of Zero Tolerance policing is concerned then with halting the progression of individual criminal careers. However, it also has a wider, symbolic function involving the imposition of discipline on the streets. As Mallon puts it, if a youth rides his bike on a pavement or drops litter in front of a police officer, "that officer must do something about it there and then" (Mallon cited in Dean, 1997b: 18) or risk losing his or her authority and, with it, public confidence. By imposing immediate discipline over unruly youths, officers may restore public confidence in the police and halt the spiral of antisocial behaviour and incivility that pervades the streets.

Significantly, however, Zero Tolerance in Cleveland has to be considered part of a wider policing strategy whose ultimate objective is the implementation of a socially informed policy of Problem Oriented Policing (POP). In this case, Zero Tolerance is regarded as a short-term approach designed to remove troublemakers from the streets prior to the introduction of POP (Romeanes, 1996): "[It] clears the ground for problem oriented policing . . . [and] . . . allows the officers to reimpose their authority in an area. . . . When you get the streets back, it is a case of what you do with them" (Romeanes cited in Dean, 1997b: 23). In April 1997, following a six-month experiment in the town of Billingham, POP was introduced to Cleveland on a forcewide basis.

The implementation of Zero Tolerance in Britain has provoked a major debate about its potential impact (Johnston, 1997; O'Mahony, 1997; Pollard, 1997; Potter, 1996c; Read, 1997; Chaudhary and Walker, 1996). First, there has been dispute as to whether reductions in recorded crime can be attributed solely to the initiative. Here, several critical claims have been made: that officers in New York fiddled the crime figures; that reductions in crime were related to declining crack cocaine use, to a reduction in the size of the young male population and to the fact that mandatory sentencing had already removed many criminals from the streets; and that organizational factors (including management reforms, the application of information technology and the deployment of increased numbers of officers) were primarily responsible for any positive effects arising from the programme. In addition, it has been pointed out that other jurisdictions—such as San Diego (Pollard, 1997)—have enjoyed similar reductions in recorded crime using very different policing methodologies. Secondly, it has been pointed out that Zero Tolerance might produce a range of negative effects: a rapid and costly expansion in the size of the prison population; a serious reduction in the scope of police officer discretion; a withdrawal of police officers from concentration on more serious crimes; and a dangerous targeting of ethnic and other minority populations that might, in turn, lead to a major deterioration in police-public relations.

To fully understand the significance of Zero Tolerance, however, it is necessary to go back to the original Broken Windows thesis (Wilson and Kelling, 1982). Wilson and Kelling's paper is, in fact, both profound and shallow. On the one hand, it argues correctly that crime, fear and insecurity are connected to matters of routine male incivility on the streets. On the other hand, it makes the erroneous assumption that the problems of a declining civic culture can be ameliorated merely by modifying the police's approach to order maintenance. Not only does this argument overestimate the reforming potential of policing, it invites the same heavy-handed modes of police activity associated with Swamp '81. Interestingly, one British commentator, having rightly depicted Zero Tolerance as "community policing with the gloves off" (Waddington, 1997), follows that definition to its logical conclusion, suggesting that the anti-terrorist stop and search powers available under the Prevention of Terrorism (Provisional Powers) Act of 1974 "should be extended to all areas plagued by street crime" (Waddington, 1996: 17). Yet, this is to invite the very contradiction between law enforcement and order maintenance identified by Scarman. As Pollard (1997), himself a chief constable, says, the emotion underlying Zero Tolerance "seems to be concentrated on aggression: on ruthlessness in dealing with low level criminality and disorderliness; of [*sic*] 'rapid response,' 'searches, sweeps and arrests' . . . and of [*sic*] the single-minded pursuit of short-term results" (Pollard, 1997: 44)

The effect of that emotion will be to increase tensions between the police and those whom they police, raising the risk that a single incident will—as in virtually all of the British riots of the 1980s—ignite the fuse of disorder. Zero Tolerance is, in other words, the site of a fundamental contradiction. Moreover, the possibility that such a contradiction may be resolved by bolting on an alternative policing methodology (POP) is, at best, unproved and, at worst, unlikely. There are two reasons for that. First, there is the problem of how to resolve the conflicting organizational demands the different methodologies will inevitably place upon police officers. Secondly, despite claims to the contrary, it is difficult to see how the aggressive and "single-minded pursuit of short-term results" is a fitting preparation for a long-term programme of socially oriented policing.

CONCLUSION

Zero Tolerance, whether combined with POP or not, is likely to exacerbate street-level disorder, thereby confirming the accuracy of Scarman's diagnosis. Having borrowed Zero Tolerance from the United States, British police would do well to learn the full extent of the American experience. For if aggressive enforcement by civil police increases the risks of civil disorder, the likely consequence will be the increased militarisation of civil policing. Kraska and Kappeler (1997) cite an illuminating comment from a local US police commander on the increased role of police paramilitary units in routine patrol:

> We conduct a lot of saturation patrol. We do . . . "aggressive field interviews." . . . The key to our success is that we're an elite fighting team that's not bogged down in the regular bureaucracy. We focus on "*quality of life*" issues like illegal parking, loud music, bums, neighbor troubles. . . . Our tactical enforcement team works nicely with our de-

partment's emphasis on community policing. (Kraska and Kappeler, 1997: 13: emphasis in original)

Zero Tolerance does not then provide a solution to the problem of Broken Windows. The assumption that civility can be imposed by any single solution—in this case the aggressive exercise of police discipline—is, like all single solutions,[6] mistaken. Incivility—together with the crime, fear and insecurity connected to it—arises within a complex of social, economic and political conditions. In Britain, these conditions include the economic exclusion and political marginalisation of some sections of society; the fragmentation of traditional social divisions and structures; the redefinition and reconfiguration of communities; the domination of socially and publicly oriented modes of governmental thinking by market-led discourses; and the reduction of local democratic influence by a state that has dispersed key responsibilities amongst a plethora of non-elected agencies. One effect of these conditions—particularly the last—has been a diminution in the role of local civil society. Incivility has then to be understood not merely as the individual pathology of adolescent males from dysfunctional families, but also as a product of long-term social, moral and governmental changes affecting civil society. The key to civility on the streets lies in good government rather than in strong enforcement. Civil society cannot be resurrected by the civilising mission of Zero Tolerance policing.

NOTES

1. The decision made by Sir Paul Condon, Commissioner of the Metropolitan Police, in 1995 to identify young blacks as the main source of street offending—without simultaneous comment on black victimisation rates—suggests that nothing much has changed. In this case, the audience to which the commissioner was appealing was probably rank-and-file police officers, rather than the London public.
2. More recent research undertaken since the implementation of the Police and Criminal Evidence Act of 1984 also suggests that blacks—especially young blacks—experience disproportionate rates of stop and search (Norris et al., 1992; Skogan, 1990).
3. "Sus," short for "suspected person," is a term used to describe legislation which allowed people to be stopped and searched merely on the grounds that they were "loitering with intent to commit a felony." The power was said to have been widely misused by the police.
4. A recently initiated scheme at the University of Newcastle provides escort services for women students walking through the city at night. Citizen street patrols may be focussed on general crime prevention (the Guardian Angels) or on the protection of particular groups (the Guardian Asians).
5. This despite evidence doubting the impact of police patrol on crime and fear of crime. For a recent discussion see Loader (1997).
6. See, for example, attempts to explain incivility and criminality in terms of those pathological family forms said to be associated with the underclass (Dennis and Erdos, 1992).

CHAPTER 3

Violent Business? Networking, Terrorism and Organised Crime

W.A. TUPMAN

The study of terrorism involves questions about the legitimacy of the state and the morality of challenging it by violent means. Although individual terrorists are charged before the courts with individual criminal acts, there is an acceptance that the phenomenon is primarily political and that it is possible to debate the relationship between a just cause and the employment of illegal means to achieve it.

At first sight, issues of legitimacy have no place in a study of organised crime. The cause is purely related to personal gain, the means used are both illegal and immoral and no serious debate is possible over the morality of the phenomenon. Free-market libertarians, however, are beginning to argue that organised crime is just another form of business, and that the cause of improving an imperfect market mechanism justifies breaking the law (Angell, 1996).

This chapter seeks to take the debate a stage further by considering the degree to which a terrorist group in order to survive will tend to obtain funds by resorting to methods copied from organised crime. It notes that, at the same time, organised crime may be copying the cellular structure associated with terrorist organisations. Implicit in the discussion is an argument that some sort of convergence may be taking place.

Other questions raised by this chapter involve the relevance to the study of terrorism and organised crime of the concept of networks, or loose associations of individuals and groups, as opposed to concepts of centralised, hierarchical organisation. For example, how terrorist is terrorism? An organisation may be called terrorist because it engages in acts of paramilitary violence. Those organisations that survive for a significant period of time, however, do so by engaging in many activities other than paramilitary violence. For instance, they have to fund themselves; they have to recruit; they have to train; and they have to engage in peaceful political activity. The individuals that engage in these latter activities are much more loosely organised than the individuals that engage in paramilitary violence, yet they are associated with them in a non-hierarchical relationship.

Similarly it is possible to inquire how criminal is an organised crime group? Increasingly it consists of networks of people who may only come together for a specific operation and the rest of the time may be engaged in completely different organisations and completely different and even legal work, especially where these individuals are lawyers or accountants. The same individuals engaged collectively in illegal activity may also simultaneously be engaged collectively in legal activity.

This in turn raises the question, how organised is organised crime? Equally, how organised is terrorism? Post-1968 terrorism in Northern Ireland has been based on five-man cells, or Active Service Units (ASUs), which are operationally autonomous. Individual cells may be engaged in their own fundraising as well as other activities quite independently of the central Army Council, the body that allegedly runs the Irish Republican Army (IRA). There has been discussion in the literature about organised crime adopting a cellular structure and copying from terrorist organisations. This leads back to the question, how hierarchical are terrorist and organised crime structures? Van Duyne has even described them as ''non-organised'' (Van Duyne, 1993: 10).

This chapter examines these issues in the UK context, while giving a general overview of UK terrorism and fund-raising activities. A discussion of how the IRA funds itself is central to the chapter. The author is engaged in a long-term study of cross-border crime and police response.

DEFINITIONS

What is terrorism? In brief, the expression may be defined as activities and tactics of which the writer or speaker disapproves. Sometimes the meaning of the word can be extended simply to cover a cause of which the writer disapproves. Writers on terrorism fall into two schools: those who extend the term to include all forms of political violence and those who use a narrower definition that relates it to political violence intended to intimidate (Arblaster, 1977: 416). Because of the polemical and ideological nature of much of the writing on terrorism, there is no universal definition of terrorism. Inconsistencies in the literature occur because most commentators wish to include some groups as terrorist and exclude others whom they see as freedom fighters, on the grounds of legitimacy.

Thus American commentators wish to exclude the mujahedeen in Afghanistan and the IRA and include the Palestine Liberation Organisation (PLO), the Vietcong and similar groups who have had an impact on US citizens. Middle East commentators have great difficulty with the notion of Islamic fundamentalism as a source of terrorism and consider the use of the term evidence of the antagonism of Western commentators towards their religion. Egyptian commentators wish to distinguish between the PLO, which they see as a legitimate group, and the Popular Front for the Liberation of Palestine–General Council (PFLP-GC), the group around Abu Nidal, which they see as illegitimate. Although the question of when it is legitimate to resort to violence and when it is not is a fascinating one and has a history dating back to Aristotle, it does serve to obscure the actuality that terrorism is merely a set of tactics neither evil nor good in themselves that are used by certain political organisations at certain times. No organisation that employs terrorist tactics will ever spend all its time engaging in such tactics to the total exclusion of all other forms of activity.

A number of issues in the study of terrorism are relevant to the themes of this chapter. The first is, what sort of violence is terrorist violence? Does it have to involve paramilitary methods and the technology of warfare, or can terrorist violence involve baseball bats, clubbings, petrol-soaked rags through doors and other less sophisticated forms of violence? This question is not only relevant to violent political activity by the extreme right wing but also to punishment beatings during the IRA cease-fire, which Protestant politicians and others see as evidence of continuing IRA activity. The second is, how organised does violence have to be to be terrorism? Are there really command hierarchies; are there autonomous systems and five-man cells or active service units, or is the whole thing much more loosely organised with individuals becoming part of particular operations at particular times but not necessarily part of a coherent permanent organisational structure? This latter question is very similar to the theoretical question, how organised is organised crime?

There are similar questions regarding organised crime. The literature is divided into one perspective that sees it as involving foreign structures within a state, another that defines it by its employment of violence as a "state within a state" and a contemporary perspective that argues that it is simply individuals who wish to make money in ways made illegal by the laws of their state (Chu, 1996): "Governments in Waiting," as a recent conference speaker put it (Angell, 1996).

As already stated, the issues are similar to those concerning terrorism: how criminal is it? How organised or hierarchical is it? How violent does it have to be? What sort of crimes does it have to be involved in? Finally, why do we wish to draw a distinction between terrorism and organised crime? Does the nobility of the cause excuse the criminality of the actions?

UK BACKGROUND

Table 3.1 reflects the author's definitional discomfort. In the real world, there may sometimes be occasions when a group of people engage totally in some form of paramilitary activity to the exclusion of all other forms of activity. Nevertheless, this is rare. Terrorism is better seen as a set of tactics used by individuals, loose associations of people and tightly organised, cellularly struc-

Table 3.1
Types of Terrorism and Terrorist Activity

Type of Group or Scenario	Examples
Domestic Terrorism	
1. Anti-colonial	None inside UK since 1922
2. Ethnic religious and cultural minorities	Scotland: SRA, SNLA, Tartan Army, Army of the Provisional Government of Scotland Wales: FWA, MAC, MOG Cornwall: An Gof Immigrant communities: BLA, Sikh groups
3. Ideological minorities, Left	Angry Brigade; Freedom Fighters for All
4. Ideological minorities, Right	SS Wotan 18, Combat 18
5. Double minorities	Northern Ireland: PIRA/INLA v. UVF/UDA/UFF
6. Urban guerrilla	None outside Northern Ireland context
International Terrorism	
7. Exiles	Spanish anarchists, PFLP, PFLP-GC
8. Exiles' auxiliaries	Angry Brigade
9. Internationalists	None
10. Catspaws	Libyan individuals
11. Counter revolutionaries	None
12. Islamic fundamentalists	None known
13. Unorganised imitators	Many in mid-1970s, few now

List of Acronyms: SRA—Scottish Republican Army. SNLA—Scottish National Liberation Army. FWA—Free Welsh Army. MAC—Mudiad Amddiffyn Cymru. MOG—Meibion Owain Glyndwr. An Gof is not an acronym. It is Cornish and describes the trade of the last leader of a Cornish demonstration. BLA—Black Liberation Army. PIRA—Provisional Irish Republican Army. INLA—Irish National Liberation Army. UVF—Ulster Volunteer Force. UDA—Ulster Defence Association. UFF—Ulster Freedom Fighters. PFLP—Popular Front for the Liberation of Palestine. PFLP-GC—Popular Front for the Liberation of Palestine–General Council.

tured political parties. Some of these people are engaged in promoting a single issue, others in seeking to supplant a government. The former are thus better thought of as armed pressure groups, the latter as armed political parties. The categorisation above derives from the European experience and in its original incarnation was intended to distinguish between phenomena on the basis of the purposes of the violence (Tupman, 1987a, 1987b). Thus categories 2, 3 and 4 form a set related to armed pressure group activity. Categories 1, 6 and 11 are more clearly armed parties. Category 5 is close to civil war, and categories 7, 8, 9, 10 and 12 are phenomena related to international relations. Category 11 has usually involved state sponsorship of groups against a recent revolutionary regime and cross-border activity. Examples are groups such as the Contras in Nicaragua, and the Iranian mujahedeen, which demonstrate that such groups are not always US-sponsored and anti-Marxist. Category 13 is simply an interesting side effect of a paramilitary campaign. Any real-world group of people or cause can move between categories over time or even overlap categories at a particular time.

The framework has been updated to recognise a generally accepted division between domestic and international or transnational terrorism (Wardlaw, 1989: 50). The analysis that follows will concentrate on UK domestic terrorism after 1968, except where there is a link between a domestic group or scenario and an international group or scenario. The main focus is thus on categories 1 through 5.

Anti-colonial groups are not a major problem in the UK in the post-1968 period. With the exception of the Irish groups up to 1922, anti-colonial terrorism within the UK has hardly existed. The imperial experience of the British security forces, however, is quite considerable. From 1950 on the Malayan emergency, the Mau-Mau in Kenya, the insurrection in Aden and the conflict in Dhofar on the borders between Aden and Oman led to the production of a number of significant counterinsurgent strategies associated with names like Kitson and Thomson. Some Americans may consider events in Northern Ireland after 1968 to be an anti-colonial "war of liberation," but this represents a major misunderstanding of the nature of the majority population in Northern Ireland. Anti-colonial struggles against other colonial powers (most frequently in recent times the cause of an independent East Timor) occasionally impinge on British politics.

The UK has suffered from a whole series of terrorist incidents associated with ethnic, religious or cultural minorities. In Scotland the Tartan Army was probably the most prominent and flourished in the mid-1970s. There have also been episodes involving the Scottish National Liberation Army, the Scottish Republican Army and the Army of the Provisional Government of Scotland. With the exception of a small cell based in Stirling University none of these have amounted to very much, and the police have found it fairly easy to identify group members and deal with them through the courts in the normal way (Degenhardt, 1983: 497–8). The major Scottish problem has, in fact, been links with the Ulster Protestant paramilitaries (*Searchlight*, 1986: 11–13; *Searchlight*, 1988: 5).

Wales, however, has suffered a greater level of activity. The Free Welsh Army was hoodwinked in the famous Fishguard trawler episode of 1967 (*Sunday Times* Insight Team, 1997); Meibion Owain Glyndwr (MOG) and Mudiad Amddiffyn Cymru (MAC) maintained a high level of activity, mostly by firebombing second homes in North Wales and later by firebombing Conservative party offices and estate agents. Police action seems to have disrupted these organisations successfully, although a celebrated trial ended in not guilty verdicts. There were allegedly connections with Northern Ireland here again, especially in the provision of explosive technology (*Times*, 14 April 1990, 17 April 1990; *Times*, 8 March 1993, 10 March 1993).

Another small group, An Gof, was active in Cornwall at various times, but the movement split in the mid-1970s and violence seems to have departed the Cornish nationalist movement. Meibion Kernow wins the odd council seat and, to all intents and purposes, satisfies Cornish aspirations by so doing (Degenhardt, 1983: 497).

Thus, the above groups, though active, have not sustained their violence over a period of time or achieved any high level of operational capability, with the exception of the Welsh firebombers. Again, with this exception, there has been no serious requirement of funding for a relatively large organisation or for the import of weaponry or explosives. Links with organised crime are possible in that one or two of the anarchists allegedly involved in paramilitary activity in South Wales have spent time in jail after being involved in various escapades in London.

One curious incident from the early 1970s illustrates the problem of differentiating between terrorism and organised crime. A group of Afro-Caribbeans were caught in the act of robbing a restaurant in South London. They promptly held the staff hostage and claimed to be the Black Liberation Army (BLA). A siege developed, known in the literature as "the Spaghetti House Siege." Subsequently, at the trial it was claimed that the BLA did not exist and that the accused were simply criminals who wished to rob the restaurant for personal gain. It was frequently said at the time among cannabis users, "If you want to buy dope north of the river, you have to deal with the IRA. South of the river it's the Black Liberation Army." The author heard this said before the Spaghetti House Siege happened. In the late 1960s there were those who argued that crime was a revolutionary act. Abbie Hoffman for instance wrote a tract entitled *Steal This Book* (Hoffman, 1971). Theft was considered an act of liberation of a piece of property, so revolutionary movements from this period did not draw the boundary between crime and revolutionary activity in the same place as the legal system does. The theft of explosives, cars or money was a necessary part of the activity of such groups.

The most serious religion-related terrorism has been in the Sikh community where Sikh temples have been intimidated into providing funding for a resistance movement opposed to the Indian government and the fight for an independent Sikh state. Deaths have occurred in this campaign, most notably during the occupation and siege of the Golden Temple in Amritsar, but there are no known links with organised crime groups in the UK. There are allegations of links between members of the organisation and cocaine smuggling rings in South America, but it is always difficult to know the degree to which this is government propaganda against their cause (*Times*, 16 June 1984; *Sunday Times*, 1 December 1995). However, the organisation has managed to continue in existence, and it appears to have sufficient funds and weaponry at its disposal. If the argument outlined below is correct then it will have done so by using the methods of organised crime to fund itself.

Cultural minorities such as new age travellers and festival goers seeking to keep alive the spirit of the 1960s have tended to possess an ideology of peaceful protest and are thus not usually relevant here, although their involvement in various activities is fairly well documented. However well the occasional violent confrontation with the police may be documented, it would be stretching the various and exotic definitions of terrorism to include a wish to live in tepees in the fields and smoke marijuana.

Left wing ideological minorities, though often stereotyped as terrorist, in fact have played little part in terrorism in the UK. Avoiding the definitional problems of left and right wing, for the purpose of this classification system, this category includes Trotskyites, Maoists and anarchists who resort to paramilitary violence. The anarchist groups, The Angry Brigade and Freedom Fighters for All, have been the only major groups to engage in bombing and issuing communiques in a significant way. The Angry Brigade appears to have funded its initial efforts by offering to carry out symbolic attacks on Spanish property for the Spanish Anarchists opposing General Franco. In return for carrying out these attacks, it would receive explosives to carry out its own agenda. Since it consisted of one, or at most two, cells there was no extensive organisation that required funding, nor was there a sustained operation over a long period of time (Carr, 1975). Freedom Fighters for All made the mistake of organising their campaign to occur simultaneously with the opening of the IRA's mainland campaign in October 1973. This group was quickly cleaned up in the heightened level of police activity that followed the more serious bombings elsewhere in the country (*Black Flag*, 1973, 1974). Again, therefore, funding does not appear to come into the equation. According to *Black Flag*, a group of anarchists was accused of conspiring to carry out a social security fraud as a means of funding persons unknown to take part in terrorist activities, but this made no major splash outside the anarchist press (*Black Flag*, 1974). It does raise the question raised earlier by the Spaghetti House siege: where the terrorists see crime as an essential and justifiable part of their revolutionary activity, can academics set a tight boundary between organised crime and terrorism?

The Trotskyite Fourth International, which elsewhere in the world went over to paramilitary activity, in the UK flirted briefly with Northern Ireland, but after the death of one or two activists returned rather rapidly to its more normal role in student agitation. There was no killing by armed police of unarmed demonstrators, which provided the impetus for violent terrorist cells elsewhere in Europe, and which usually bore the name of the date on which the demonstrator had been killed, such as June the 2nd or May the 15th.

Right wing violence, contrary to the work of most authors on the subject, has been much more widespread in the UK than violence by the ultra-left. It tends to be ruled out as terrorism because it is rarely paramilitary in the sense of involving high-technology attacks. It consists mainly of attacks on individual members of ethnic minority communities, bookshops and prominent left wingers, the intention of which is to intimidate these communities as a whole. This certainly fits in with at least one definitional school of terrorism. *Searchlight* documented a horrifying number of attacks of this sort, and numbers of individual groups of right wingers were brought to trial (*Searchlight*, 1985). This was not depicted by the press or academics as a whole as terrorism, although Paul Wilkinson did write a short book entitled *The New Fascists* (Wilkinson, 1981). Funding on the right has tended to come from prominent wealthy retired or semi-retired sympathisers, but according to *Searchlight*, the British Movement under Michael McLaughlin became very much involved in business activities. Later, McLaughlin set himself up as a wholesaler of militaria and survivalism supplies and retired from leadership of the British Movement (*Searchlight*, 1983: 5).

All this pales, however, in comparison with the Northern Irish groups, which fall into the double minority category—a category not of this author's invention but an adaptation of Robert Moss's coinage in his book *Urban Guerillas* (Moss, 1972). The problem of Ireland is that the Protestants form a minority in the island as a whole, which is predominately Catholic, but in the six counties that form Northern Ireland, the Protestants form the majority and the Catholics the minority. Thus both sides can claim to be the majority. On the side of the cause for a single 32-county state in the island of Ireland, the Provisional IRA (PIRA) and the Irish National Liberation Army (INLA) have been the main paramilitary protagonists, although INLA split at one stage, and Saor Eire has also been significant at times. On the side of continuing union with the United Kingdom, the Ulster Defence Association (UDA), with its *nom de guerre* of the Ulster Freedom Fighters (UFF), and the Ulster Volunteer Force (UVF) have been responsible for the majority of violence. There have also been other groups, such as the shadowy Ulster Resistance Movement and the Red Hand commandos.

IRA FUNDRAISING

In the late 1980s or early 1990s, Rowan Bosworth-Davies and Barry Rider persuaded the author to produce a series of presentations on money laundering and terrorism. From this emerged a spoof prospectus for the IRA PLC (Public Limited Company), which has recently been shamelessly plagiarised by journalists without attribution. Table 3.2 represents an updated version of the prospectus.

The problem with discussing the income and expenditure of the IRA is propaganda. It clearly suits the security forces to portray the IRA as no more than another organised crime group. This is of course a distorted picture of the IRA, which is not primarily in business to make money but needs to make money in order to stay in business. Indeed, although ''IRA PLC'' is a catchy title, it would be more correct to talk of ''Republican Movement PLC.'' Indeed Irish politicians prefer this latter term. The former title gives the impression that the IRA controls all branches of the Republican movement, and this cannot safely be asserted. Sinn Fein, Cumann nam Ban (the women's movement), social clubs, Gaelic Sports associations, the Catholic ex-Servicemen's Association, prisoners' support groups and various businesses are all organisations within a broader movement. Who controls whom, who interacts with whom and how are not only matters for research but occasionally matters disputed before the courts. The money-making ventures alluded to in the prospectus may or may not be under the control of the Army Council, may or may not pay a percentage to the Army Council and may or may not take place in areas considered to be under Republican movement control.

Related problems may indeed appear frequently on the agenda of IRA Army Council meetings. How far should they engage in fundraising, and how far in armed operations? Should the same personnel be involved in both? Should they be kept totally separate? How can they be used against the movement as propaganda? The essence of every act of terrorism is propaganda. Terrorism could be said to be simply armed propaganda. So fundraising in itself presumably could be used as a weapon to undermine the British state. Fraud committed against the Northern Ireland Housing Department would be legitimate, as would fraud against the Ministry of Agriculture, Food and Fisheries, customs duties evasion and similar activities. Fraud against domestic Irish credit unions would presumably be unacceptable.

Dealing drugs in the UK might also be acceptable, while dealing drugs in Belfast would not be. Discussions by the author with senior police officers have indicated that the Royal Ulster Constabulary (RUC) denies any involvement in IRA drug dealing, whereas police officers from further south are certain that IRA personnel are involved in trafficking if not in street dealing. Certainly the IRA has taken a leaf out of the pages of their Basque colleagues Euskadita Askatasuna (ETA) in gaining popular support by kneecapping or placing orders of exile on well-known drug dealers in Belfast, Derry city and elsewhere. Similarly, what the British security forces would call protection rackets, the IRA would say are in the nature of a revolutionary tax, again following the Basque model.

Another problem discussing this subject is the nature of the sources. Various officers of the RUC and Garda Siochana have kindly briefed study groups led by the author in the past, but where documentary material has been shown, it

Table 3.2
IRA PLC Company Report

IRA PLC
Company Activities

A small international company providing executive and leisure services to the British Isles and North West Europe. Overseas offices in the United States and Australia. Courier services available to various parts of the world.

Subsidiary companies provide construction and demolition services. IRA PLC also franchises clubs and a "get you home" service. Private security services also provided for housing estates. Insurance quotations against bomb damage can also be brokered.

The company has recently secured a niche in the import-export market, particularly of livestock and CDs.

Statement of income

Contributions from overseas subsidiaries		£1,500,000
Shebeen subsidiaries: bar and machines		£4,275,000
Import-export business		£2,250,000
Fire and bomb damage insurance [Protection PLC]		£6,150,000
Construction		£5,000,000
Involuntary bank and post office contributions		£1,250,000
	Total cash	£20,425,000
Non-cash contributions		
Demolition equipment and executive toys		£1,500,000

Statement of expenditure

Executives in UK [4]	Salaries		£80,000
Warehouse and support staff in UK [20]	Salaries		£400,000
Transport and accommodation			£200,000
		Sub-total	£680,000
Executives in Northern Ireland	Salaries		£400,000
Warehouse and support staff	Salaries		£600,000
		Sub-total	£1,000,000
	Balance		**£1,680,000**
Pay-outs from executive family insurance fund			£2,000,000
Semi-retired staff in Eire [50]			£1,000,000
	Balance		**£4,680,000**
Investments			£15,000,000
	Balance		**£19,680,000**
Petty cash fund			£745,000
	Total		**£20,425,000**

has been on a confidential basis. The figures given in Table 3.2 have had to be justified by reference to press sources, and these are often dubious. At one stage the stories were all about security forces' successes against the IRA's financial network, at another the IRA's links with the US were exaggerated to pressure visiting US politicians. At all times stories are exaggerated to sell newspapers, and the *Sunday Times* clearly thinks IRA scare stories keep its readers interested. Nevertheless, it has received a number of major security forces leaks over the years and devotes more space and depth to Northern Ireland than its broadsheet rivals. The truth problem needs to be borne in mind constantly when considering the pseudodata in the IRA-PLC prospectus.

Returning to the main theme of crime and terrorism: post office and bank raids throughout Ireland appear to be acceptable ways of blooding recruits and finding out how serious their commitment may be. Unattributable briefings given to the author allege that 50% of post office and bank raids in the south have some form of IRA connection. The figure in the table above reflects the total amount stolen in post office and bank raids in Ireland; 50% of that total has been calculated and entered in the table as income (unattrib., 1995).[1]

The figure of contributions from overseas subsidiaries reflects published statements of the North American organisation, Noraid, which vary annually from $160,000 to $800,000 (Bishop and Mallie, 1988: 297). Added to this are contributions from the UK and Australia. Early in the 1970s contributions were also made by Libya (Bishop and Mallie, 1988: 305). This is generally presented as money raised for the welfare of prisoners' families, and it is balanced in the statement of expenditure by an estimate that money to prisoners' families costs the Republican movement as a whole £2 million. This is of course where the problem starts in discussing the legal and illegal aspects of the business of the Republican movement as a whole. Noraid would presumably claim that to support the families of prisoners is legitimate business and in no way relevant to the IRA as an armed illegal organisation. Nevertheless in the table, both these categories are included in the statement of income and expenditure.

Contributions from overseas obviously fluctuate. When the British security forces have carried out high-profile operations, such as the killings in Gibraltar, the contributions tend to rise significantly. Collections are regularly made in various public houses in English and Scottish cities as well as by more formal fund-raising organisations in the United States and Australia. These contributions probably amount to at least £1.5 million. However, very little of this money would have been used to buy weaponry or bomb making equipment in the 1980s, and perhaps the 1970s, because of the munitions smuggled in from Libya during this period (unattrib., 1996). Libya apparently admitted to shipping 130 tonnes of weaponry between 1985 and 1987, of which about half has been found by security forces (*Sunday Times*, 24 December 1995). Iran has also been accused of maintaining a £20 million slush fund in the mid-to late-1980s, of which some went to the IRA (*Sunday Times*, 21 August 1994).

Shebeen subsidiaries are one of the curious consequences of the troubles. During the early 1970s most pubs were bombed out by the Republican side or the loyalist Protestant side. Most pubs were in fact owned by Catholics. As a result shebeens, or illegal unlicensed drinking clubs, grew up as places where the community could drink safely. In the 1970s it was very difficult to tell to what degree these were actually owned by the paramilitaries on either side. It is thus impossible to work out how these enterprises were used for fundraising or for money laundering. In 1989 new regulations were brought in by the RUC anti-racketeering unit to try to estimate the income of gambling machines and other commercial activities to social clubs and compare it with figures reported by the legal accounts of these businesses for taxation purposes (*Sunday Times*, 1 August 1993). Again it is hard to determine where the Republican movement ends and the IRA begins. Where these bars are run by committees from the community, and everything is done in a legal fashion, they may simply be paying protection to the IRA.

The heading ''Import-export business'' in Table 3.2 covers the increasing allegations that the IRA is involved in the import of counterfeit computer software, videos and music CDs. The security forces apparently attribute this to their success in clamping down on the drinking clubs, which they estimate has cost the IRA £7 million per annum (*Sunday Times*, 1 August 1993) Therefore, the figure given in the table may be an underestimate for up to 1989 and an overestimate after that date. This introduces the issues about the degree to which the IRA shades into northern and southern Irish organised crime groups and the degree to which propaganda is being engaged in to discredit the movement with the community. Nevertheless an early attempt to estimate income from these activities alleged £1 million per annum from fraud and extortion, £2 million from smuggled goods and video piracy, £750,000 from the black taxis,[2] £500,000 from fruit machines, £250,000 from charities and £250,000 from overseas sympathisers (*Sunday Times*, 12 March 1995).

The Unité de Coordination de la Lutte Anti Fraud (UCLAF), the fraud investigation unit of the European Commission, has alleged that the IRA is also involved in the movement of cattle across the border between Ulster and Eire to attract import subsidies and evade various forms of duty (*Irish Independent*, 21 January 1994: 11). If this is being carried out by individual members of families normally associated with IRA membership, it may not necessarily follow that these individuals consider the activity to be IRA activity rather than private enterprise. Again the *Sunday Times* and the *Times* proper linked the IRA to a South African fraud of £41 million (*Times*, 20 May 1995), a US heist of $7 million (*Times*, 15 November 1993), a London bond robbery of £292 million and a US bank fraud of £150 million (*Sunday Times*, 22 May 1994). Table 3.2 above gives a more sober figure.

The *Sunday Times* also has the IRA smuggling £2 million a year in stolen antiques to dealers in the British Midlands; selling illegal growth promoters for cattle, counterfeit designer jeans, computer games and videos; and engaging in major building-site fraud (*Sunday Times*, 1 August 1993). Again, these activities may be taking place, but the IRA is unlikely to have the time or the personnel to run them all. It is much more likely that, like legal businesses, illegal businesses pay a licence fee to the IRA to operate. This is one way of explaining the different signals coming from the security forces on drugs. Indeed, there are suggestions that, in the case of drugs, some of this licensing was freelance. During the cease-fire, the IRA turned to attacking drug dealers to keep its activists battle-hardened, but it was possible to pay local commanders to prevent your name being put forward as a target to be approved by the Army Council (*Sunday Times*, 31 December 1995).

''Fire and Bomb Damage Insurance'' refers to the allegation that various businesses pay money to the IRA to protect themselves from a bombing campaign. The *Sunday Times* alleged that a major bakery chain, for example, paid £2 million a year to the IRA through an international security consultancy to prevent its bakeries from being destroyed. In fact it appears that this was not an annual payment but related to the kidnapping of Don Tidey, an executive (Coogan, 1987: 659). A one-off payment of £2 million for one large business suggests that a total of £6 million for all businesses to insure against kidnapping and bombing is not actually that high, and the income in this area may indeed be higher. The same paper, the *Sunday Times*, in one of its colour supplements, quoted a meeting of black-taxi drivers at which attendees were called on to raise their weekly contribution to £8 (*Sunday Times*, 1996). That would give a contribution figure of £400 per driver per year. Multiplied by the number of drivers a substantial sum of money is involved. Similar calculations may be made for other ad hoc groups of individuals, as well as for small and large businesses, both legal and illegal, around Northern Ireland. But as already mentioned above, the same newspaper has quoted security force sources as calculating an income of £750,000 annum from taxis.

The heading ''Construction'' refers to fraud carried out against the Northern Ireland Housing Office during the reconstruction of bombed buildings. An estimate of £15 million lost has been given in newspapers. There have also been allegations of IRA involvement in social security fraud on the British mainland. Again the problem is that anything with an Irish connection is going to be called IRA.

Turning to the expenditure statement in Table 3.2, the category of ''Executives in the UK'' is based on the assumption that the IRA has moved away from the totally independent five-man cell ASU as their basic unit. They now use surveillance and intelligence teams whose job is to set up particular operations. These are represented by the category ''Warehouse and Support staff.'' Such support staff tend to operate in pairs when actually carrying out a bombing or shooting. The assumption made in the table is that full-time staff would be provided with an income of £20,000 per year, and that the whole team would have access to a budget for hiring, as well as stealing cars, and for obtaining legitimate accommodation.

These figures may be high; on the Northern Ireland side they have been halved on the assumption that the individuals concerned are drawing unemployment benefits or obtaining income from legitimate sources. The security forces estimate that there are about 100 full-time genuinely-IRA units.[3] Table 3.2 doubles that assumption, seeking to err deliberately on the high side. Fifty are allocated to the south of Ireland, 24 to the UK and 100 to Northern Ireland: 40 in the executive role and 60 in the warehouse and support role.

This may be a complete misunderstanding of the way the IRA operates, and the idea that there genuinely are 100 full-time personnel is probably a security force's fantasy. Such an assumption leads to the conclusion that all that has to be done in Northern Ireland is to lock up the 100 people and everything will stop. This is clearly not the case. The notion that there is such a thing as a full-time IRA operative is not borne out by memoirs that have been produced from within the organisation (Collins, 1997). Occasionally it has been alleged that three-quarters of all the personnel in prison for IRA membership in the north of Ireland had actually been in legitimate employment at the time of their imprisonment. On the other hand, the notion that the IRA consists of unemployed personnel hanging around street corners waiting for a bombing to be suggested is a newspaper, rather than a security force's, fantasy.

The obvious point to be deduced from Table 3.2 is that the IRA is actually quite a cheap organisation to run. As the Libyan weapons and explosives cache is exhausted, this will of course change. The second point is that it is a profitable operation. Those profits have been invested somewhere.

The figures given are of course purely speculative, and other more official sources would put the figure at £10 million profit per annum (unattrib., 1995), whereas the estimate here is closer to £15 million. To reiterate a word of caution, these figures probably refer to the Republican movement as a whole, and it *may* be a mistake to leave the reader with the impression that the IRA runs the whole Republican movement. It is certainly a matter of importance to the propagandist.

TERRORISTS IN PRISON: EXCHANGING IDEAS WITH ORGANISED CRIME

The IRA has a long history of involvement with various forms of what we now call money laundering and fraud. Between 1916 and 1922, money was raised for the independence of Ireland, and according to Tim Pat Coogan's biography of Eamonn de Valera, a large proportion of it was siphoned off by de Valera to found a newspaper under his own control. Not only did it remain under his own political control but because he was the majority shareholder, it became his family's business and this lasted until the early 1960s (Coogan, 1993: 417–21). Tim Pat Coogan discusses the legality and morality of this. He also discusses the role of the famous American fundraiser, Joe McGarrity, who kept the IRA going during the 1930s and 1940s (Coogan, 1993: 193–94). There is further discussion of the role of members of the Irish government in the setting up, funding and arming of the IRA after 1968 in another of Tim Pat Coogan's books, simply called *The IRA* (Coogan, 1987).

Certainly the leaders of the Provisional IRA had mostly been in prison during the 1956–1962 campaign and mostly held in English jails because of a refusal to treat them as political prisoners (Coogan, 1987). Without reading their memoirs, if they ever come out, it is impossible to know to what extent they formed links during that period. Joe Cahill, allegedly the IRA's financial expert, was in jail during this period (*Sunday Times*, 28 March 1993). It is more certain, however, that the members of the IRA and other Republican groups arrested during the mainland campaign after 1973 and held in British and Irish jails, rather than the H-blocks, would have had the opportunity to make links with organised crime circles. The criminal spirit of the 1970s and 1980s was certainly entrepreneurship. Research may eventually demonstrate that the real intermediaries were the cannabis dealers of the early 1970s, who saw themselves carrying out an ideological commitment to change society rather than being simply involved in the process of making money.

Howard Marks's autobiography suggests that such thoughts did motivate people like himself, and entrepreneurs in the cities of Cork, Limerick and Dublin would almost certainly have been motivated similarly. His autobiography also describes a network of connections between himself, Jim McCann of the IRA and Dutch interests in the early 1970s (Marks, 1996: 77–107).

Marks actually claims to have pointed out to McCann that, if you can smuggle arms, you can smuggle drugs. The last four shipments from Libya were brought in by a professional smuggler, who was paid a £100,000 fee for arranging shipment (unattrib., 1995). The US fiasco alluded to above also involved an arrangement with an alleged professional arms dealer (Bishop and Mallie, 1988). The arms trade is thus another source of contacts between terrorism and organised crime.

Increasingly in Dublin, Limerick and, to a lesser extent, other towns in Ireland, the IRA finds itself coming into conflict with domestically based organised crime. The shooting of Martin Cahill, ''the General,'' in Dublin in 1994 by the IRA was a clear warning to organised crime that the true holders of the monopoly of violence were neither the state, nor the state within the state of non-political organised crime, but the Provisional IRA (*The Independent*, 12 May 1996). There were allegations in the 1970s that a street career structure went as follows: join the Provisionals as a 16-year-old, graduate to the Official IRA in your mid-20s and move on to crime in your late 20s (unattrib., 1995).

In addition, although it was found by the courts to be a case of CIA entrapment, during a US trial, links were claimed between the American branch of the Republican movement and a figure close to the Mafia in a conspiracy to supply arms to the IRA. The USA is thus another possible place where connections to organised crime might have been created (Bishop and Mallie, 1988: 298).

The business of trade and traffic in drugs needs more research. The cannabis dealers of the late 1960s and early 1970s tended to see themselves as Robin Hoods with leftish political affiliations, tweaking the nose of capitalism and forming part of the process of creating an alternative society (Marks, 1996). They may have contributed to the funds of the IRA in the 1970s, particularly in the post-internment period of 1972 when feelings ran high in both southern and northern Ireland. Obviously it is difficult to research relationships in this or any other period until people start writing their memoirs. Nevertheless, it is alleged that the Provisionals did, briefly, lose a lot of street credibility in the 1970s when they were identified with heroin dealing in Belfast ghettoes and had to remove themselves from the trade very quickly (unattrib., 1995). That they were involved in heroin suggests that they had been involved in other drugs previously, and certainly it has been alleged that they remain involved in trafficking and wholesaling, but not in retailing and street dealing, both south and north of the border. This has been alleged equally of Protestant paramilitaries, and there have been allegations that in drug terms all the paramilitaries actually work together and have the turf well divided up in Northern Ireland (unattrib., 1995). Protestant paramilitary organisation would presumably also reach into the west of Scotland, and IRA organisation reaches down into the south of Ireland. If the intelligence organisations of the paramilitaries are as efficient as they are supposed to be, it is hard to believe that drugs can be sold in the areas under their control without their knowledge.

Like organised crime groups, the IRA seems to have turned increasingly to fraud as a low-risk, high-profit activity. It is a matter for serious research to ascertain whether ideas were exchanged in prison, or whether accountants and lawyers taught the IRA's fundraisers these techniques. In organised crime circles, it often appears that the children of criminals have been trained in these trades and have initiated changes in the modus operandi of the crime families. Perhaps the same family upward mobility operates within Irish Republicanism.

ORGANISED CRIME AND CELLULAR STRUCTURE

The Provisional IRA was in many ways a new organisation and represented a break with previous organisational structures. Most of the political agitators went off with the Official IRA when the split occurred (Beresford, 1979). The hierarchy of the IRA tended to split on family lines—relatives becoming part of the same organisation. On some occasions, a particularly charismatic individual kept a particular area organisation intact and took it into whichever organisation he chose, the Official or the Provisional IRA. Indeed, for some time after the split, in some areas individuals from the two organisations worked together on particular paramilitary operations without any problems (Beresford, 1997). Internment, however, removed most of the old cadres, and a new, younger leadership took over and created a completely new structure.

In the period after the Sunningdale talks of 1973 and the collapse of power sharing in 1974, the Provisional IRA reorganised itself into a series of small ASUs modelled on the classic five-man guerilla cell. It is not clear to what degree this structure ever actually took hold, and to what degree this simply facilitated the move to a much looser network of associations. There still appear to be individual organisations for different parts of the border area. For example, South Armagh appears to be organisationally coherent, as does South Tyrone and perhaps Newry. The organisations in the border areas appear to be suspicious of their nominal superiors in both Belfast and the South and may keep their own fundraising and smuggling operations quite separate from those of the Army Council. (Collins, 1997:ch. 18). It is not clear whether these units are typical or aberrant.

As noted above, there is some evidence of movement away from the ASUs and of the emergence of a network of different individuals specialising in different roles. To that extent, the structure of the IRA appears to be converging with the changing structure of organised crime. A network of specialists is coordinated by some central planner for a one-off purpose or for a more long-term enterprise. Just as organised crime has its enforcers, its specialists in violence, so too does the IRA. Equally, organised crime has its smuggling or transportation specialists. The IRA either has its own specialist or a contract with a specialist from organised crime, as it did to move the consignment of arms and explosives from Libya (unattrib., 1995).

Organised crime increasingly consists of different types of operatives related in different ways to a central organisation. In the area of drugs, for example, there are different levels of dealers down to the non-professional street pusher; the next level up may be the apartment-based dealer, who sells larger quantities to specialist consumers, and the upper levels consist of retailers, wholesalers and even importers. The street dealer may be considered part of the organisation in that there are rules that he will be punished for breaking. On occasion he may find that he is given a particular task to perform by the organisation. Where organised crime groups have created "no go," or high crime, areas, a number of different criminal activities take place. Traditional academic views were that this produced a pyramidal structure of parallel functional hierarchies held together by the violence disposed of by the criminal leadership. Ianni and Ianni (1994) began to demolish this view in *Black Mafia*; now much looser specialist structures and relationships exist, characterised by the nature of the business opportunity.

Similar analytical structures can be applied to Republicanism. In its early street fighting days the bottom of the pyramid was composed of the youngsters who could be relied upon to follow the call to throw stones or to riot—a tactic copied by drug dealers in inner-city areas to keep the police at bay. Above them were the paper sellers and the Sinn Fein members in general, who during the hunger strikes became active in canvassing and other forms of political work.

Above them were the councillors, and in a lateral position, or somewhat above, came the various paramilitaries: logistic specialists (quartermasters with an expanded role), intelligence and reconnaissance specialists, bomb makers and designers and actual bomb planters and assassins.

This picture still presents too hierarchical an impression. In Republican areas today, individuals perform specialist roles; they are not part of a hierarchical command structure. Since the cease-fire, the picture needs to have added to it the "baseball bat enforcers" of community discipline and "the law," in a distortion of community policing. Just like traditional organised crime elsewhere in the world, the IRA increasingly finds itself responsible for law and order and obedience to rules in a particular estate. To some extent the nature of the housing estate structures both the IRA and the organised crime group. With the collapse of policing between 1968 and 1974, and the problems of gaining legitimacy for a paramilitary Royal Ulster Constabulary after 1974, the Provisional IRA found itself charged with more than simply providing the housing estate with security from attack by Protestant gunmen. It also found that it had to increasingly take on police roles such as dealing with petty property crime and anti-social behaviour. The forms of punishment it chose began with tarring and feathering and then developed into a series of different forms of kneecapping. Indeed the IRA is now moving into housing estates north of Dublin by providing vigilante security and policing services. It has always been a truism that where you have organised crime you have very little petty crime, because petty crime is frowned upon by drug dealers and racketeers. This is an area in which there is definite convergence between organised crime and terrorism. The dynamics of excluding police personnel from a given territory produces a need to provide alternative policing structures akin to vigilantism.

Similarly the IRA has had to turn to the methods of organised crime to raise money. At one time armed robbers were the aristocracy of organised crime, and for a period the IRA obtained its funding by committing robberies. As mentioned above this still goes on, but like organised crime groups, the IRA flirted with drugs and now has followed organised crime into the much lower-risk area of fraud—especially cross-border fraud—and the importing of counterfeit products. It has also been suggested that, to obtain guns, vehicles and forged documentation, IRA operatives on the British mainland have begun to pretend to be normal criminals and have "infiltrated the criminal infrastructure" (*The Independent*, 4 March 1996).

THE PROTESTANT PARAMILITARIES

The Protestant paramilitaries had no need to exist between 1922 and the mid-1960s as the forces of law and order were very much behind the Protestant ascendancy. With the advent of the civil rights movement and the conciliatory response from the then Prime Minister of Ulster, Terence O'Neill, the Ulster

Protestant Volunteers were created by the Reverend Dr. Ian Paisley, now (since 1997) the leader of the Democratic Unionist Party (Bruce, 1994: 3).

In 1966 the Ulster Volunteer Force (UVF) was recreated as an urban working class based organisation that did not support Orangeism and other aspects of traditionalist loyalist politics. It drilled, collected weapons and robbed shops and an armoury. Its leadership then languished in jail until 1974. From the inter-communal riots that drove the RUC from the streets of Belfast, the Ulster Defence Association (UDA) emerged as a vigilante organisation.

Both groups engaged in sectarian murder of Catholics during the 1970s but went into decline after the resurgence of the reformed RUC after 1976. The UDA rapidly became synonymous with its *nom de guerre*, the Ulster Freedom Fighters, in whose name the sectarian murders were carried out (Bruce, 1994: 9). These organisations at this stage had very little need for funding because there were many legally held weapons in Protestant hands, and they were able to join the new Ulster Defence Regiment and gain access to training, weapons and intelligence (Bruce, 1994: 14). After the Hillsborough Agreement of 1985, however, many Protestants began to feel betrayed by the RUC, and there were cases of the burning of homes belonging to the police.

Networks of drinking clubs had begun to emerge as early as 1970 and provided a funding basis for the organisation. The rough-and-ready accounting systems of the clubs were used to launder the proceeds of bank robberies, and the Protestant paramilitaries began to branch into other areas: notably, a protection racket on building sites, which brought in hundreds of thousands of pounds (Bruce, 1994: 17). There are allegations of involvement in a whole series of rackets, including prostitution, drugs and pornography as well as the above-mentioned bank robbery and extortion. There is evidence of a tendency for "some of it to stick to the fingers of those that raise it" (Bruce, 1994: 17).

There was also a flirtation with the old apartheid South African government, which linked with the Protestant paramilitaries, made an attempt to obtain British-made Rapier missiles and beat the arms embargo. This particular plot was foiled and the leaders arrested. More recently, allegations have been made in the press that Protestant paramilitaries have either begun to copy the IRA or even to cooperate with them in the sale of counterfeit products to the community.

CONCLUSIONS AND THOUGHTS FOR FURTHER STUDY

Obviously, a great deal of further research is required, and the information on which much of this chapter is based is both controversial and unreliable. Nevertheless, the area requires further study. Long-lived terrorist groups clearly rely on wider popular movements to sustain and support them. Relationships between the members of these groups, who may be families, associates or merely residents in the same area are complex and non-hierarchical. The existence of a central paramilitary organisation means that coercive sanctions are available to impose discipline upon the wider movement, if necessary, although at the same time, there always exists the possibility of rival gangs emerging based on different territorial areas.

The shared political cause can impose an illusion of organisation but can also create the possibility of ideological splits over the goals or the pace of the campaign. This creates a variable distinguishing these groups from organised crime, which may split over which leader to follow, or which business to prioritise, but will never find ideology getting in the way of business. The greater the devotion of manpower resources to fund-raising activities, however, the greater the likelihood the political group will become an organised crime group in fact, though not in name.

Evidence suggests that the form of organisation adopted by both organised crime and terrorism is dictated partly by the nature of police response. The interest in cellular structure and network arrangements is partly to make prosecution on the basis of "shared purpose" difficult to prove. The nature of the business will affect the organisational structures of organised crime as a whole but will affect only the fund-raising structures of terrorist-related movements. The structure of the coercive apparatus will be governed by the relationship between the number of people required to deliver a violent event and the requirements of internal security. The specialised nature of a paramilitary arm of a political movement may make it attractive for organised crime to employ such a group for the purpose of contract enforcement on an occasional basis, but there is no evidence of this as yet. However, there have been allegations that individuals have been used to provide armed escort for consignments.

A group may set out with a political aim. If it cannot raise money, it will not survive. This chapter has discussed many small groups that passed briefly across the British political stage. On the other hand, if a group is successful in raising money but cannot find a peaceful political role for itself, it will increasingly take on the character of the organised crime groups whose methods it copies. History demonstrates that the Triads began with the aim of restoring the Ming dynasty after the Manchu invasion of China in 1644. They have transformed themselves 350 years later into a loose network of cross-border crime groups (Chu, 1996). Similarly the Mafia as a group began by opposing the imposition of a French dynasty on the kingdom of Sicily. Today they too have branched out into other businesses. Could it be that the profit motive will always conquer political goals?

NOTES

1. The citation *unattrib.* refers to a series of unattributable briefings given to the author and his students by individual members of the Royal Ulster Constabulary and the Garda Siochana during study visits to both organisations.

2. A "black taxi" is a term used in Northern Ireland to describe a licensed taxi cab, in appearance the same as a black London taxi. Because of the dangers of sectarian assassination, there are Protestant and Catholic varieties that have largely replaced public transport due to the frequent use of buses as burning barricades. Cab drivers have been killed for sectarian motives and thus genuinely see themselves as in need of protection from the paramilitaries.

3. This estimate has occasionally led to some army and RUC officers telling me, "If the politicians would only let us take 100 of them out, this nonsense would all be over."

CHAPTER 4

Policing in England and Wales

IAN K. MCKENZIE

INTRODUCTION

In 1960, Bruce Smith, a contemporary commentator on American policing, quoted the words of an unnamed chief constable of an English Police Force who told him:

> If the members of an English force were assigned to police an American city, they would all be kidnapped within twenty-four hours; and if American police were transferred to an English jurisdiction, they would promptly be placed under arrest for abuses of police authority. (Smith, 1960: 11)

These words seem to suggest that the alleged benign and avuncular style of the English[1] bobby would be a disadvantage when contrasted with what Reiner (1986) calls the ''freewheeling more aggressive style of policing'' in America, and that the forceful ''in-your-face'' style of American cops would be anathema to a quiet, pacific nation of animal loving hot-tea-with-milk-and-sugar addicts.

In the close to forty years that have passed since those words were spoken, the world has seen much change: wars and rumours of wars, social and societal upheaval, changes in the political map of the world and since, as Bailey (1977) points out, police institutions do not exist independently from their social environment, consequent changes in policing and police activity.

It is the purpose of this chapter to examine the current nature of policing in England and Wales and to attempt (where appropriate), by comparing and contrasting it with contemporary American police literature and experience, to assess the extent to which the words of Smith's anonymous chief constable remain, at the end of the 20th century, an accurate description of the distinction between police activity on *either side of the Atlantic Ocean.*

To that end the chapter examines four principal areas: the structure and organisation of policing, the legal context of policing, the definition of the scope of police work in both countries and the application of force and deadly force.

THE STRUCTURE AND ORGANISATION OF POLICING

Hirschel and Wakefield (1995) point out (in what might almost be called, were they not American, British understatement) that ''England possesses a lengthy historical heritage.'' Those authors start their time frame with the building of Stonehenge almost 4,000 years ago. It is tempting to operate within such a time frame in a discussion of modern policing. However, whilst one may be permitted to tip-one's hat at Saxons, Normans, Tithings, watchmen and Bow Street Runners, an examination of policing in England and Wales should properly start with the foundation of the Metropolitan Police in 1929. (See Hirschel and Wakefield (1995) for a useful overview of police history to that date.)

Although Robert Peel's ''Bill for improving the police in and near the Metropolis'' was passed by Parliament largely unopposed, it is well known that Peel, then the Secretary of State for Home Affairs, more commonly known as the Home Secretary, had overcome substantial opposition to achieve that end. The Metropolitan Police Act of 1829 was the culmination of years of wrangling and infighting, much of the resistance emanating from fear that an organised police would inevitably become ''effective in a manner defined by government rather than the people, and would thus become a vehicle for controlling and subjugating the working class'' (McKenzie and Gallagher, 1989: 17).

It was Peel's inspired decision to appoint two commissioners to the new police: Colonel Sir Charles Rowan, a soldier, and Sir Richard Mayne, a lawyer. Thus, in combination with his formidable political skills, Peel laid the ground for the development of policing strategy in London based upon the tenets of organisation (military skills), equitable and lawful behaviour (legal skills) and public relations (political skills).

Initial resistance to the new police was strong. As McKenzie and Gallagher (1989) put it: ''Hostility was fuelled and possibly orchestrated by a campaign in the press. The Times was strongly critical of the concept of central control . . . because of the apparent increase in powers it gave to the government'' (McKenzie and Gallagher, 1989: 18).

There is also some evidence that the population at large saw the police (and some of the content of the Metropolitan Police Act of 1929) as an exemplar of the notion that the aristocracy was attempting to subjugate the proletariat. The Act, for example, made criminal offences of ''kite flying,'' ''knocking at doors without reasonable excuse'' and ''hoop-rolling'' (Metropolitan Police Act, 1829, s.54), although it also included genuine attempts to address public health concerns. For example, the Act prohibited the ''throwing or laying of dirt, ashes, litter, carrion, fish, offal . . . into any sewer, pipe, well, stream, watercourse, pond or reservoir for water'' [Metropolitan Police Act, 1829, s.60 (3)]. The population's anxieties are reflected in the nicknames given to the new police, in particular "Mr Peel's Bloody Gang" and "The Crushers."

Robert Reiner (1985, 1992), pointing to the potential for bias, refers to the "cop-sided view" of police history: a view that sees as the seminal, attitude-changing event in this police-public relations arena the death (or more properly the inquest on the death) of Constable Robert Culley in 1883. Cully had been stabbed to death following a disorder at a public meeting. There was some confusion about whether the assembly was legal, and that confusion was sufficient ground for a coroner's jury to return a verdict of justifiable homicide. Members of the jury were later presented with a medallion (the foreman got a cup) each engraved to the effect that the mementos would "serve as a Perpetual memorial of their Glorious Verdict of Justifiable Homicide on the body of Robert Culley, a Policeman, who was slain while brutally attacking people while peacefully assembled."

The cop-sided view is that public horror at this turn of events "directly influenced the movement towards acceptance and legitimation" (McKenzie and Gallagher, 1989). It is Reiner's view (1986, 1992), however, that the true driving force toward legitimation was the predetermined combination of military, legal and political skills, noted above, to create a specific strategy to ensure the acceptance of the legitimacy of an organised and paid police presence in London. (See Reiner [1992] for a full exposition of this idea.)

The deliberate creation of a policing policy for London is, as McKenzie and Gallagher put it, "far removed from the development of policing in the USA where an essentially *ad hoc* process has spawned a complex, multi-layered and multifaceted body of police whose function may differ markedly from that of policing in the UK." (McKenzie and Gallagher, 1989: 20).

However, following what became viewed as the success of the Metropolitan Police, legislation and local initiative led to the development of a large number of police bodies, which were usually based upon geographically defined areas such as towns, cities, boroughs and counties. In towns, cities and boroughs, the principal legislation driving these initiatives was the Municipal Corporations Act of 1835. As Wall (1996) points out, although this act "was not too popular at first due to its financial implications for local government," by 1853, 155 out of 178 boroughs had fully installed a force. Only six had failed to do so completely, and the rest had carried out least part of the requirements of the Act.

Later reform of the police in the counties was driven by the County Police Act of 1839, an Act of Parliament that met with more resistance than had resulted in the boroughs and cities from the earlier Municipal Corporations Act. For example, by 1856 only 25 out of 55 counties had installed police forces (Wall, 1996). Within each force, constables had the power to arrest offenders only within the boundaries of their force area or, in the case of "instant" or "immediate" pursuit, within six miles of that boundary.

In 1856, Parliament passed the County and Borough Police Act. The Act was developed as a consequence of the deliberations of a Parliamentary Select Committee on the Police (1853), which had examined the effectiveness of policing arrangements in the country and had concluded that by and large an organised police was a "good thing." The new Act mandated the introduction of police in both counties and boroughs. At the same time, conscious of the need for supervision of police activity, the Act introduced an Inspectorate of Constabulary and made financial arrangements such that the Treasury, on certification by the inspectorate, was to pay half of the costs of the pay and uniforms of all police forces. The Act also encouraged crime record keeping. In addition as Wall (1996) puts it, the Act "forced the very small boroughs to amalgamate with the local county force thus reducing the overall number of very small independent police forces (some were as small as two or three officers)."

By 1860, there were 226 police forces in England and Wales, and in 1866 Parliament passed a second Act, which had the effect of reducing the number to 183. Much later, in 1919, following a disastrous strike of police officers in some of the principal cities in the country, a Police Act was passed, which whilst spawning representative bodies for police officers (in particular the Police Federation) also had the effect of starting a process of removing full autonomous control of individual police forces from the local population, placing it in the hands of central government bodies—in particular, the Home Office. The Act allowed the Home Secretary to make regulations governing the pay and conditions of service of police throughout England and Wales and also introduced a standardized discipline code. Although local police supervisory bodies (then known as Watch Committees and now called Police Authorities) could be involved in the selection of chief police officers, restrictions were imposed upon who could be considered for a post in the first place, and selections were required to be approved by the Home Secretary or his representative. The bitter pill of lost autonomy was sugared by an agreement that central government would pay half of the full cost of policing, not just the pay and uniforms as stipulated under the previous arrangements.

By 1960, the number of police forces in England and Wales had fallen to 125. Following a series of *causes célèbres* (Reiner, 1986, 1992), a Royal Commission on the Police of England and Wales was established. Known as the Willink Commission (after its chairman), this body, among many other recommendations, proposed that the number of forces should be substantially reduced (RCP, 1962). Therefore, in two rounds of amalgamations, the existing 125 forces were reduced to the current 43 by 1974. Many of the recommendations of the commissioners were later incorporated into the Police Act of 1964, which in addition to requiring the proposed amalgamations also gave police officers the jurisdictional authority to act as such anywhere in England and Wales.

The Act also further defined the relationship between central control and local autonomy through the definition of the responsibilities of the Home Secretary, the Police Authority and the Chief Constable. In the last 30 years this has, in practice, led to the development of a system in which 76% of the local police budget is, in fact, paid through central government funding. Although in theory, the central government contribution made by the Home Office stands at 51%, additional monies are made available through a combination of that direct police funding and a special grant (the Revenue Support Grant) paid to local authorities by the Department of the Environment (Jones, Newburn and Smith, 1994). In exchange for that purse, the Home Office may now exercise a degree of centralised control by limiting force establishments, by encouraging the inspectorate to become more systematic in its examination of forces, and by what Reiner (1991) describes as the "controlling" of the career opportunities of chief constables.

Thus over the years, a large body of individualised police forces has been reduced to a manageable number. This has taken place—or at least it appears to have done so—at the same time as the centralisation of the overall supervision of forces has been increased. However, this view would be misleading, for it fails to take into account the extent to which chief officers and their forces remain autonomous: free to make unilateral decisions about internal matters—most particularly if the decisions relate to operational matters. It also contrasts markedly with the position in the bulk of municipal and state police organisations in the USA—that is that the democratic control of policing, including the setting of objectives, hiring (and firing) of senior staff, recruitment targets and a plethora of other matters considered to be the domain of either the community as a whole or of their elected representatives. Whilst that approach is not without problems (see Greene, 1993 for a more complete discussion of this area), as a matter of underlying principle, "he who pays the piper calls the tune."

The rather strange position in England and Wales, in which the body providing the bulk of the funding for policing has a limited say in how the money is spent, is exacerbated by a similar problem in arrangements for local accountability in policing. Once centred in Watch Committees, the local supervision of policing is now conducted through Police Authorities. These bodies draw their membership from a combination of elected and appointed individuals drawn from the local community. The area for consideration by the new authorities is to identify local policing objectives, to review performance, to produce an annual report and to develop the final draft of a Policing Plan (Loveday, 1996). There is little doubt that, seen in those terms, there seems to be a degree of both local and national accountability. However, this fails to take into account the existence of the legal construct of "constabulary independence": the notion generated by Lord Denning that constables (including chief constables) are immune from political interference, still best described in the words of Denning himself:

> No Minister of the Crown can tell [a Chief Constable] that he must or must not keep observation on this place or that; or he must or must not prosecute this man or that one. Nor can any police authority tell him so. . . . He is answerable to the law and the law alone. (R.v. Metropolitan Police *ex parte* Blackburn, [2QB, 118, 1968])

Following Denning's words, a sometimes heated debate arose in which chief officers contended that the defining factor of the *dicta* was that operational matters were for the chief officer whilst policy matters could properly be the domain of others, including the police authority. Lustgarten (1986) argues that there is a false distinction between police policy matters and police operations (arguably the sole subject of Denning's *dicta*), and police authorities and others, "generally found chief constables willing to discuss the former but steadfastly refusing to speak about the latter" (Lustgarten, 1986: 20). The remit of the new police authorities does nothing to relieve that situation.

Although some contemporary commentators suggest that the changes are working well and that the disputes are a thing of the past, Butler (1996), a serving chief constable, suggests a different scenario. He argues that the introduction of the new remit for police authorities and in particular the requirement to produce a Policing Plan raises—not lowers—the potential for conflict. He writes: "The Policing Plan can be seen as an instrument through which the Home Secretary and the police authority may seek to test the limits of the control on the operational aspects of policing. . . . Although key national objectives are in the policing plan, the chief constable, by statute (The Police and Magistrates Courts Act 1994) *needs only to have regard to them*" (Butler, 1996: 223: emphasis added). The groundwork appears to have been laid for continuing dispute.

THE LEGAL CONTEXT OF POLICING

Sykes (1993: 300) writes that "traditional policing in America was often stereotyped as corrupt, repressive and inefficient. The 'watchman' style of policing and its informal 'street justice' practices represented a target few reformers could resist."

In the USA and a number of other nations, the existence of a formal written document (or formally linked group of documents) containing the detail of the nation's constitutional structure, particularly where that document lays down the procedures through which various constitutionally dictated rights are to be enforced, may have a significant effect upon the nature of policing and criminal justice.

In the USA, the Constitution and its amendments (especially the Bill of Rights) have laid down the procedures for the management of a constitutional democracy. In England and Wales, however, (and in the whole of the UK) there is no single constitutional document, nor is there a Bill of Rights in any formal sense of those words. There is what McKenzie and Gallagher (1989: 34) describe as "a hotch-potch of legal documents, gentlemen's agreements and democratically agreed statute law." This does not mean, however, that the population is bereft of rights. The United Kingdom is a parliamentary democracy. Put in the simplest terms, this means that the population may assume that rights exist subject only to the will of Parliament, that there is liberty for the nation's population. Sometimes known as the "liberty of the subject," this means, for example, that such a freedom of "freedom of speech" is assumed to exist *without it being spelled out*, and that people may go where they like, say what they like and do what they like, provided they do not break the law. Parliament may restrict the scope of that freedom through legislation but would be unlikely to achieve any success in seeking to remove it completely.

However, the existence of a constitutional structure with formal procedures, which is interpreted by a supervisory body (in the USA, the US Supreme Court) also provides the opportunity for procedures (processes) to be extended into significant areas of the social infrastructure, including the criminal justice system.

The Fourteenth Amendment to the US Constitution reads, in part, "nor shall any state deprive any person of life, liberty, or property, without due process of law; or deny to any person within its jurisdiction the equal protection of the laws." From this clause, the power to control and manage policing and the criminal justice system in the USA emanates. Although the Fourth, Fifth, Sixth and Eighth Amendments also have a role, it is the due process requirement of the Fourteenth Amendment, developed by the US Supreme Court during its "due-process revolution," which had the most substantial effect in moving the informal street justice practices noted by Sykes (1993) into something more formal and controlled.

By contrast, the less restrictive crime control model of criminal justice, until recently, held sway in the UK. The crime control model, which is closely associated with the Watchman Role, leads to a "prominent police profile, incorporating assertive patrol activity, high-level visibility, extensive use of stop-and-search powers, the likelihood of abrasive street contacts, and, on occasion, a casual attitude towards civil rights (Newman, 1984: 62). In the next section it will be argued that the crime control model, remains a key feature of the street work undertaken by police officers in England and Wales. It will also be argued that the constitutional dictates that shape the law in the USA also shape the expectations of both the public and the police about the police role.

One important feature to be borne in mind during a reading of the next section is the effect of the exclusionary rule, which does not exist to any significant level in the UK, on policing in the USA.

POLICE WORK

The nature and scope of police activity is difficult to define. Although some scholars (e.g., Reiss, 1971; Packer, 1968) consider the principal defining factor of police work to be the "virtual monopoly" of the police of the legitimate use of force, others (e.g., Wilson, 1968; Goldstein, 1977; Banton, 1964) point to the "multiple functions" of police work. Weber Brooks (1993: 142–43) classifies these as the "law enforcement" role—crime detection, taking criminal complaints, writing reports, making arrests, investigating, protecting crime scenes, questioning and frisking persons—and the "non-criminal" role—settling disputes, providing transportation, giving directions, investigating suicide threats, rescuing sick and injured animals and providing medical treatment. She suggests that "this non-criminal component is referred to in different terms in the police literature (e.g., keeping the peace, order maintenance, service, etc.), and all [writers] do not agree on the exact nature of these non-criminal activities" (Weber Brooks, 1993: 142).

This is a much simplified version of the true position, however, conflating as it does the "peace keeping/order maintenance role" of the police with that of the provision of service. Indeed, in the earlier quoted definition of non-criminal police activity, the uneasy juxtaposition of "providing transportation" or "rescuing sick and injured animals" with "settling disputes" and "investigating suicide threats" is problematic.

This is because, although there may be some overlap between order maintenance and law enforcement, both are to be distinguished from the "service" role of police. Order maintenance (the Watchman role [Wilson, 1968]) is, in comparison to law-enforcement, a low-level police activity. It is, in essence, a crime prevention, community-oriented and proactive facet of police behaviour. It is police activity that is defined by an officer's (or police department's) perception that the role is one of peacekeeping rather than strict enforcement of the law (the "Move along" or "Go away before I have to arrest you" approach [McKenzie and Gallagher, 1989]). Such discretionary activity steps outside the bounds of legalistic law enforcement behaviour when police choose to ignore compelling evidence of the commission of offences for the greater good, but nevertheless remain concerned with limiting *the effect* of such breaches of the law.

By contrast, the law-enforcement role (i.e., Legalistic role [Wilson, 1968]) is a pragmatic, high-level, "catching bad guys" activity, driven, even in relatively low-level encounters, by a belief that the key feature of the role is that illegal activity must be dealt with through a strict and direct strategy: "Because the law, and that's me, says so" (McKenzie and Gallagher, 1989).

The key feature that binds these two elements together is that both are, in practice, albeit through different methodologies, addressing the same aims. In 1829, Sir Richard Mayne, one of the first two commissioners of the Metropolitan Police wrote:

> The primary object of an efficient police is the prevention of crime: the next that of the detection and punishment of offenders if a crime is committed. To these ends all efforts of police must be directed. *The protection of life and property, the preservation of public tranquillity* and *the absence of crime* will alone prove whether those efforts have been successful. (Cited in the *Instruction Book of the Metropolitan Police*, 1961: par. 2: emphasis added)

Mayne clearly believed that the three elements noted above were inextricably linked; that they were at the core of police work; and that they supplied the rationale for it. He appeared equally to believe that crime prevention was a higher order aim than was crime detection.

If this is a correct statement of the role of police, then order maintenance and law-enforcement activities both address the same problems. The protection of life and property, the preservation of public tranquillity and the absence of crime will be achieved through the application of both or either of those strategies. However, the social role has been deliberately tacked on top of that, Reiner (1992) suggests, as a public relations strategy.

Thus, Weber Brooks's (1993) notion that (for example) solving disputes and investigating suicide threats are in some way separated from core police activity (law enforcement) is mistaken. Some police officers in the UK, making the same error, have rejected, by labelling the cases rubbish, their involvement in domestic disputes (PSI, 1983), believing that the only true policing activity—the *raison d'être*—is "feeling collars," that is, arresting offenders.

Nevertheless, it is fair to say that Peel's insistence upon the social dimension of police activity both softened the impact of an organised policing body and added immensely to its scope. Activities such as dealing with stray and injured animals, taking in lost (as opposed to stolen) property, providing medical aid to those who are not the victims of crime and even reporting motor vehicle accidents in which there has been no breach of the law (i.e., for insurance recording purposes) are all aspects of the social role of the police, the Service style (Wilson, 1968). Such activities do fall outside the scope of *both* law enforcement and order maintenance—that is, core police activity. But they are not, and cannot be, fully separated from core policing.

Describing Police Activity

The continuum model: Traditionally the relationship between the law enforcement, order maintenance and public service functions of policing has been graphically defined as a continuum along which an operational police officer moves depending on the situation with which he or she is dealing, selecting eventually the appropriate style, Legalistic, Watchman or Service, that fits the circumstances. Referred to as the continuum model by McKenzie and Gallagher (1989), the paradigm is often used to define the difference between hard and soft policing. It is represented by a horizontal line with the Legalistic/Law Enforcement approach at one end and the Service/Social role at the other. The Order Maintenance/Watchman role lies at the mid-point of the line.

In describing the behaviour of one officer at any given moment, or of a police department's philosophy in a slice of time, such a one-dimensional model is perfectly adequate. But, by presenting a complex piece of human behaviour on a continuum of discrete units, it is a simplistic picture of police activity. It is not really a case of either/or, but of a balancing act between the components. The balance will shift over time, and variations in individual psychology or departmental politics and policies will make it something altogether more dynamic.

Wilson (1968, ch. 9) argues that much of the style of the police department is *a consequence of the discretionary behaviour* of the patrol officer, albeit that such behaviour is, to some extent, controlled and directed by departmental executive decisions and policy. But discretionary behaviour is not either/or, it is a complex, multi-faceted exercise in which the officer balances his or her own attitudes and values against a perception of the attitudes and values of the society in which he or she works. The balance at any one time is as much a matter of an officer's perceptions of the public's *expectation* of the role as it is of departmental philosophies.

McKenzie and Gallagher (1989) argue that the dynamics that produce a policing style are related to a nation's psychology, sociology and history. In addition, they argue that the process of law making; the interpretation of the law; and legislative, judicial and popular expectations (based on past experience) of police behaviour and style have a marked effect on the overall behaviour of police.

Undoubtedly Wilson (1968) was right in defining certain police departments as *typically* Legalistic-, Watchman- or Service-orientated. In the same way McKenzie and Gallagher (1989) argued that individual police-officer style may be identified using similar parameters with the proviso that personal shifts in style can occur, and individual policing style, like individual personality, is dynamic.

The balance model: The problem of defining the style of a nation is no different. The overall paradigm of the process and practice of the police of the two countries under discussion is best described by a two-dimensional model that allows movement in two defined but separate areas and that sees the public service function not as the end of a continuum but as an orthogonal line on the continuum of law enforcement and order maintenance as in Figure 4.1.

Because, by definition it must be a generalisation, a national picture of policing style is less obviously dynamic than that of an individual officer or even a single city. For this reason, McKenzie and Gallagher argue that, although there is, as Wilson found, individual and municipal variation, overall, American policing is typified by a balance between the Law Enforcement (due process/ Legalistic) and Public Service functions. In contrast, policing in England and Wales is typified by a balance between Order Maintenance (crime control/ Watchman) and Public Service.

McKenzie and Gallagher (1989) suggest that the expectations of the legislatures, the courts (which administer, in the USA, a substantially due process model of law) and the public is such that the style of the American police officer is of a Legalistic/Service nature. As a consequence, principally because their work is surrounded by procedural *rules of law*, officers, of necessity, think of themselves as law enforcement personnel. On the other hand, expectations of their English counterparts are influenced by Parliament, the courts (who by and

Figure 4.1
The Two-Dimensional Model of Policing

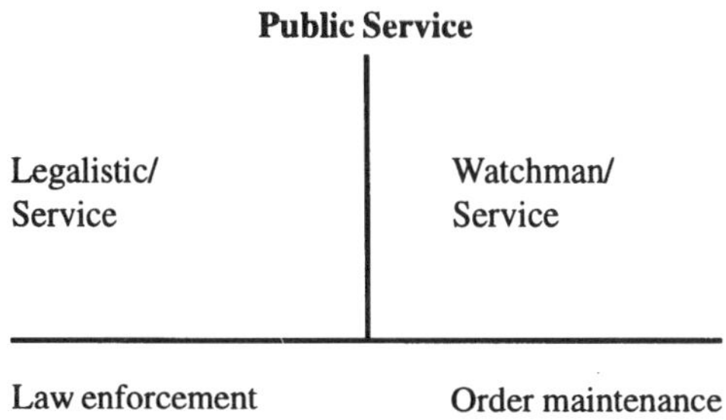

large administer a crime control model of law) and the public, which results in a Watchman/Service style. Largely unencumbered by procedural rules (until the Police and Criminal Evidence Act of 1984, the effect of which will be discussed below), and merely given advice and guidance (for instance, through The Judges' Rules), such an expectation leads English officers to think of themselves as part of the Police *Service*. It remains to be seen whether that Service orientation can be maintained.

The Legalistic/Service role in American policing: McKenzie and Gallagher (1989) have argued that police officers in the USA are expected to enforce the law first and provide help and assistance second. This is evidenced by the history of policing in the USA (law enforcement following the pioneers); the construction of laws (American laws are usually concerned with strongly legalistic issues rather than order maintenance or crime prevention issues); the activity of the courts (a concentration on due process rather than on crime control dimensions); the nature of the ethnic and cultural mix in the USA; and a huge concern about the constitutionality of police behaviour and the role of police in a democracy.

In a typical example, California police officers called to a bar to end a disturbance were held to be not liable for failing to provide emergency medical assistance to people found injured following a shooting. The court stated that such an obligation only arose when they (the police) caused the injuries or caused the parties to rely on their help. According to the court, "They have no obligation to offer assistance to injured people who are not arrested" (Rose v. County of Plumas [119 Cal. Rptr. 842 (App. 1984)]). Thus, in the face of legal decision making, the social role of police comes in a very poor second.

None of this, of course, denies the empirical evidence that as much as 70 to 85% of police time on both sides of the Atlantic is spent in dealing with non-crime related matters. There is, of course, a service role to American policing. But the dynamics are a constant shift of emphasis within the left quadrant of Figure 4.1, the balancing of a Legalistic, Law Enforcement style with a Public service/social role style. As Johnson et al. (1981) point out: "The myth of the fight against crime as the sole element of the police responsibility is accepted by the typical citizen and *by the bulk of working police personnel* in the USA'' (Johnson et al., 1981: 15; emphasis added).

The fight against crime becomes a battle against criminal activity. The fight *against crime* is a prevention/crime control philosophy: the battle against *criminal activity* is a *post hoc* individual and enforcement philosophy. They are, it has been argued, both the same side of a coin, core police work. Because of the propensity for police officers to see themselves as law enforcement personnel (some even refer to themselves as LEOs—the aggressive animalistic tone of which might have provoked Sigmund Freud into comment), the whole of the police role is seen in that way. Therefore, there is much resistance to community policing, with its connotations of softness and sensitivity.

The belief in ''crime fighting'' as the *raison d'être* of policing, not surprisingly, colours expectations of future performance and perceptions of past performance and reinforces and expands the law enforcement element. Placed against a background of public fear of police and governmental power (which is common in the USA), and the development of externally imposed rules (Supreme Court decisions), this is to be expected. Consequently the Legalistic/Service role develops and flourishes.

The Order Maintenance v. Service role in English policing: English police officers have a different perception of their policing role than do their American colleagues. In the UK, there is a history of Watchman-type policing; judicial decisions are primarily based on crime control rather than due process; the public has accepted a social role for the police from its inception; and society is prepared to tolerate a high level of government involvement in personal lives. There also remains a strong insistence that ''the primary aims and duties of the . . . police are to uphold the Rule of Law, to protect and assist the citizen and to work for the prevention and detection of crime and the maintenance of a peaceful society'' (Metropolitan Police Instruction Book, 1985). Thus, the nature of national policing in the UK is typified by a balance within the right quadrant of Figure 4.1: the maintenance of the Queen's Peace with a strong Service role element.

There is, it should be noted, movement in England and Wales towards the Legalistic/Service role and many people, some of them police officers, would like to see such a movement occur with more haste. The increasing existence of outright hostility to the police in certain communities, allegations of racism and overt criminal activity are stretching the patience of many officers who see such lawbreaking take place and are impatient to deal with it at whatever cost to the peace. (See Johnston, Chapter 2, on Zero Tolerance policing.) It is nevertheless the case that concentration on the Watchman/Service role has given policing throughout the country its unique flavour since the time of Robert Peel. It remains to be seen if such a stance can be maintained.

The result of the movement towards a more legalistic style in the UK is that legislators are responding in much the same way as they did in the USA. In 1986, the Police and Criminal Evidence Act (PACE) came into force. The Act contains much that places more power into the hands of the police, but at a cost. The cost was the development of a series of Codes of Practice that have the effect of creating a due process environment for English police officers. Some sections of the Act itself fulfill the same function. These legislative initiatives prescribe rules for how things must be done. If the rules are not followed, evidence may be excluded, court cases may be lost and possible disciplinary action may be taken against recalcitrant officers.

The advent of the PACE may have an unexpected consequence. It may be the first concrete step towards the creation of a policing style—this time dictated by society (or at least Parliament acting on its behalf)—which will be more Law Enforcement- than Watchman-orientated. As seen above, police behaviour affects legislators and vice versa, and by and large, the old police saying still holds true: "The public get the kind of police they want" (or in some areas) "the police they deserve."

THE USE OF FORCE AND DEADLY FORCE

Although as discussed above, some writers (Reiss, 1971; Packer, 1968) consider the principal defining factor of police work to be the virtual monopoly of the police to legitimately use force to undertake their role, it has been argued that other dimensions are just as, if not more, important. However, it is here argued that the use of force, and most particularly the use of deadly force, is the ultimate application of the law *enforcement* role, albeit that there is within it a substantial element of self-protection and self-preservation.

Although there is dispute about it,[2] the police in England and Wales feel themselves to be the victims of an increased threat of firearms. Similarly, there is some evidence to suggest that the level of assaults committed against police officers during the execution of their duties is increasing (see Moxey and McKenzie (1993) for a summary of some of these data). Regardless of whether the figures are accurate or not, that the police believe them to be so is sufficient. Studies of victimisation repeatedly suggest that some groups in society (e.g., the elderly) commonly overestimate the threat posed to them by criminals. Often, the risk of victimisation is relatively low, but the impact of a crime (including the fear it generates) is high (Mawby and Walklate, 1994). Thus, in the face of apparent increases in violence against them, the police themselves become victims of the fear of crime.

According to Bonnifacio (1991), with the exception of having one's partner killed, sustaining a serious injury is the most traumatic experience in police work. The self-concept of officers, their view of themselves as people who are prepared to place themselves in a dangerous position and not flee, is damaged each time a colleague falls victim to the gun or is in some other way seriously injured. Thus, because they are in a "special position of jeopardy . . . and seek to reduce their vulnerability" (Sargent, Brown and Gorlay, 1995: 243), they seek enhanced protection.

The two-year period between 1994 and 1995 was a watershed in this debate. Against a background in which fear of gun violence took a paramount position in the minds of police officers, there was an augmentation—particularly in London and Manchester—of the availability of firearms to the police. In May 1994, Sir Paul Condon announced an increase in the number of Armed Response Vehicles (ARVs) in the Metropolitan Police Area from 5 to 12. This decision was coupled with an announcement that the officers manning these vehicles and others carrying firearms would, henceforth, be permitted to do so openly (*The Independent*, 18 May 1994). Within weeks of Condon's announcement, James Sharples, Chief Constable of Merseyside, and the outgoing chairman of the Association of Chief Police Officers' (ACPO) firearms committee, speaking at the ACPO conference in Bournemouth, said that armed routine patrols could "come sooner rather than later," and that

> Firearms incidents are increasing. . . . In the past, armed professional criminals would normally be the culprit. Increasingly now, it is the young hooligan going into the corner shop, bank or building society. It is the drug dealer seeking to protect territory or turf. There is a wildness about the scene. More sophisticated weapons. We are seeing Kalashnikovs, Armalites and Uzis, on a fairly regular basis. (Bennetto, 1994: 3)

In part the movement towards a more heavily armed police was driven by the Police Federation (the police union in England and Wales). As a part of the general outcry, the voices of a few Police Federation members had been heard, declaring that the level of firearms use against officers was at an all-time high, and claiming that, in the interests of the protection of officers on the street, arming was becoming essential.

Fred Brougton, then vice-chairman of the Police Federation, told a gathering of Police Federation conference delegates in Brighton that they were "like cannon fodder from the first world war" and that it was not enough to have "more ARVs on the street" (McMahon, 1994). Substantial play was made of the alleged desire of a large number of officers to carry guns (Leppard, 1994). Later, when in 1995 the Police Federation conducted a wide-ranging survey examining police officers' ideas about arming, self-protection and training, much of the argument was revealed to be hyperbole when federation members showed far from unanimous approval of such a proposition.

Overall, the 1995 federation survey suggested that 83% of respondents supported the proposition that "Firearms should *not* be issued to all police officers," but a similar proportion of respondents felt that "More officers should receive appropriate training and be issued with firearms as and when necessary." Sixty percent of respondents expressed dissatisfaction with their self-defence training.

However, between 1993 and 1997 steps were taken for enhanced protection. These took the form of increases and improvements in officer-safety training, the introduction of extendible sidehandled batons (ESHBs) and other long-batons of various designs, the introduction of rigid handcuffs, the provision of some protective body armour and the testing and introduction of personal issue CS spray canisters.

Of course, this tooling up of street duty officers, whilst an adequate response to the concerns of the police themselves, may have a down side. Bayley (1977) suggests that, "as long as police [officers] are afraid of being shot they will favour pre-emptive action," but that whilst the police may be afraid of being shot, "the citizens will be afraid of being shot by mistake." The presence of guns, he writes:

> adds a real but incalculable amount of emotion to any police citizen encounter. . . . The gun on the hip is a visible reminder that the police have other things to do, that non-enforcement activities are a distraction from main purposes. . . . A disarmed police will be better prepared to provide mediation not involving enforcement. (Bayley, 1977: 222–223)

Whilst the gun on the hip remains a relative rarity, the overt carrying of CS spray and long-batons is commonplace. There is some evidence to suggest that, particularly with the application of CS spray, police officers are indeed favouring pre-emptive action (*Police Review*, 30 August 1996), events that have resulted in calls for the guidelines for the use of CS spray to be reviewed. Similarly, following the death of a man after the application of force with a long-baton, a coroner called for "all officers who have been trained to use a baton to be taught the specific dangers, the after-effects and potential signs and symptoms that can follow a blow to the head" (Potter, 1996a).

The image of the British bobby has changed forever. Although the likelihood of a police more completely or even more regularly armed with guns has receded somewhat,[3] the police continue to seek a compromise between what they want (more protection, more firearms-trained officers, more officer-safety training) and the recognition that to move too far in those directions will permanently damage the image of an order-maintenance/mediation-based, avuncular, pacific, fair-yet-firm policing style with an added dash of social conscience.

Perhaps compromise lies in the direction outlined by John Kenny. In a letter to *Police Review* (16 August 1996), he wrote:

> No police officer can anticipate whether he is going to come up against an armed person around the next corner. By the same token no villain should be able to assume that all patrolling police officers walk around unarmed.
>
> Specially selected officers could be daily and randomly issued with state of the art concealed weapons and body armour so that villains would never know what they were really taking on when confronting an apparently unarmed officer in the street.

CONCLUSION

This chapter opened with the observations of a chief constable in the 1960s about the relative fates of officers from each side of the Atlantic were they to be deployed in each others' countries. In an effort to establish the current position in each nation and the truth of those prognostications, this chapter has discussed the development of policing in England and Wales, issues of accountability, the nature of police work, issues associated with the legal environment in which the police operate and, to a limited extent, the current position vis-à-vis the equipping of the police for their legitimate application of force.

The police officer deployed from the USA to the UK would find a political structure very different from that experienced at home. The absence of overt political manipulation of police chiefs through hiring and firing decisions made by mayors and city councils, the complete absence of any local say in senior appointments (no public meetings, no elections) might be surprising. The officer would find himself or herself with powers of arrest that could be used all over the country and would find that training in each of the 43 English police forces was virtually identical. The work undertaken would be remarkably similar to that previously undertaken. A key difference would be, however, in the perception of the role to be played.

If the analysis in this chapter is correct, then the US officer might well find that, particularly in the absence of a gun on the hip, the Law Enforcement/Public Service role requires some moderation. The nature of the Order Maintenance/Public Service role requires a slightly less "in your face" set of behaviours than are common in US policing.

Although, in many police departments in the USA, a continuum or hierarchy of force is commonly taught, much of the teaching is confined to the use of weapons of force: impact weapons, chemicals and firearms. It remains unusual for teaching to concentrate much on the weapons of persuasion: body language (including stance, posture and eye contact) and verbal control (Cleede and Parsons, 1987). However, as Fyfe (1989) states:

> Violence occurs when police lack the eloquence to persuade temporarily disturbed persons to give up their weapons, but shoot them instead. It occurs when, instead of pausing to consider and apply less drastic alternatives, officers blindly confront armed criminals in the midst of groups of innocent people. It occurs when officers called to quell noisy but non-violent disputes act in a way that provokes disputants to violence to which the police must respond in kind. In short it occurs when well meaning police officers lack—or fail to apply—the expertise required to resolve as bloodlessly as possible the problems their work requires them to confront. (Fyfe, 1989: 467)

The quelling of noisy but non-violent disputes, and other similar events, is core to the order maintenance role.

The question is still begged. How would an officer from each nation cope in the opposite society?

Perhaps the only solution to this question is to allow that the 'USA to England' outcome remains unclear. However, there is some evidence which may be be brought to bear in the other direction.

One person who has seen policing on both sides of the Atlantic is Gina Haynes, now a lieutenant with the Sacramento Police Department in California. She was once a constable in the Leicestershire Police in England. Gina found that the talking skills, and order maintenance skills she had learned in police training and on the beat in England held her in good stead. She argues that the skills of talking to people are just as important as those associated with the use of force: "In England I had learned to use myself as a weapon—my voice, my posture, my gestures. What I learned in America was how to use lethal weapons—guns, batons, mace and so on" (McKenzie, 1996: 23).

The skills associated with the use of force are increasingly being taught in the UK. Perhaps that would enable an officer to avoid kidnap!

NOTES

1. Throughout this chapter, except where stated, the use of the words, "English" or "England," may be assumed to include Wales.

2. "Although there is widespread concern about the criminal use of firearms, and the public perception, or at least the media portrayal, is of a relentless rise in the incidence of armed crime, it is salutary to state at the outset that the use of firearms in crime is comparatively rare in England and Wales. According to *Criminal Statistics* for 1992, the most recent year for which data are available, about 0.2% of recorded notifiable offences involve a firearm, and one-third of these were cases of criminal damage, often trivial in nature, over 90% of which were caused by air weapons" (Morrison and O'Donnell, 1994: 1).

3. The introduction in 1996 of legislation to limit the number of privately held handguns, *may* have an effect here, although indications are that the frequency of use of illegally held guns in crime is unlikely to be reduced, however draconian the legislation.

CHAPTER 5

Ethnicity in Criminal Justice

SIMON HOLDAWAY

INTRODUCTION

Anyone who wants to get to grips with the question of whether racial discrimination is found within criminal justice institutions is faced with a considerable body of statistical evidence, which can be bewildering. Typically, academic commentators review the available evidence and literally reach a measured conclusion. However, a particular method of research lies behind each review. Statistics do not speak for themselves; like any data, they always require interpretation. An understanding of the benefits and limitations of particular methods of research and, just as important, the assumptions about the nature of reality on which they are based, helps us to understand criminological and policy-related disputes about the nature and extent of racial discrimination in criminal justice institutions.

A number of the examples from research used in the chapter are therefore representative of ways of arguing and assessing evidence more than definitive statements of knowledge. In this vein, the final part of the chapter is concerned with race relations within the police, considering how the occupational culture of the lower ranks constructs and sustains negative relations between majority and minority ethnic officers.

THE STANDARD RESEARCH TEMPLATE

Criminological analyses of racial discrimination in the criminal justice system are usually shaped by a carefully designed template, which is crafted precisely to identify differences of treatment for the members of different racial groups. The template is applied like this: First, calculate the proportion of ethnic minorities within the whole prison (or other criminal justice) population. Secondly, compare this proportion to the proportion of people of ethnic minority origin in the general population. Remove the template and take stock.

An overrepresentation of ethnic minorities within the prison population in relation to their proportion of the national population might indicate racial discrimination, which is as far as some commentators go. The mere presence of, for example, a larger proportion of black people, by which in England we mean people of Afro-Caribbean origin, in the prison population than in the general population is sufficient to identify racism. Members of pressure groups, politicians and a host of rhetoricians use this kind of prison population argument as adequate proof of discrimination, but in fact it is inadequate. The presence of a disproportionately large number of black people in prison is not an indication of racial discrimination or racism. There could be a host of reasonable and unreasonable explanations for the overrepresentation of black people in prison.

Take the statistics of black men in prison during 1995, the most recent available figures as this chapter is written, as an illustration. Official government figures indicate that in June 1995 there were 8,000 people from ethnic minorities in prison service establishments. The figure of 8,000 represented 17% of the total male inmate population and 24% of the total female inmate population (Home Office, 1996c).

These figures represent a far greater proportion of ethnic minority prisoners than ethnic minorities in the national population and could therefore be indicative of discrimination. However, the two figures are not comparable because the prison population figure includes foreign nationals. We are not yet comparing like with like. When foreign nationals are removed, and the prisoner population is broken down into different ethnic groups, we discover that 10% of the male prison population in 1995 was black, 2% was Asian[1] (which in England means South Asian), 1% was from other minority ethnic groups and 87% was white.[2] Among female prisoners, 11% were black, 1% were Asian, 2% came from other minority ethnic groups and 86% were white.

Now we are more able to compare like with like, meaning a comparison of the proportion of particular ethnic minorities in the prison population with the proportion of the same minorities in the national population. The 10% black male representation is to be compared to a 1% representation in the national population and the 11% female black prisoner population to a 1% representation in the national population. When these figures are contextualised with the same proportions for white males, 87% and 95%, and white females, 86% and 95%, we can see that there are indeed disproportionate numbers of black men and women in prison.

The tone is deliberately dispassionate here because, with the standard "finding-discrimination" template guiding the analysis, we have so far discovered no more than a disproportionate number of black men and women in prison. We *appear* to have discovered discrimination that leads to a disproportionate number of black men and women imprisoned, but we do not yet know how this has occurred. In relation to their number in the population, not least when compared to the proportions of white men and women imprisoned, black men and women are imprisoned disproportionately. If all members of all ethnic groups within the population began from the same starting point, we would expect there to be somewhat similar proportions of people from different minority ethnic groups imprisoned. In 1995, 87% of the whole population of England and Wales was comprised of white men, while 95% of the national prison population was comprised of white men. This contrasts sharply with the 1% and 10% figures for black men. The disparity suggests that we may have identified racial discrimination.

It is, however, one thing to identify an overrepresentation of members of an ethnic group within the prison population but another to explain it. Prison staff do not decide who is to be imprisoned, and the cause of discrimination cannot be laid at their door. We therefore have to ask some more questions, redesigning the template to include other decision makers—such as sentencers, prosecutors and police officers. Is the ethnic composition of the prison population explained by differential sentencing practices by judges or magistrates? Perhaps we should focus upon differential decisions to prosecute. Or is the imbalance more to do with differential arrest patterns by the police? Should we rule out the possibility that black people might commit more crime than white people and, in relation to the amount of crime they commit, are proportionately represented in the prison population? Maybe a combination of discriminatory practices at all or some of these decision-making points has led to the overly large prison population of black men and women.

SIFTING AND SORTING STATISTICS—RACE AND CRIME

Retaining the standard research template to guide our analysis, we first need to track back from the prison population to the earliest possible point, which is the committing of offences, and try to establish whether or not black people commit more crime than white people. This has been an area of considerable contention, not least because of the danger of suggesting that there is an innate reason why black people per se commit crime and, therefore, of fostering a view that there is a connection between biology and action, which is racism. Debate about this question has consequently been animated "empiricist haggling over official statistics," as Paul Gilroy put it, which becomes part of "the development of the new racism for which the link between crime and blackness has become absolutely integral" (Gilroy, 1987: 74). Gilroy's argument has been dismissed by the "empiricist hagglers" because, save by the application of their research template to the numerical data, they cannot find any other way of proving or disproving the existence of disproportionate offending, racial discrimination or anything else within criminal justice institutions.[3]

In 1971 the House of Commons Select Committee on Race Relations and Immigration decided that there was no evidence to suggest that any ethnic minorities were disproportionately involved in offending (Lambert, 1970; Select Committee, 1971–1972; Benyon, 1986). In 1976, however, the committee returned to the subject and pondered further over evidence submitted by the Metropolitan Police (Newing and Crump, 1974; Select Committee, 1976–1977). The Met argued, ''Our experience has taught us the fallibility of the assertion that crime rates among those of West Indian origin are no higher than those of the population at large'' (Newing and Crump, 1974: 182).

Their evidence did not claim a causal link between race and criminality; neither did it deny the social disadvantages faced by black people, which may have an impact on levels of offending. The Met's concern seems to have been to draw attention to new statistics of differential offending rates, especially for street crime—and presumably to accept the consequences of doing so.

The Select Committee noted the Metropolitan Police evidence but did not fully accept it. Their primary concern, which drew on Home Office advice, was that the police statistics used were not controlled for sex and age, which could affect offending and therefore arrest rates. Further research taking this and other factors into account was suggested and later pursued by Philip Stevens and Carole Willis from the Home Office Research and Planning Unit (Willis and Stevens, 1979). It should also be pointed out that the statistics used to argue about the extent of black peoples' involvement in crime were arrest statistics, which could be an indication of police discrimination against black and other ethnic minority people as much or more than an indicator of offending rates.

Stevens and Willis were concerned with trying to unravel the various factors that might explain any relatively high rates of offending, if they exist, among the ethnic minorities. Age, unemployment rates, household tenure and social class were controlled. The single control for age left black youth considerably overrepresented in most categories of indictable crime, especially robbery, other violent theft and assault. Asian youth, though slightly overrepresented in arrests for assault, were found to be arrested less frequently than might be expected given their number in the population.

Controls for socio-economic factors were then introduced, and an association was found between social deprivation and levels of arrest, but the particular features of social deprivation differed when the figures for each ethnic group were considered.

> For both the black and Asian arrest rates no single indicator emerged as strong as the white employment rate for white arrests; but the best indicator of high arrest rates for blacks, for violent crime, appeared to be a low rate of home ownership whilst that for Asian arrest rates appeared to be a high proportion of Asians in the lowest socio-economic group. (Willis and Stevens, 1979: 41)

These findings indicate that there are particular social characteristics that refract the impact of social deprivation on ethnic minorities, *or* the activity of the police is a strong factor in constructing an arrest rate *or* both are important. The age structure of the minority ethnic populations surveyed and other socio-economic factors explain some of the higher arrest rates, but not all.

Stevens and Willis then considered the explanation that all the remaining differential arrest rate was the result of an extrinsic factor, in particular police activity, which leads to the greater number of arrests of black people. This marks a slight move away from the statistical analysis of variables to consider whether or not police action has constructed an appearance of reality in which black youth commit more street crime than white youth. But, as stated by Stevens and Willis:

> To explain the 1975 arrest figures in terms of differential success in clearing up black and white crime, it would have been necessary for police to arrest 66% of all black offenders but only 21% of white offenders. Such an imbalance is implausible, given that the ethnic identity of offenders is unknown at the outset. . . . It can be calculated that if 75% of all black arrests and only 19% of white arrests in 1975 had been mistaken ones, it would be possible to reconcile the 1975 arrest rate with the hypothesis that rates of underlying black and white crime were identical. . . . Mistaken arrests alone do not look like a plausible explanation of the difference between black and white arrest rates, although they might of course explain some part of it. (Willis and Stevens, 1979, 34)

These arrest statistics seem to indicate that when population, socio-economic factors and aspects of police discrimination are taken into account, some of the differential arrest rates and assumed crime rates are explained. High levels of assault, robbery and other violent theft remain, but as Stevens and Willis construe, these are offences that incorporate many different types of acts that are open to some degree of police discrimination (Walker, 1987).

This Home Office research clarified rather than settled any final answer to the question raised by the 1976 Metropolitan Police evidence to the Select Committee. Importantly, the methods of research used demonstrate some of the benefits and drawbacks of statistical analysis. Researchers are able to point to differential rates of offending and to separate variables that together form a cluster of factors leading to crime, but whilst valuable, the identification of these variables—such as age, gender and social class—does not explain why, as seems to be the case, young black men are arrested more often than expected from their number in the population. Researchers indicate and clarify in quantitative terms that some structural phenomena have an impact on police action and on people from minority ethnic groups but do not explain their relationship to the action of the police or to people from minority ethnic groups, young black men for example. They also do not describe or analyse social processes that reconstruct and sustain racial relations, and it follows, the phenomena we conceptualise as "society." The statistical approach provides a numerical picture, but the quest to isolate the proportion of the arrest rate that results from police discrimination and the proportion that results from offending by ethnic minorities has really led in two directions. Some criminologists will continue to pursue these types of study against Robert Reiner's view, for example, that "It is inconceivable that this approach could ever conclusively establish racial discrimination" (Beatty, 1994: 5). Other criminologists will perpetuate a "police discrimination or ethnic minority crime" form of debate. This is the point at which Jock Young's realism is needed.

CRIMINOLOGICAL REALISM

The finding that black youth are overrepresented in some offence categories formed the starting point of John Lea's and Jock Young's contribution to the race and crime debate (Lea and Young, 1982, 1984). At the heart of their argument is the view that too little attention has been given to human creativity; to the richness and diversity of cultural forms created by minority groups; and that research should be as much concerned with heterogeneity as with homogeneity.[4] An explanation of offending rates should take into account both the impact of structures of social inequality on minority ethnic groups *and* the diverse responses found within such groups. The diverse, widely drawn cultures of the country from which migration originates; the more specific sub-cultures of those who migrate; and sub-cultures that develop within Britain are all integral to understanding the situation of black youth (Lea and Young, 1984: 125).

There is no straightforward transfer of a monochrome culture from one generation to another, just as there is no single response that can be characterised as "black culture" or "Asian culture." Within the black population, for example, various responses to settling and being born in Britain have been identified, some oriented around religion, some around status and some around hustling (Pryce, 1979; Rex, 1982). If we take into account the diversity and creativity within and between different minority ethnic groups, as well as the common effect of structural factors, including ways in which social deprivation can lead to crime, it is not surprising that an element of criminal activity is *one* adaptation amongst a small number of the members of *one* minority ethnic group (Pryce, 1979; Rex, 1982).

A challenge to this explanation is that there is no significant adaptation by black youth to the racialised context of British society. The gift of creativity is owned and crafted by police officers, whose discriminatory strategies construct the appearance of a higher rate of offending amongst black youths (Lea and Young, 1982). Lea and Young have replied to this by arguing that, on the basis of the police evidence to the 1971 Select Committee, it is assumed that a type of positive discrimination has influenced, and continues to influence, police action towards Asians since the late 1950s, because they are not subjected to the high arrest rates experienced by Afro-Caribbeans and whites. The stance towards black, but not white, youth has changed. Why? Were the police acting within a framework of positive discrimination in the early 1970s, or has crime by some black youth increased? The critique has to account for police action increasing in relation to a small number of crimes, especially street robbery, not crime and criminality *per se*. Further, if police discrimination is the sole explanatory factor to explain arrest rates, it is necessary to assume that all ethnic minorities have identical crime rates, which seems very unlikely. As far as the political character of crime is concerned, Lea and Young, along with other commentators, point out that most crime is intra- rather than inter-racial, and therefore is not related to a kind of quasi-political redress of experienced prejudice and discrimination.

The conclusion of Lea and Young's work is that a perception of relative deprivation leads some black youths to commit more crime than white youths. Police prejudice and discrimination respond to this real rise in crime—to be associated with economic circumstances—in inappropriate ways, such as making arrests of black youths who have not committed offences, partly leading to a construction of higher crime rates.

> The notion that increasing youth unemployment, coupled with a high young population in the black community, and the effects of massive, well-documented, racial discrimination and the denial of legitimate opportunity, did not result in a rising rate of real offences is hardly credible. (Lea and Young, 1982: 167–68)

Lea and Young's argument remains a significant one. Importantly, they move us on from an either/or type conclusion to consider the interplay of a range of factors. They introduce a note of rational calculation into arguments often based wholly on conjecture.[5] However, they may have placed an inadequate emphasis on the ways in which the media and other institutions construct an image of the atypical as typical and, therefore, understate the ways in which their rational argument might not reflect how the criminality of black youth per se is fostered by the routines of a range of institutions.

The notion of a greater rate of black offending might be further reviewed in the light of evidence from a recent self-report study dealing with samples of black and white youth aged between 14 and 25 (Graham and Bowling, 1996). These researchers found that there was no difference in rates of self-reported crime for black and white youths. However, the sample research was very small, and there are pretty obvious limitations to the methods of self-report studies, in which people are asked to state how much crime, if any, they have committed in a recall period.

TAKING STOCK

One of the main purposes of this chapter so far has been to explain the methods of research that criminologists have used to determine whether there is racial discrimination within the criminal justice system. The chapter has deliberately not reviewed all the available statistical evidence. However, readers would benefit from some information about the findings from this type of research. Therefore, these findings are briefly summarised below, virtually verbatim, from a very recently published paper by David Smith (Smith, 1997: 169–172). On the basis of a very thorough review of the evidence, Smith concludes that

- Ethnic minorities—both blacks and South Asians—are found to be at higher risk of crime victimisation than white people.
- Black people are about seven times as likely to be in prison as white people or South Asians.
- The pattern of offences for which black people have been arrested and imprisoned suggests that they tend to be the targets of proactive law enforcement.
- There is some evidence of discrimination in the targeting of police resources; the decision to prosecute people; and the sentencing practices of the Crown Court.
- At various points, black people are placed at a disadvantage by the application of apparently neutral criteria—consideration of social background and of decisions to plead not guilty, for example.
- There is no evidence of a cumulative effect of bias as black people move through the decisions that proceed as a case is processed within criminal justice institutions.
- All the evidence suggests that there is no bias against South Asians within criminal justice institutions, though they are differentially victimised by racial attacks.

All of these conclusions are qualified by a recognition of the inadequacies of the data available and the less than satisfactory design of many studies that have been published. Smith's concern is mainly to strengthen the standard template, though he acknowledges that the wider context of racial inequalities and the nature of criminal justice institutions are important factors in an analysis of racial discrimination. However, it is not evident in his or similar work that the notion of race is socially constructed, a matter that needs to be considered further.

UNDERSTANDING RACE

These various template-based studies provide evidence of racial discrimination at various points in the criminal justice system. Given the loose coupling between institutions within the criminal justice sphere, however, it is inappropriate to think in terms of a tightly integrated system of justice that systematically disadvantages ethnic minorities. Institutions certainly have a life of their own; they are more than the sum of their parts; they endure and solidify. It would be a misperception, however, to attribute a collective mind to criminal justice institutions, assuming that, together, their personnel form a collective, rational mind, a systematically calculated mind that consciously works to the necessary disadvantage of ethnic minorities. One of the extraordinary features of criminal justice institutions is how they fail to integrate as a system. This is not to minimise the moral taint of racial discrimination or to underplay its serious effects on individuals or groups. It is to recognise that research has found a lack of coordination between criminal justice institutions when they work together in inter-agency partnerships, and a lack of common policy (Bowling and Saulsbury, 1992).

A further basic point is that we should be wary of assuming that once we have identified statistical discrimination at one or more points of the criminal justice system, we understand what is happening to disadvantage the members of different minority ethnic groups. We do not. All we can say is that there is a measure of statistical discrimination against people from different ethnic groups. We have documented the outcome of a host of decisions by various personnel working in the criminal justice system, but we do not yet know anything about the taken-for-granted assumptions they make about minorities, about how they work—about their common-sense reasoning.

For this and other reasons, quantitative studies that have been concerned with racial discrimination within criminal justice institutions have often been unable to move us forward to an adequate explanation. They cannot because they are devoid of a sociological theory to assist an analysis of the social context within which their statistics of outcomes have been constructed. Take, for example, Roger Hood's large study, *Race and Sentencing*, in which he undertook a detailed statistical analysis of sentencing patterns within the West Midland's Crown Courts. Hood's final chapter carefully summarises differential patterns of sentencing found within the West Midland's courts generally and between individual courts within the one circuit. He then ponders the reasons for the overall treatment meted out to Afro-Caribbean males, concluding that:

> One is left wondering whether it is not a result of different racial stereotypes operating on the perceptions of some judges. The greater involvement of black offenders in street crime and in the trade in cannabis, their higher rate of unemployment, their greater resistance to pressures to plead guilty, and possibly a perception of a different, less deferential, demeanour in court may all appear somewhat more threatening. And if not threatening, less worthy of mitigation of punishment. It was significant that being unemployed increased the risk of a black male getting a custodial sentence, but not, in general, for a white man or an Asian offender. . . . But without research which would allow the investigation of judicial attitudes towards, and perceptions of, racially related differences in crime patterns and in cultural responses to the criminal justice system, all this for the moment must remain speculation. (Hood, 1992: 188–89)

In other words, Hood describes patterns of sentencing but does not and cannot explain them because to do so he would be to have to make some analytical links between wider structural features of contemporary British society (rates of unemployment, for example), the ideas some judges have about black and other minority ethnic people, and the culture of the courts within which judges act. Hood begs a sociology to inform his research, not least to make some sense of the relationship between structure and action within the sphere of criminal justice he has researched.[6]

To go further we need to look at the social processes that produce discrimination. Social research in this area has led scholars in two basic directions. First, they have looked at the wider social context of race and related relations within a society and extrapolated what occurs in criminal justice institutions from their wider social structural analysis. Secondly, and usually alternatively, they have looked at the ways in which the cultures of criminal justice institutions lead personnel to think and act in particular ways that mould particular patterns of racial discrimination.

Both of these perspectives are based on a sociological understanding of race. Race is not a biological phenomenon. It is not possible to divide people into distinct biological races. There are stock physiological differences between groups of people, but they cannot be used as adequate criteria to define distinct biological races (Banton, 1967). There is much variation within and between such groups and no relationship between membership in a biologically defined race and in a culture.

Race nevertheless is real. People in contemporary Britain categorise each other by their racial identity. We talk confidently about race relations. Conflicts exist between the members of different racial groups, and the recurrence of genocide, based on hatred between different races, indicates how powerful a notion race remains.

So, race does and does not exist. Some sociologists have argued that we therefore need to jettison the notion of race completely. Robert Miles, for example, argues in this vein (Miles, 1989). He understands race to be an ideological ruse, shielding inequalities created by the labour market, in which black and Asian people are afforded discriminatory, differential opportunities. The economic conflicts of capitalism require a cheap labour force to sustain high levels of production and the extraction of profit. Migrant workers have served this end and, in the context of contemporary Britain, black and Asian people, the former rather more than the latter, have met the need for cheap labour. For various other reasons, these minorities have been subjected to continuing disadvantages within the labour market and, therefore, in the housing, consumer and other markets too. Social processes articulated by a capitalist economy thereby create and sustain a class of low-waged migrant workers defined by criteria of race and by ideas about inferiority and the dominance of white people (Miles, 1989). A link between biology and action is constructed and lives as a feature of a capitalist society. Racism is the notion that there is a link between biological traits associated with particular races and the culture and action of the members of those races.

Stuart Hall and his colleagues have argued similarly in *Policing the Crisis* (Hall, Critcher et al., 1978; Jefferson, 1993). They have pointed out that in the mid-1970s young black men were increasingly sentenced to harsh punishments, not least for robbery, and characterised in the press, in the minds of sentencers and, it is implied, in popular consciousness, as "muggers." Crime and black youth became all but synonymous. Black youth were criminalised by the concerted action of the police, who established special squads to deal proactively with muggings; by judges who disproportionately sentenced them to custody; and by journalists, indeed, by the whole apparatus of the media, who by dramatising one or two cases, created powerful icons of black youth as muggers and as all but inherently criminal. A range of powerful ideas about black youth and by implication about black people per se created a criminal group. Crucially, this was a construction articulated within the context of a particular historical moment of an economy in recession, high unemployment and minimal prospects for speedy economic recovery.

Hall, Critcher et al.'s analysis forges a link between this material context and the ideas associated with it. Ideas direct attention towards a scapegoat—black youth—and, crucially, away from the troubled economy, the responsibility of government and business. Ideas, an ideology, and material factors harmonise to construct a notion of race that sustains a particular form of society. Race is not real, but it becomes real and potent within the context of a capitalist economy in crisis. The crisis has to be policed by the construction of a demonised group, perceived through the lens of race relations.

In this type of analysis, wider structures of racial inequality and resonant ideologies articulate the criminal justice system. The link between biology and action is severed completely. A secure link is forged between social structures, ideas and the action of criminal justice personnel.

However, there is an assumption made that people's ideas are all but determined by the structures of an economic system, which is unsubstantiated. There are also remaining questions about the extent to which these types of analyses, and Hall's in particular, have allowed theoretical presuppositions to select and interpret the evidence presented (Holdaway, 1979; Waddington, 1986). Theoretical licence has dominated, and a balance between evidence and theory needs to be restored. Importantly, we need to introduce a more adequate theory of human action into the analysis (Giddens, 1979). Wider structures of inequality are integral to a comprehensive analysis of racial discrimination within the criminal justice system, but they act as a framework for action, not as a straightjacket.

CULTURE AND ACTION—THE DEPLOYMENT OF RACE WITHIN THE POLICE

A rather different approach to understanding discrimination has been developed by criminologists and sociologists who have focussed on the cultures of criminal justice institutions. These studies are very few and far between, but they are linked by an interest in the ways in which shared ideas, perhaps particular to an occupation like policing, might foster racial prejudice and discrimination. Research in this vein has not used the template that has guided so much statistically based research. The quest has been to get much closer to the ordinary world of the police, for example, and to document by firsthand evidence the ways in which ideas about ethnic minorities are moulded within routine police work, at times leading to discrimination. To illustrate this approach it is useful to consider the experience of ethnic minority police officers.[7]

Racial prejudice and discrimination have been found to be abiding elements of the occupational culture of the police rank and file (Manning, 1977; Holdaway, 1983; Reiner, 1993; Holdaway and Barron, 1997). Although the relationship between ideas and action, between racial prejudice and discriminaon, is not direct, there is sufficient evidence to argue that the lower ranks work in an environment in which derogatory language about ethnic minorities is a commonplace and in which discriminatory action is likely. The task here is to consider how the occupational culture moulds the experience of ethnic minority officers, especially black and Asian officers. This in turn demonstrates some of the ways in which mundane social processes that are basic to the occupational culture of policing construct and racialise the employment experience of black and Asian officers.

The evidence used in this section is drawn mainly from the author's two studies of serving and erstwhile black and Asian police officers, about 70 in total. They were interviewed about their experience of a police career, from thinking about joining the force to, in the case of one study, their resignation from the police (Holdaway, 1991; Holdaway and Barron, 1997).

These studies were prefaced by a smaller project, in which 15 black and Asian serving constables were interviewed about their reasons for joining the police (Wilson, Holdaway et al., 1984). They made it clear that the most significant barrier they had to overcome during their consideration of recruitment into the police was the attitude of future colleagues, suggesting that race relations within the police were of as much and probably of more concern than the attitudes of their ethnic peers and other factors. In a subsequent study of serving officers, thirty ethnic minority constables were interviewed, and just four did not mention racist comments and jokes as a regular feature of colleagues' conversation (Holdaway, 1991: 135–156). One of the four had recently joined her force, two identified a specific incident but did not find it to be of major significance and the other had no comment to make.

Prejudice and discrimination were a routine feature of these officers' experience of police employment. The problem was not one of racist individuals, unchecked by colleagues and supervisors, but the culture of the rank and file that formed a framework for police employment. To understand this situation we therefore need to place race within the social context of the police as an organisation, with its distinctive occupational culture. We can then try to analyse how taken-for-granted features of this culture, which may affect all or a range of other minorities within the work force similarly, construct negative racial relations between ethnic minority and ethnic majority officers.

The statement below is from a person interviewed during the study of black and Asian officers' reasons for resigning from the police service. It makes the general point that being treated differently is not just the fate of members of minority groups. However, most minorities are regarded differently by the rank and file.

> No, they didn't treat me differently, not necessarily because I was black, the thing is it's down to attitudes really. . . . It wasn't just about blacks, it was about women who were beaten up, it was about women who were raped dressed up in loud clothing shall we say, it was about Irish people, it was just about everybody—and I just didn't, I didn't really share the ideas, I didn't really.

White resigners made similar comments, but a difference between white and minority ethnic officers' views became clearer when they talked about the power of the occupational culture and its particular relevance to black people, and to women. The following quote is from a white male officer, whose view was challenged by the majority of black, Asian and white female officers interviewed. If you are not on the butt end of prejudice you can afford to say that you "never felt it was racist and it was never sexist." When you stand as a target, your perception is rather different.

> But I always felt that it was never racist, and it was never sexist, it was simply part of—I mean they'd take the mickey out of a man who's fat, and they'd take the mickey out of a man who's bald. It's part of just seeing how far they could push you and, you know, making sure you understand. And the lads who work out on the unit, they want you to understand them. They want to know that they can trust you, that you're there and that you're not going to blow up every time you talk.

The occupational culture is an oppositional culture that engenders negative views among the rank and file. Rather than placing a primary emphasis on positive and hopeful aspects of police work in which social order is preserved, people helped, crime prevented and community bonds affirmed, its heart is a triumphant defeat of what, by rank and file definitions, is not normal and taken for granted. Minority ethnic officers therefore have to weigh the value of the negative views that surround and at times influence them.

> Yes, unfortunately. There are some aspects of it that aren't very savoury but by and large it tends to indoctrinate you, well brainwash. Because the police culture, it applied even to me. I found myself regurgitating and spewing it up at home. It was like I was a third person. I could actually see myself making all these comments, thinking, "Well, that's not quite right." I found myself doing it. I mean, specifically, I started picking people, putting them into little compartments. I found myself thinking, "Well, that's not quite right," perhaps coming from an ethnic minority myself and having experiences at first hand, I should know better but I found myself doing it.

Time and again the resigners interviewed talked about the all-embracing way in which the occupational culture had formed a framework for their experience of work, whatever ethnic group they came from. Race, however, was manifested in particular ways, and in this chapter two ways in which racial relations were constructed and sustained will be considered.[8]

Stereotypes

The essence of a stereotype is a rigid and one-dimensional presentation of a more diverse and multi-faceted phenomena. Stereotypical thinking has been identified as a characteristic of rank-and-file police thinking *per se* (Manning, 1977; Chatterton, 1992; Keith, 1993a). Stereotypes are different from what sociologists call "typifications," rounded and therefore somewhat inaccurate résumés of information about people, situations and places of relevance to a social position, the position of police officer being the case in point (Schutz, 1967). The complexity of the social world requires us to simplify information to some extent, to disregard in some measure evidence that is contrary to our own beliefs, to justify the relationship between our ideas and actions with a retrospective gloss of constancy rather than inconsistency. Conversation would be endlessly laced with qualifications if we did not routinely use typifications. Typifications, however, are not stereotypes, which are less complex, more rigid and virtually irrefutable, except in extreme situations. Being particularly rigid, stereotypical ideas are difficult to challenge, and they become increasingly entrenched within organisational thinking. Where stereotypes are left unchallenged, when there is no organisational strategy to change them through the implementation of a consistent and concerted policy, life within the police work force remains difficult for black and Asian officers.

When researchers have asked serving black and Asian officers about their occupational identity, respondents have stressed that they regard themselves as police officers who happen to be black or Asian (Wilson, Holdaway et al., 1984; Holdaway, 1991). Their colleagues regard them rather differently, as black and Asian people who happen to be police officers and therefore as different from the mainstream.

From the perspective of many white rank-and-file officers, to be a police officer is to be white (Her Majesty's Inspectorate of Constabulary, 1992). In the most routine of situations, race as a social category that summarises differences seems to be of immediate relevance to white officers. This is a black officer describing his colleagues who regularly talked about black and Asian people in derogatory terms:

> I would say, "I don't think you should be saying that" and those people that said, "Sorry, I didn't know you were there" would say, "Well you know what it's like, you get used to it." "Well get un-used to it then," I would say, "You wouldn't like it if I said, "You so-and-so, I mean how would you feel if I said that to you?" . . . They like to put people in boxes. If someone was black they could call them some derogatory name but instead they put us in boxes. They were just trying to identify us with the sort of person that was socially deprived or any person that's black. But I should say they

should just give it a bit of thought before they open their mouth and that's what I told them. I don't know, I sort of give up. I never got any sort of commendation because I'd said that. Nobody takes any notice.

The prevalence of stereotypical thinking within the rank and file therefore amplifies racial prejudice and, possibly, discrimination. It is a stable feature of the occupational culture but one with particular implications for the tenor of race relations within the police work force.

Team Membership

Rank-and-file officers define police work as team work. There are without doubt occasions when groups of officers work together to a common end, when an individual needs to urgently call on the assistance of colleagues and be sure it will be forthcoming. The bulk of police work, however, is not of this type, because officers mostly work on their own.

Their notion of being the member of a team has a further implication. Team membership implies acceptance of the rank-and-file definition of police work, the ways in which it is practised and the values that underpin it, including stereotypes of members of minority groups. This does not mean that an officer joining a shift from training school, who places primary emphasis on community-based crime prevention, for example, will be completely shunned by colleagues. The point is that most colleagues' assessment of such an officer will be compared to their stereotypical view of what constitutes a police officer and police work, including attitudes and beliefs about minority ethnic groups.

Membership in the work group implies a significant measure of acceptance of the rank-and-file culture, including its racial elements, which makes it difficult for a black or Asian officer to find an agreeable reception from colleagues. Stereotypical thinking and team membership go hand in hand.

Various routes lead officers into team membership. One is by demonstrating the acceptance of an occupational trait with a higher status than one relevant to race. An ability to use physical force to protect a colleague is such a value, and the following illustration is concerned with a black officer who found a greater measure of acceptance amongst colleagues precisely because he demonstrated physical prowess when dealing with an offender. Not all colleagues at this officer's station placed the same degree of credibility on defensive skills, and the officer's skills were not entirely unrelated to police work. If the chapter argued thus, the occupational culture would be presented as a stereotype. The officer quoted here has nevertheless found himself integrated into his team of colleagues since he demonstrated he could "handle himself." The irony of his remarks is that in his colleagues' minds he has moved from one stereotype to another. At first he was straightforwardly perceived as a black person. Once integrated he is *the* officer who can deal with difficult situations requiring physical force. Also notice that being the member of the police team is, in the officer's words, "being one of the lads.'' At first he talks about the way in which colleagues assume he and his parents were born in Jamaica, that all black people are unintelligent, and that derogatory language about black and Asian people is acceptable. The situation then changed.

> But then finally another one of these breaks. One night there was quite a bad disturbance in the town centre, and we actually had to wade in. One of the officers was overpowered so to speak, and he was getting a damn good pasting. Now, because I had done quite a lot of self-defence, and I'd done quite a bit of martial arts, I didn't find any problems. I was able to dig him out and get him back to the van. And from that point onwards I was one of the lads. . . . That was it. I was one of the lads because I'd actually gone out and proved myself in a situation, and they thought well that's it for us, he's one of the lads. And from that point onwards I was always being dragged off, ''Oh we need someone to come with us. Call Bob, go and find Bob, wherever he is, go and find Bob.'' You know, if I was sat at the station desk doing something else, ''Can I have Bob to come with me please?''

Another sign of acceptance by the team draws us beyond the working day to socialising after work and the implicit expectation lodged in the occupational culture that officers will congregate for a drink.[9]

Probationer constables joining the shift in a pub after work are eased into membership of the team of colleagues; an invitation to socialise is a sign that closer team membership is being offered. The problem for many Asian officers, however, is that for religious reasons they do not consume alcohol and, although the same is true of some white people, it is more likely to be the case amongst Asians. This makes the drinking route into team membership difficult because, although it is perfectly feasible to drink non-alcoholic beverages in a public house, it seems hardly commonplace for police officers. This Asian officer describes how be believes abstinence has contributed to his experience of policing:

> Even those I had a good rapport with probably wanted to draw a line and after tour of duty, that was it. I mean after a while I talked of going to pubs and things. Some people would obviously have social occasions in their homes and things and I wasn't invited to some of these things—because ''What's S* going to do, he doesn't drink, he's not going to have a piss-up.'' I felt a little bit isolated at that time.
>
> I tried a hell of a lot to, or I feel I tried a hell of a lot to, integrate myself. The first Christmas that we were there, for example, we were on duty. ''Ok, what are we going to do this Christmas?'' People were starting to talk. I can prepare quite nice stuff so I prepared an Indian meal for everybody. I got my parents to do this, bought it out of my own pocket. I didn't get them to pay. We had a really fantastic meal, and it was a good time. Everybody enjoyed it. So I wanted to say, ''Look, I want to join in with you.''

Team membership, another stock feature of the occupational culture, places particular obstacles in the path of black and Asian officers. Interwoven with stereotypes that structure so much of police thinking, team membership is fully afforded to probationers on the basis of criteria that are unrelated to the quality of their formal work performance, equal opportunities, justice, fairness or any other stated grounds. Rank-and-file definitions and perceptions of black and Asian officers compared to those of white officers structure membership of, and relationships within, the rank-and-file team.

The analysis of these qualitative data strengthen the notion of race as socially constructed through mundane processes. Officers did not separate their construction of racial relations between minority and majority ethnic peers from their routine work. The negative occupational culture formed racialised relations between majority and minority ethnic officers, and the processes analysed have led to the continuing underrepresentation of ethnic minorities within the police. Social processes therefore lead to outcome measures of recruitment, which remains at around 1.5 to 2% minorities, compared to the approximately 5.5% representation of ethnic minorities within the general population. To understand these figures, and to reform the police to change them, it is necessary to go well beyond the template type of study and document the social processes that construct and sustain race as a phenomenon.

CONCLUSIONS

By focussing on different types of research, it has been possible to understand the ways in which the phenomena ''race'' has been studied by criminologists and sociologists. Their methods of research assume a theory of the nature of social phenomena and of their social context. For some, race is conceptualised as a variable that can be measured to identify racial discrimination. For others, race is constructed, and the research task is to document the social processes that constructed it, as well as the functions race fulfills.

We have not been able to analyse any data within the constraints of a zero-sum notion of power, in which all ethnic minorities or all members of one racial group are dealt with similarly (Mason, 1994). The experience of South Asians is different to that of blacks, black women to that of black men, and so on. To describe Britain and its criminal justice system as uniformly racist is a shorthand that obscures a patterning of relationships. Such a catchall analysis does not assist reform.

If a research focus is placed upon the analysis of the outcomes of decision making, and differential treatment for majority and minority subjects is identified, we have done no more (or less) than discovered discrimination. Outcomes are the end result of a complex moulding of social processes that lead to discrimination. This is a key point, both in terms of its theoretical implications and the requirements of policy reform. The task is to understand mundane social processes that construct the phenomenon of race. The more we do this, the more opportunity there will be to create equality between different ethnic groups coming into contact with criminal justice institutions.

NOTES

1. In Britain, the expression "Asian" refers to people with ethnic roots in the Indian subcontinent. By contrast, the American expression "Asian" refers to people with ethnic roots in such countries as China, Vietnam and Korea.

2. The foreign national figures cannot be straightforwardly discarded because they represent a very considerable number of people who have been arrested and, for one reason or another, placed in prison. This provides a glimpse of attitudes to immigration and asylum-seeking that constitute part of the attitudinal framework within which ethnic minorities are perceived in England.

3. There is much more to Gilroy's argument and its rebuttal than can be presented in this chapter. See Holdaway (1996: 89–90) for more discussion.

4. Paul Gilroy was one of the writers Lea and Young criticised in *What Is to Be Done about Law and Order*. His ideas have now been revised and the diversity of culture is at the forefront of his analysis (Gilroy, 1992).

5. There is not scope to develop this point. A full discussion of it can be found in Holdaway (1997b).

6. This point is also of relevance to the reform of criminal justice agencies. It is one thing to identify and describe patterns of discrimination but another to recognise its phenomenal forms and, therefore, to be able to develop policies to assist in its amelioration.

7. One good reason for changing the subject of discussion is simply that there are no studies of the type described that deal with the actual impact of cultures on relationships between criminal justice professionals and ethnic minorities.

8. This section draws on the author's forthcoming book (Holdaway and Barron, 1997).

9. Other occupations also have unwritten rules about the use of alcohol, and a willingness to consume alcohol is of course part of a broader value placed on consumption by men. There is nothing about this point that is intrinsic to the police.

CHAPTER 6

The European Dimension

PAUL NORMAN

INTRODUCTION

In the last decade the boundaries and scope of international police cooperation in Europe have been dramatically transformed. During this time the UK's access to international policing networks, and the development of an international police function, has graduated from low-level informal links and associations to a coherent span of institutional arrangements. The progressive internationalisation of elements of the police function shows few signs of abating given the contemporary mobility of people and the financial opportunities available to those who offend transnationally. The global reach of the International Criminal Police Organisation (Interpol) is now evident, and it is apparent that the European Union (EU) is developing a strategic orientation to its policing function that also extends beyond European regional confines. In addition to these institutional loci of police cooperative activity, there are others of a specifically bilateral nature, whilst the traditional informal associations of senior officers and police experts continue to exist.

It will be seen below that the way that international policing is organised in Europe is clearly gaining some coherence. For example, the European policy structures of Interpol were developed substantially during the late 1980s. Latterly, the EU's law enforcement functions have gained an increasingly integrated character. Importantly, the EU's developing criminal justice policy domain—and its efforts to coordinate related policy sectors—potentially provides a comprehensive approach to international and transnational offending affecting the Member States. But the model of international cooperation is clearly under development and currently fractured by the EU's three treaty "pillars."[1] The practice has occurred because the European Commission has the right of initiative in the EC pillar but not in the JHA pillar. Other negative factors may also emerge as the "EU-centric" approach—underwritten by the power of aid and trade links with other regions and countries—contrasts with Interpol's apparently neutral respect for national sovereignty.

The EU's locus of policing activity forms the ascendent part of the current matrix of international police arrangements available to the police in England and Wales. However, the support for international police operations provided by Interpol and Europol has been affected by two main European regional factors. The most significant has been the changes in the European geopolitical order triggered by the revolutions in the countries of Central and Eastern Europe (CCEE). These tumultuous events—followed by the breakup of Czechoslovakia and Yugoslavia—led to a dramatic expansion in the number of nation-states able to exercise their full political sovereignty. At the time, this raised (largely unfounded) Western fears of large-scale irregular population movements from the far side of the Iron Curtain. The second factor was the high-profile campaign of the European Community (EC) to establish an area "without internal borders" in the Single European Act of 1987.[2] The counter to these freedoms is, however, the "fortress Europe" concept. This factor has largely been obscured by obliging the CCEE to act as buffer states, but the ideological pitch remains one of exclusion—a stance that sits uncomfortably with efforts to encourage closer international police cooperation. But given the prospect of free movement within the EC, the idea of a Europol was established—specifically for the EC Member States—to investigate those within, and those seeking to enter the community, who sought to abuse the newfound freedoms for criminal ends.

Other less visible aspects of this technocratic EC security solution to the problems of the free movement of persons were apparent. Crucial was the expansion and formalisation of the EC's former "Trevi" intergovernmental police cooperation structures into the "third pillar" of Justice and Home Affairs (JHA) (Bunyan, 1992) within the Treaty on European Union (TEU). In addition, an organised police technology industry emerged to service their newly internationally-mobile enforcement clients as the traditional military markets became less lucrative and new enemies were projected across national horizons (Norman, 1996: 74–75).[3] Thus global communications, computerised information systems and the intelligence function have become a reality for European criminal policing, not the specialised preserve of those police and secret security service agencies concerned with politically-motivated violence and national security. More contentiously, but in common with other European states, the agendas of all three of the UK's security services now encompass "the prevention and detection of serious crime" (HMG, 1994: 1.[2][c] and 3.[2][c]; HMG, 1996: s.1[1].[4]

The organisation of the UK's police structure is continuing to undergo change to ameliorate the impracticality of more than 50 police forces operating within an international policing context. In addition, both Interpol and Europol require their members to have a single national office. Before examining the national police structures that support international policing in England and Wales, it is important to analyse the forms of international policing that are now apparent, and the impact these changes have had upon the police per se.

THE DEVELOPMENT OF THE UK'S INTERNATIONAL POLICE FUNCTION

The term "international policing" covers a number of different levels of police activity. In relation to information exchange, international policing could include bilateral exchange of evidence or other policing information relating to a specific investigation. Similarly, the phrase could refer to the automated multilateral exchange of information on specific categories of crime between a defined number of states such as that seen in border control databases—for example, the Schengen Information System (Baldwin-Edwards and Hebenton, 1994: 137–57) and the proposed EU European Information System.[5] It could also embrace the national collection and supranational collation, analysis and dissemination of police intelligence data via a central agency such as Interpol or Europol.

International policing also covers other categories of police actions, such as transnational police surveillance operations. In addition, investigations by a state on the territory of another state, and the conduct of subcontracted (Dorn, 1993: 443–45) or reciprocal police surveillance operations at the request of another state (Bruggeman, 1987; Cannings, 1990: 160–64; Norman, 1996: 219–22), introduce a higher level of international police activity.

Finally, international policing may refer to the multilateral coordination of police operations (Joubert, 1995: 309–13; Tabarelli, 1987: 79–84), such as controlled deliveries of dangerous drugs across a number of jurisdictions, either in a single case or through regular ad hoc arrangements, that are mediated by an institution such as Interpol or the Europol Drugs Unit (EDU). A crucial mechanism for achieving many of these forms of international policing is the deployment of the national liaison officers of one state to another state. These officers can facilitate many of the above forms of police cooperation, from information or intelligence exchange to operational cooperation. The differing European liaison officer networks will be examined in greater detail below.

Many formalised international police arrangements are predicated on bilateral and multilateral agreements but are, in character, transnational. They relate to the pursuit of cross-border offending extending beyond, but affecting, the nation-state. Importantly, this feature places the principal burden of control and accountability within, rather than outside, the respective national domains. Outside the realm of supranational intelligence analysis in a future Europol, the principal features of police cooperation will remain predominantly transnational until states agree to relinquish substantive control of elements of their international police function to a supranational enterprise. Such opportunities may present themselves, but it is clear that arrangements are more likely to evolve from existing arrangements, and will progressively involve a number, but not necessarily all, of the Member States.

In the UK, the initial state of uncertainty about the nature of European crime problems, and the impact of border controls in the late 1980s, resulted in a "recoil effect" (Hebenton and Thomas, 1995: 104), which as some have argued, allowed the police service to promote compensatory policies in a relatively unfettered fashion. This is witnessed in the shopping list of compensatory security measures that the police felt would be needed if the border controls between the UK and the rest of the EU were relaxed (Home Affairs Committee, 1992: app. 9). Objectively, these proposals can only have been predicated upon anecdotal evidence and unsubstantiated police perceptions of the threats posed by illegal immigration, the growth in serious transnational crime (Gregory and Collier, 1992; Levi and Maguire, 1992: 168–72; Levi, 1993: 60–61) and the uncertain role that border controls may play (Gregory, 1991; Butt, 1991).

In any assessment and analysis of such growth of international and transnational crime there needs to be a body of knowledge relating to the current form and scale of cross-border crime, the extent to which border controls have been effective in countering it, and the proactive police measures that could limit any possible growth. But data collection for these assessments has not been traditionally regarded as part of any official or police function. For example, in 1992, Levi and Maguire noted:

> There is almost no hard information available about cross-border crime for gain in Europe. Because police forces and national governments define their responsibilities for the production of statistics in terms of crime occurring within their own jurisdictions . . . no data are routinely collected. Nor are there any specific research studies which demonstrate with any accuracy the proportion of all offences which possess a crime-border dimension. (Levi and Maguire, 1992: 171)

Levi and Maguire suggested that the exceptions to the lack of data collection were terrorism and drug trafficking.[6] As recently as 1995, the police in England and Wales were only citing drugs and credit-card fraud as providing reliable data, whilst it was admitted that there were still no comprehensive statistical data on cross-border crime affecting the UK, or any systematic research being undertaken into the nature or scale of cross-border crime (ACPO, 1995: 10).

In any analysis of the international police function, account must also be taken of the intra-national pressures bearing upon the organisation of policing. These can be seen in (albeit limited) efforts to traverse the traditional demarcation lines between national enforcement bureaucracies. This process was initiated by the creation of the National Criminal Intelligence Service (NCIS) in 1992, which covers both police and seconded customs officers (and lately, immigration officers) and requires the integration of diverse police intelligence functions into this agency. Another important initiative involving inter-agency operational cooperation is the Metropolitan Police's Joint Action Group on Organised Crime composed of more than 25 investigation, prosecution and regulatory agencies that form small clusters to cooperate on specific crime problems (Norman, 1995). Similarly, proposals for task forces extending beyond the police would bring much needed financial expertise to bear on police investigations (Pacey, 1995) and could easily encompass other countries.

Before examining the role of Interpol and the EU in facilitating international police cooperation, the regional and national police agencies in England and Wales will be outlined. These agencies form the principal police response to serious and internationally organized crime and are undergoing significant institutional change in response to international police developments.

THE ORGANISATION OF REGIONAL AND NATIONAL POLICING

In England and Wales there are 43 local, or geographically-based, police forces. However, outside London these forces only engage in international police activities against serious crime to a limited extent. The principal police agencies involved in the policing of internationally mobile offending are the six Regional Crime Squads in England and Wales, and the NCIS, with its six Regional Offices in Britain. The Regional Crime Squads are operational police agencies composed of police officers seconded for a limited period from the constituent police forces. They are primarily self-tasking police agencies but also act on intelligence supplied by the NCIS. The Regional Crime Squads target known and suspected serious mobile offenders and are increasingly engaged in international police operations, particularly in the European region (Norman, 1996: 33–62). Recent legislation will result in amalgamation of the six Regional Crime Squads—which until 1997 had no legislative basis—into a National Crime Squad covering the whole of England and Wales in 1998.[7]

Similarly, the NCIS has now gained a statutory mandate as a UK-wide criminal police intelligence agency, formalising its role as the conduit of international police enquiries by local police forces. It acts as the interface with both Europol and Interpol, and is also now responsible for tasking the UK's Security Service in its work against serious crime (Home Office, 1996). Using these sources of intelligence, NCIS's primary function is to provide intelligence packages on serious national and international offenders for operational police action by the Regional Crime Squads and local police forces.

THE ROLE OF INTERPOL

In 1989 the International Criminal Police Organisation (ICPO, more commonly known as Interpol) had 150 members, 26 of which were within the European Region (International Criminal Police Review, 1989). But the 1989 revolutions in Eastern and Central Europe subsequently presented Interpol with an opportunity to expand its European membership and to shift its activities to a more symbolically balanced position away from Western Europe. Thus by 1997 Interpol had truly gained global coverage as the total number of members rose to 176 (NCIS, 1996b), 46 of which comprised the European Region.

Interpol's purpose is to facilitate the investigation of international crime between member countries' police agencies by the mutual exchange of information. The organisation is unique in that it operates on the basis of universality, respect for national sovereignty and equality. But to function on the basis of these principles,[8] it "cannot have teams of detectives with supranational powers who travel around investigating cases of different countries" (Interpol, 1992: 7). Instead a General Secretariat houses a central support structure for the member countries' National Central Bureaux (NCBs), which are linked by a secure global communications network operating in the four official languages of French, English, Arabic and Spanish. Since 1992 the UK's NCB has been part of NCIS.

Interpol's organisational structure is split into two main parts: the official policy-making deliberative organs and the operational permanent departments. The policy structure consists of the General Assembly, which annually elects the thirteen members of the Executive Committee. The Executive Committee is composed of the President of Interpol, three vice-presidents and nine other members geographically representative of the overall membership of Interpol. Annual regional conferences result in decisions and recommendations, which are submitted to the General Assembly for approval (Interpol, 1992; 8–9). Interpol's operational police cooperation departments consist of a three-tier hierarchy of the General Secretariat, the three sub-Regional Bureaux and the NCBs of each member. The Secretary General of Interpol is in overall control of the operations of the General Secretariat and the sub-Regional Bureaux, but not of the NCBs, which remain under national control.

Interpol's recent institutional development in Europe has now put into place a dynamic process of decision-making focussed upon the European Regional Conferences. These commenced in 1967 (Bossard, 1990: 136), but since the early 1980s the European Regional Conferences have become important bodies in the development of international policing policies and practices in Europe. Given that each member of Interpol is responsible for its own NCB facilities, the wealthier Western European countries have improved their facilities qualitatively above those of other poorer regions of the world. This higher level of resourcing has contributed to further innovation within the European Region and in deepening forms of operational police cooperation. Interpol's European regional structures have provided a forum for the circulation of ideas about the development of a Europol-type agency. For example, at the 1981 European Regional Conference, the German delegation suggested the creation of a regional bureau specifically for Europe. This eventually resulted in the creation of a working party, which reported in 1984 (Anderson, 1989: 170). The following 1985 European Regional Conference implemented many of the working party's proposals, sanctioning the creation of a European Secretariat and a Technical Committee for Cooperation in Europe (TCE), with both units coming into operation in 1986. At that point, central control was maintained by the Secretary General (Interpol, 1992: 12).

The European Secretariat's initial role was limited to the general aim of improving cooperation within the European Region, while the TCE had a more practical brief (Baun, 1987: 27). However, this was an embryonic structure with as yet little formal strategic direction. By 1988 the situation had begun to change as the General Assembly approved the extension of the European Secretariat's function into the facilitation of operational police cooperation in Europe (Interpol, 1989). This initiated a process that changed the nature of police cooperation within Interpol (in Europe) from information and experience exchange to the facilitation of police operations—exemplified by the creation of a European Liaison Bureau in October 1989 (Interpol General Secretariat, 1990: 12). The bureau's aim is to enhance operational police cooperation, particularly in relation to drugs, as "the European Liaison Bureau . . . combine[s] in one place a team of experts in the linguistic, legal and organisational characteristics of the European members . . . covering all languages used in Europe" (Home Affairs Committee, 1990: 34–35). There was, therefore, a formal commitment to create a specific infrastructure for the European NCBs, based at Lyon but autonomous from the General Secretariat, using only two of Interpol's four official languages, namely French and English (Baun, 1987: 26). Other measures were implemented by Interpol to underpin its operational role in Europe. For example, at the request of the General Secretariat, in January 1988 19 European NCBs nominated an officer to help with day-to-day cooperation (*International Criminal Police Review*, 1987). This group became known as the European Contact Officers System (ECOS). The initial Western orientation of the scheme was gradually redressed as many of the CCEE joined Interpol and subsequently entered ECOS (Bresler, 1993: 207–8).

Within the developing institutional and operational structures, it was becoming apparent that senior police officers within the TCE were performing a de facto executive function for the European membership. They sought to improve both the information technology and crime analysis services provided by Interpol's General Secretariat, whilst deepening operational police cooperation within the European membership. The ad hoc institutional development of Interpol in Europe precipitated a major review of structures in 1991, the same year the German Chancellor formally proposed an operational Europol to the Luxembourg European Council. The review resulted in the renaming of the TCE as the European Committee "to examine strategies, policy and practical issues" (Interpol, 1991: 30) and an increase in its membership to eight, with the addition of a European representative from Interpol's Executive Committee, which formalised the body and ensured policy coordination.

The European Secretariat and Liaison Bureau continued, but to the disappointment of the General Secretariat, the expected rapid expansion in its membership did not occur (Home Affairs Committee, 1990: 35; Cameron-Waller, 1993a: 13). This was partly due to lack of resources within the CCEE, which prevented the deployment of their nationals as liaison officers, whilst Western Europe was already well represented. Thus in 1993 the Liaison Bureau was combined with the separate network of national Drug Liaison Officers, who were based at the General Secretariat (Cameron-Waller, 1993a: 14). This consolidation was represented as a practical move but also indicated the gradual integration of the roles and functions to allow the concentration of expertise, languages and countries within a combined multipurpose cooperation and coordination unit. The new European Liaison Officers (ELOs) were clearly detailed to support police operations in Europe (Interpol, 1991: 30), each being assigned responsibility for a number of countries in one of three geographic areas within Europe (Cameron-Waller, 1993a: 14). In an effort to enhance the representation of the CCEE, a sponsorship scheme was established, enabling Polish and Russian ELOs to join in 1993 (Home Affairs Committee, 1994: 156). By 1994 there were 16 ELOs, though only 3 were from countries outside the EU.

These central initiatives by Interpol clearly deepened operational cooperation, but further measures were required to elevate the quality of service provided by the NCBs and to stave off encroachment of its international police functions by the EU. Traditionally, there have been wide variations between NCBs due to their variable status within each country (Anderson, 1989: 81–90). This has affected their resources and their access to other policing agencies within the state. In 1993 Interpol started to address this problem because in its view "the efficiency and effectiveness of the National Central Bureaux in obtaining and passing on information has a considerable bearing on the ability of the General Secretariat to provide quality crime intelligence" (Cameron-Waller, 1993a: 4). To redress the variable quality of service between NCBs, the European Committee formulated a "rolling 4-year Business Plan for Europe," which developed into more detailed practical measures to provide extra resources to the NCBs of CCEE that would enable them to function at a certain level of minimum service (Cameron-Waller, 1993b: 9–10; Home Affairs Committee, 1994: 156–57). Five areas were outlined in the Business Plan for Europe:

1. Minimum standards of service at NCBs.
2. The development of an Information Systems and Technology Strategy for Europe.
3. The introduction of performance measures.
4. Common data standards for crime reporting.
5. Support for the establishment of effective NCBs. (Cameron-Waller, 1993a: 4)

In 1994, "17 common standards of service" were promulgated for all of Interpol's members to aspire to (NCIS, 1995: 18). However, it is by no means certain that all members will be economically able to comply in the short term, given the wide variations in resources.

If coordinated effectively, it is obvious that all European NCBs would capitalise upon the Business Plan for Europe, raising the possibility of a European criminal intelligence system mediated regionally by the European Liaison Bureau (ELB). This was clearly the important contextual background to the floating of the Europol concept by the EU—which powerfully rivalled the institutional development and information technology investment programme of Interpol in Europe. Interpol's long-term future was clearly uncertain given that one-third of Interpol's annual budget is provided by EU Member States. However, Europol's development proved to be faltering, and by the time the Europol Convention was agreed upon in 1996, a formal role for Interpol was provided for, and the initial conflictual relationship between the two organisations at the political level has now become—at least temporarily—more cooperative (Norman, 1997).

THE ROLE OF THE EUROPEAN UNION

On February 7, 1992, the Member States of the EU formalised their ad hoc intergovernmental police cooperation arrangements into a third pillar, Justice and Home Affairs (JHA) (Council of the EC, 1992). Although this agreement sought to create a locus of activity around a European Police Office, or Europol (Art. K.1 [9]), it was more than three years before the Member States could agree on a convention. This document detailed the role of Europol in the prevention and combat of crimes ''where an organised criminal structure is involved and two or more Member States are affected'' (Council of the EU, 1995b: Art. 2.1). Moreover, Europol cannot be established until the extended process of national ratification by each of the Member States has been completed.

To appreciate the breadth of current forms of practical police cooperation within the EU, it is important to understand the detailed rationale behind today's concept of a Europol. This has stimulated international police cooperation within the whole European region, and at many different levels aside from the prospective supranational police intelligence function. Ultimately the idea for a Europol derives from the Single European Act, where the policing and security elements of the abolition of internal border controls highlighted the importance of control at the EC's external borders. But the debate over closer police cooperation rapidly became embroiled in non-border policing issues concerning compensation for the so-called security deficit. This meant that efforts to enhance police cooperation between the Member States were directed both at the effectiveness of border controls to create a ''hard outer shell,'' and the increased transnational mobility afforded to potential offenders. This intergovernmental cooperation was originally conducted informally through the secret Trevi Groups, remaining secret when ratification of the Treaty on European Union formalised the process in November 1993. The overall breadth and complexity of cooperation within the third pillar created a complex organisational structure in which significant changes to the investigation and prosecution of international and transnational offending were to be achieved. But as was seen above, the new focus on mobile offending trespassed upon many of the functions of the much more broadly based Interpol, threatening its position within Europe and providing a further stimulus to Interpol's modernisation of information technology and institutional relations with national police authorities.

The precursor to Europol, the Europol Drugs Unit (EDU), started operating in February 1994, on the basis of an informal Ministerial Agreement (TREVI Ministers, 1993). The initial work of the EDU was limited to drug investigations and resulted in exchange of information between Member States and an increasing number of police operations, including controlled deliveries, across national borders (Norman, 1996: 211–13). Slow progress in gaining agreement on a Europol Convention led the European Council (Essen) to extend the remit of the EDU in December 1994. This resulted in the first formal Joint Action of March 10, 1995, broadening the role of the EDU to

(a) illicit drug trafficking;

(b) illicit trafficking in radioactive waste and nuclear substances;

(c) crime involving clandestine immigration networks;

(d) illicit vehicle trafficking together with the criminal organizations involved and associated money-laundering activities. (Council of the EU, 1995a: Art. 2.2)

Agreement was finally attained on the Europol Convention in July 1996, but national ratification procedures—perhaps lasting a further two years—led to a further Joint Action in December 1996 extending the role of the EDU to "combatting the trafficking in human beings" (Council of the EU, 1996b). This progressive extension of the EDU to other crime sectors—a developmental model sustained in the Europol Convention—raises organisational issues, given that in each Member State a number of agencies would have to operate through their National Units to enable this cooperation. In the UK, these issues have been tackled by seconding non-police officers to NCIS's International Liaison Unit: from Customs and Excise at its inception in 1992; from the Immigration Service in 1993; and in respect of "illicit trafficking in radioactive and nuclear substances" (Council of the EU, 1995a: Art. 2.2.[b]), from the Security Service in 1996. The latter's location within NCIS also dovetails with its controversially extended role in "the prevention and detection of serious crime" (HMG, 1996).

By June 1995 the 15 EU Member States had deployed 32 Europol Liaison Officers, supported by over 50 EDU support staff, including intelligence analysts. The distinctive advantage of the EU's initiatives over Interpol's lies in the possibility of creating a focussed international intelligence analysis function. Formally, intelligence analysis is currently restricted to the "preparation of general situation reports and analyses of criminal activities on the basis of non-personal information supplied by Member States or from other sources'' (Council of the EU, 1995a: Art. 2.3[b]). This strategic intelligence analysis of patterns of crime affecting the EU also makes use of developing relations with other sources, including the United States. This can be seen in the New Transatlantic Agenda, a wide-ranging cooperation agreement signed in December 1995 by the EU and the USA, accompanied by a detailed Joint Action Plan. The Plan details measures such as ''establishing interim cooperative measures between competent US authorities and the Europol Drugs Unit and . . . implementing the possibilities provided for in the convention on EUROPOL'' (EU-USA, 1995: 24). By 1996 the JA Council was considering a formal protocol entitled ''Access of the United States to the data held by the Europol Drugs Unit'' (Statewatch, 1996: 2). Similar third-party agreements are extending the reach of the EDU/Europol as seen in the subsequent EU-Canada Action Plan (Statewatch, 1997: 4).

Whilst examining the EDU's international police function it is important to recognise that, for the purposes of control and accountability, the unit is formally split between actions undertaken by the EDU proper, and those undertaken by the Team of (national) Liaison Officers. In reality, however, the police functions of the EDU staff and the Europol Liaison Officers are intermingled, particularly when acting in support of specific operations against offenders. Until ratification of the Europol Convention, the EDU staff are unable to establish a central database of offenders and perform a truly supranational police intelligence analysis function. However, tactical intelligence analysis of offenders is being undertaken by the EDU personnel as long as it is requested by National Units and relates to one of the EDU's specific crime categories (EDU, 1995a: 7–8). This is short of the future Europol system of police intelligence analysis where National Units would systematically send all their relevant intelligence data on offenders to EDU to be centrally stored and analysed.

The Crime Analysis section of the EDU is composed of two units, one charged with Strategic Analysis and the other with Operational Analysis (EDU, 1995a: 23). Operational intelligence analysis at the EDU would involve the temporary storage and analysis of personal data, but the third-pillar Working Group on Europol has advised that this can be undertaken bilaterally (EDU, 1995a: 7). As one senior UK officer has put it, the Europol Liaison Officers ''from each of the European nations are beginning to contribute effectively, both at the intelligence level and in terms of operations. I am afraid this is a question of police officers having to run ahead of the politicians in order to make that work'' (Venness, 1994: 104).

Indeed, this flexibility is also allowing ''all the plans and computer work . . . [to] get underway as we will need years to get data processing going'' (Storbeck, 1995) before ratification of the Europol Convention. Currently, the Liaison Officers have access to an internal EDU electronic information exchange system and to their own databases, which are in turn linked to their national police intelligence systems (EDU, 1995b: 7).

In preparation for the complex Europol supranational intelligence analysis system against international offenders, a range of more basic technical issues are being addressed in a number of EU third-pillar working groups. This involves agreeing on common definitions for crimes, terminologies, standardised intelligence reports and intelligence analysis techniques. The difficulties of accomplishing this type of work across the EU were demonstrated by comments within the JHA Council about the lack of comprehensive official knowledge about how organised crime is affecting the EU (Home Affairs Committee, 1994: 96). The ad hoc International Organised Crime (IOC) Group presented a detailed series of recommendations to the Council, which included the production of an annual report on international organised crime. The report noted:

> Production of the [annual] report and analysis of the information contained in it will eventually fall to Europol. . . . The report will be based on information about specific investigations into the activities of particular international criminal organisations. Further work is to be undertaken to determine which international criminal organisations should be covered and to agree the detail of the information to be collected. (Home Affairs Committee, 1994: 98)

By 1995 the Working Group on Drugs and Organised Crime had devised a list of characteristic features indicative of an organised crime structure. If a group of offenders displayed six out of ten of these characteristics, then it was to be denoted as an organised crime structure. In the UK a three-month pilot scheme involved the Regional Offices of NCIS, the six Regional Crime Squads, a number of police forces, Customs and Excise and the Benefits Agency. In April 1996, the scheme was applied nationally (NCIS, 1996a: 2–3). These national assessments are now combined with those of other EU Member States for presentation to the JHA Council every six months. But these are not published, which prevents academics from analyzing their results and estimating the prevalence of organised crime.

Much of the police cooperation work in the EU third-pillar has been, and will remain, concerned with the harmonisation of police intelligence practices so that an EU intelligence system can be effectively established centred upon Europol. The importance of recognising the penumbra of third-pillar activities focussed on the EDU/Europol has been recognised for some time. As Fijnaut observes:

> A more dynamic process of growing police cooperation for its part also will enhance the harmonisation of the internal structures, the operational methods, the technical equipment and even the legal powers of the police forces in the Member States of the European Union. The interplay between co-operation, harmonisation and integration must not be underestimated in this field. (Fijnaut, 1994: 614–15)

These dynamics are already observed in the EDU/Europol concept but are now taking a more structured form. Demand for sources of information from inside and outside the EU—including Interpol—will entail the progressive linking of current and planned databases of personal information to Europol and Europol access to other sources of information from the public and private sector.

One notable area of police intelligence gathering is the EU's development of telecommunications infrastructures, which qualitatively enhanced opportunities for surveillance. Objectively, these can only be of benefit to international police investigative action if the procedures are in place to enable their speedy mutual provision. This need was recognised in a 1990 Trevi document, *The 1992 Programme of Action* (Trevi, 1990), which outlined the police measures required to overcome the perceived security deficit created by the impending abolition of EC internal border controls. As a result of the Programme of Action, ministerial approval was granted in December 1991 for "a study of the relationship between Community legislation on telecommunications and possibilities at a national level for judicial interception of telecommunications." (Netherlands Presidency, 1991). This type of work has been promoted by the EU's ad hoc IOC Group, which presented a detailed series of recommendations to the JHA Council in November 1993, resulting in agreement on a JHA Council Resolution on the interception of telecommunications (Home Affairs Committee 1994: 98–99; Council of Ministers, 1995: Annex XI[a]). By the end of 1994, the JHA Council had further agreed that requests for the interception of communications should be "acted upon in all cases in which similar measures could be taken at the request of a country's own authorities" (*The Guardian*, 1994). In England and Wales, a warrant would still be required for the interception of the content of telecommunications for another state, but this would be lodged at the Operational Support Unit at NCIS, before signature by the Home Secretary.

This international infrastructure of police cooperation, and ultimately police intelligence gathering capability, cannot replace the need for police-to-police contacts at the operational level to create the trust necessary for the exchange of police intelligence and for the conduct of joint international police operations against offenders. Both inside and outside the EU, this is being accomplished by the deployment of police personnel as liaison officers in foreign jurisdictions.

THE ROLE OF LIAISON OFFICERS

Liaison officers are a recent innovation for the UK. In 1989 there were just four police Drug Liaison Officers (DLOs) based at British Embassies or Consulates (Home Affairs Committee, 1989: 116). However, by 1994 there were 34 police and customs officers based in more than 20 countries worldwide (NCIS, 1994). The DLOs organise their work into two regions: Europe and the rest of the world. The European DLO network contains police and customs officers who report directly to the International Liaison Unit (ILU) of NCIS, whereas DLOs outside Europe report directly to Her Majesty's Customs and Excise.

In Europe, there are 15 UK DLOs in eight countries. These officers "work in the field of drug trafficking and associated money laundering. They liaise closely with their host countries' relevant law enforcement agencies, exchanging information and building up intelligence on individuals, groups, smuggling routes and so on" (NCIS, 1996b: 15). The ILU acts as a focal point for all international intelligence gathering, coordinating the activities of UK's police and customs liaison officers in Europe, and receiving intelligence reports from the increasing number of foreign Overseas Liaison Officers based at NCIS.[9]

The high cost of deploying liaison officers, with remote information technology systems and the expense of a foreign location, is offset by the enhanced speed of delivery of intelligence to the UK, the possibility of exchanging sensitive intelligence directly and the cultivation of close professional contacts with the host agencies, which will in turn help intelligence gathering and the coordination of police operations. Analysis of DLO activities by NCIS shows that around a third of the officers' time is spent in support of police operations and a third on proactive information gathering on offenders. In 1995/96 the ILU received more than 11,000 intelligence reports from overseas sources and disseminated over 13,000 reports abroad (NCIS, 1996b: 20). The increasing integration of international police roles, witnessed by the broadening role of the Europol Liaison Officers described above, has been acknowledged by the most recent NCIS deployments of what are now termed "Crime Liaison Officers"—who are responsible for all aspects of serious crime.

The concept of liaison officers, acting at the outposts of national police units abroad, was pioneered by the Scandinavian countries, who established DLOs in their efforts to combat drug trafficking and foster closer police and customs cooperation (Fode, 1993: 66). Examination of the Scandinavian liaison officer system shows a close relationship between the respective national authorities that has been absent from subsequent deployments by other EU Member States. The Scandinavian liaison officers systematically supply police intelligence to the participating national authorities directly, irrespective of their nationality, enhancing the speed of communication of intelligence, and reducing the need for duplication of posting (Fode, 1993: 66–67).

In late 1996, the Council of the EU sought a more coordinated system for the deployment of the variety of Member States' national liaison officers (Council of the EU, 1996a). This Joint Action provides for a (voluntary) framework for the deployment of national liaison officers by establishing an EU register (Arts. 3 and 6). The agreement states that where liaison officers are posted to the same third country, they "shall assist one another" (Art. 5[2]), and when members are deciding upon a specific deployment they "may take account of tasks already performed . . . by liaison officers posted by other Member States" (Art. 4[3]) and perhaps may agree on the mutual use of their liaison officers by other Member States (Art. 4[1]). However, the agreement is markedly weaker where a liaison officer discovers information of interest to other Member

States who are not represented in the country concerned. In this case, they "shall assess, according to the seriousness of the threat, whether the States concerned should be informed" (Art. 5[3]). The Joint Action specifically encourages deployments to the CCEE, particularly where there is a drug or organised crime problem. In the drugs field, there is further encouragement to deploy liaison officers to the Andean Region, after the EU's recent conclusion of an agreement that, in part, seeks to combat drug abuse and trafficking.

CONCLUSION

The arrangements for international policing in England and Wales have undergone significant change in the last decade, and a number of trends are now apparent. These can be summarised as a move from informal international police relations to more formal relationships mediated by international police organisations. In addition, the movement to utilise sophisticated police surveillance and intelligence gathering technologies to combat international organised crime is now apparent in the EU and is a common feature of policing strategies in Western Europe and North America generally. But at the level of police structures, important issues of control and accountability are now becoming apparent. The traditionally distinct cleavages between national and sub-national police agencies are becoming less artificial in a move towards more open relationships based upon the reciprocal delivery of police services and greater inter-agency law enforcement cooperation at the national and international level. These changes are a direct consequence of the internationalisation of crime and policing where the traditional geographically bounded arenas of action are becoming increasingly irrelevant.

The first dynamic of development, from one characterised by informal police initiatives in the international sphere to those mediated by the institutional arrangements of international police organisations, has been manifest. Both Interpol and the nascent Europol have accelerated the cohering of international police arrangements at the operational level—but within a framework that attempts to create a broader international police culture based on a structured approach to reciprocal police action and policy coordination. Thus police agencies in England and Wales have developed their breadth of action by moving from a reliance upon limited international deployment of crime-specific liaison officers, and ad hoc informal contacts with overseas jurisdictions, to a situation where they act at a number of levels within larger networks. This engenders an expectation that police expertise, resources and access will be shared in a routine manner. In Interpol, this was most keenly seen in the broader European region from the late 1980s, but since the 1990s the EU's third-pillar police cooperation structures have qualitatively improved the terrain of international action, and this is only the starting point. As police intelligence practices are developed further, those participating in EU institutional arrangements will sustain the internationalisation of police surveillance practices and joint police operations and forge closer relationships between a broad range of law enforcement agencies, security services and other public and private agencies.

The breakdown of organisational cleavages between the police when operating at the international level has been quite clear in England and Wales. This has been stimulated by institutional reforms as well as changes in working relationships. Thus the creation of NCIS in 1992, and the impending creation of the National Crime Squad, have necessitated police-to-police cooperation on a routine basis to ensure intelligence exchange and maximisation of the limited resources of NCIS by police forces and the Regional Crime Squads. The honing of relationships between different police agencies has clearly been stimulated by the wider police reforms to quantify and cost police services and establish distinct policing priorities, which have resulted in a common ''service culture'' among police forces, the Regional Crime Squads and NCIS. These internal police changes have perhaps been the most difficult to attain—and are by no means universally accomplished—but are accepted as essential in England and Wales to ensure that a federal police agency for the UK is effectively dealing with international and transnational offending.

The further advance of close working relationships with other law enforcement agencies and the security services, at the national and international level, raises more serious consequences for police accountability and control. The investigation of serious crime, and international crime involving a number of criminal justice agencies, are clearly difficult—and underresearched—areas for the agencies concerned and for the wider criminal justice system where the identities of informants, sources of information and locus of investigation and prosecution decision making are much more occluded. These factors are likely to become more important as the international police function becomes routinely embedded in the work of all levels of police in England and Wales, and their intelligence-led policing strategies gain transnational and—with Europol—supranational features.

NOTES

1. The (Maastricht) Treaty on European Union established three ''pillars'': pillar one consisted of the original treaties that founded the European Coal and Steel Community, the European Economic Community and the European Atomic Energy Community (as amended); pillar two concerned a common foreign and security policy; and pillar three related to intergovernmental cooperation in justice and home affairs.

2. Article 13 of the Single European Act amended Article 8A of the Treaty of Rome 1957, seeking to create ''an area without internal frontiers in which the free movement of goods, persons, service and capital is ensured.'' This Article was renamed Article 7a by the Treaty on European Union, Article G(9).

3. In the UK, an offshoot of the Defence Manufacturers Association was created in 1987 at the request of the Home Office. It expanded rapidly, becoming a separate agency with over 150 members in 1993: the Association of Police and Public Security Suppliers.

4. These are the Security Service (domestic), the Secret Intelligence Service (overseas) and the Government Communications Headquarters (eavesdropping).

5. The European Information System (EIS) will fulfill the EU's (police, security service, border control, immigration and asylum) information exchange requirements of the draft External Frontiers Convention and the agreed-upon Asylum Convention. In practical terms, the EC has agreed that the established Schengen Information System will be extended to all EU Member States to form the EIS.

6. The statistics on drug trafficking are an estimate based on data on drug seizures, and a guess about what proportion this is of the total drugs smuggled into the UK.

7. The Police Act of 1997. Part II relates to the formation of the National Crime Squad (for England and Wales), whilst Part I places NCIS on a statutory footing.

8. The full list of Interpol's "Principles" appears in Home Affairs Committee, 1990, 31.

9. In 1995/96 there were six Overseas Liaison Officers, five from EU countries.

CHAPTER 7

Prisons and Alternatives to Prison

MIKE NASH

> It was once believed that prison, properly used, could encourage a high proportion of offenders to start an honest life on their release. Nobody now regards imprisonment, in itself, as an effective means of reform for most offenders.
>
> (Home Office, 1990: par. 2.7)

> The government firmly believes that prison works. By taking offenders out of circulation it prevents them from committing yet more crime and it protects the public from dangerous criminals. Prison—and the threat of prison—also acts as a deterrent to would-be criminals. Finally, time spent in prison can be used to rehabilitate offenders.
>
> (Home Office, 1996)

These two statements, separated by six years, reflect a significant U-turn in penal policy in England and Wales that took place over a relatively short period of time. Not only do they represent a reversal in policy, but they also indicate a government reversing its own policies—policies for which it had been claiming success as recently as 1993. These policy shifts have had a significant impact upon both prison and its alternatives over this period. This chapter will attempt to convey a flavour of this policy development through a brief historical account.

In England and Wales, the death penalty may technically be imposed for treason and piracy. For all other criminal offences, a term of imprisonment remains the ultimate penalty. Since the 1991 Criminal Justice Act (CJA), imprisonment can most accurately be regarded as the ultimate deprivation of liberty. In considering both the history and present state of prison and its alternatives, it is crucial to note the primary position that imprisonment has held in the penal system for nearly 200 years. Despite the ever expanding range of community sentences, the continued prominence of custody has meant that these penalties have been seen as alternatives to prison rather than as sentences in their own right. This led the government in the 1991 CJA to introduce the concept of a graduated deprivation of liberty and, in so doing, effectively to abolish the idea of an alternative to custody: "No other penalty can place the same restrictions on liberty as a custodial sentence; if it did, it would be another form of custody: so there can in reality be no 'alternative' to it" (Home Office, 1990: 18).

It could be argued that the relative use of imprisonment or community penalties reflects the level of society's tolerance at the time. Authors such as Garland (1985) argue that, in periods of relative affluence, the centrality of punishment recedes, whereas at times of recession, punishment becomes a more dominant discourse (Sparks, 1996). A greater use of custody could indicate a harsher public attitude, whereas an expansion in community penalties could perhaps be a sign that forgiveness and a belief in rehabilitation dominate. Yet the work of writers such as Foucault (1977) and Cohen (1985) offers a different perspective on punishment in the community, a perspective that points towards increasing levels of social control that rely on the services of so-called soft agents, such as teachers, social workers and doctors. The decline in the use of community disposals in England and Wales in the 1970s could have reflected this view among practitioners as well as the courts' loss of confidence in these alternatives. In the late 1990s, punishment has not only returned to the top of the agenda but has also spread its net over custodial and community disposals. This chapter will chart the interplay between custody and alternative sentences over time, portray the present situation in England and Wales and comment on the similarities with the North American experience.

PRISONS—AN OVERVIEW

In late 1996 there were approximately 140 prison service establishments in England; and the total number of prisoners was over 57,500, a record number. Not content with this, Home Secretary Michael Howard announced on October 25, 1996 that 12 new super-prisons would be privately built and run to house another 11,000 inmates (*The Guardian*, 26 October 1996). This growth, however, has to be seen in the light of projected cuts of 13.3% over a three-year period, which were announced in 1995. These cuts could result in the loss of 3,000 prison officer jobs and a severe curtailment of regime activity. The new prisons would be needed to hold the expected increase in the prison population arising from new mandatory penalties announced in the Crime Bill (see below), which reflects the prison works policy announced by Howard in 1993. The size of the prison population, or the "crowding crisis" as it is known in the USA, determines the conditions under which sentences are served. This has been at the heart of the debate concerning prisons and its alternatives for many years now. Indeed, as Newburn (1995) claims: "It is the growth in prison numbers . . . that has set the tone for much that has happened in criminal justice policy-making since 1945" (Newburn, 1995: 15).

However, it is not the size of the population that has caused the most alarm but its location and the consequent severe overcrowding in particular parts of the system. For example, in March 1995, more than 8,700 prisoners were sleeping two to a cell (Cavadino and Dignan, 1997: 13). Prisons in England and Wales are classified by security categories, according to the risk presented by the prisoner if he or she were to escape. Therefore those prisoners deemed to need the highest security category (A) are those from whom the public are said to need the greatest protection. Prisoners categorised as follows:

Category A—prisoners whose escape would be highly dangerous to the public or the police or the security of the state. These prisoners are held in prisons with high perimeter security, high staff ratios, electronic surveillance and dog patrols as well as restricted visits.

Category B—prisoners for whom the highest conditions of security are not necessary, but for whom escape must be made very difficult.

Category C—prisoners who cannot be trusted in open conditions, but who do not have the ability or resources to make a determined escape bid.

Category D—prisoners who can reasonably be entrusted to serve their sentences in open conditions where there is little physical security. At this level the prison is in effect open; in other words, there is no external security and inmates could, in essence, simply walk out if they wished.

All prisoners including unconvicted prisoners on remand, are allocated within these security categories. Prisoners serving sentences from life imprisonment and those serving a few days for defaulting on fine payments may well be in the same establishment. Prisoners are allocated within the national prison system, according to their security classification, the length of sentence, prison vacancies and to a certain extent the geography of the area in which they are sentenced (rather than their home address). This tends to put most of the pressure on local prisons, which are invariably Category B, as these are required to accept anyone committed by the courts. Locals generally hold short-sentence prisoners from a particular locality or those awaiting allocation to training prisons and are usually the older facilities of the prison service estate; most were built in town and city centres during the Victorian period. Crucially, these prisons often hold those on remand, either awaiting conviction and therefore innocent, or awaiting sentence (some 21% of the total population in 1996). These prisoners invariably endure some of the worst prison conditions. As stated by Morgan: "The consequence is that those prisoners whom on any criterion should have been given the least oppressive conditions, the untried subject to the presumption of innocence, have typically had the most impoverished regimes (Morgan, 1994: 918).

Almost a quarter of the prisons in England and Wales were built during Victorian times when the "less eligibility" doctrine ensured that prison conditions were as punitive as the deprivation of liberty. Indeed this doctrine appears to have been rediscovered in the 1990s. The Home Secretary's wife stands accused of influencing the new prison austerity developments in a television programme, *World in Action* (24 February 1997), when she claimed that prison food was too good for inmates. It could be argued that the best conditions exist in the maximum security prisons, some of which form the "dispersal system," which was created following the deliberations of a committee chaired by Sir Leon Radzinowicz (Advisory Council on the Penal System, 1968). The report of the committee recommended against a previous report from Lord Mountbatten, which had proposed keeping top security prisoners in one institution, to be known as "Vectis" and to be built on the Isle of Wight off the coast of southern England. The Radzinowicz recommendation was to build several maximum security prisons, among which Category A prisoners would be dispersed, thereby diluting their influence and making it easier to transfer them in the event of trouble. In dispersal prisons the inmates enjoy single-cell accommodation and a range of work and leisure facilities (although these have increasingly been cut back since the late 1980s). It could be argued that the fault of the dispersal system is that it not only provides excellent facilities to low-security prisoners but also wraps them in unnecessary internal and external security measures. The cost is hard to justify when average dispersal places cost £36,736 per annum compared with less than £22,000 for a training prison. Older dispersals such as Parkhurst, which has just lost its Category A status, were costing nearly £63,000 per annum. This is one of the reasons why there has recently been a move away from the dispersal system to multifunction local and training prisons that may have special secure units for Category A prisoners. This replicates the provision for female Category A prisoners, who are held in a special wing at the male Durham prison. However, in the wake of recent escapes from maximum security prisons and the report of the investigation into one of those escapes at Parkhurst (Learmont, 1995), the government is once again considering building a new super maximum security prison (super-max) to hold all dangerous prisoners, estimated at approximately 200 inmates (Sparks, 1996a: 119). Indeed, Learmont is proposing to introduce six security categories, 1 being exceptional risk and 2 being great risk. The remainder of the prison estate is more modern. It was generally built on green-field sites after the late 1940s, a time when the crime rate began to grow significantly. Many of the open prisons (Category D) are former military establishments or large country houses introduced as a cost-effective solution to the need for more accommodation in the post-war period.

To a large extent the conditions in which staff work and prisoners live not only determine the type of environment and disciplinary structure offered but the spirit in which the prison works. It is difficult to imagine a creative and positive regime being provided in conditions that the Council of Europe Committee for the Prevention of Torture described as "inhuman and degrading"

(Morgan, 1994: 919). Such conditions will be seen as an important, but by no means the only, contributor to the riot at Strangeways prison in Manchester in 1990 (and which spread to 20 others elsewhere). (See Cavadino and Dignan (1997) for an account of the multiple causes of this penal crisis.) The Strangeways riot triggered the most far-reaching inquiry ever into the prison service in England and Wales. The following section describes the background, results and recommendations of this inquiry, which was chaired by Lord Justice Woolf.

THE WOOLF REPORT

The riot at Strangeways prison resulted in the death of one prisoner and the injury of 147 officers and 47 prisoners. The eventual cost of the repairs was £30 million. It is difficult to pinpoint a single cause for the disturbances; probably one does not exist. It reflected crises represented in most penal regimes around the world, which are characterised by rising populations, escalating costs, overcrowding and poor conditions, and concerns about the purpose of internal discipline in prisons (Sparks, 1996: 207). A potential for serious prisoner disorder was not fully acknowledged until the 1970s, when the Home Office warned of "the potential of unrest in an organisation which has the complex aims of both containing and rehabilitating" (Home Office, 1973: par. 147). This complex aim perhaps lies at the heart of the difficulties within the prison system. Containment and rehabilitation are not easy bedfellows and the mix of people coming into prison, as well as the reasons they are there, makes the enterprise a difficult one for which to set easily defined and understood mission statements. Morgan (1994) identifies three legal uses for imprisonment: *custodial*, for remand and unsentenced prisoners; *coercive*, for those imprisoned for default of unpaid fines; and *punitive*, for those serving a sentence of the court. Much of the prison system in England and Wales is dominated by a mix of these purposes and, therefore, a corresponding mix of prisoners under one roof.

The integration of different prisoner types in relatively small institutions makes the production of coherent regimes a difficult task. Laid upon this are the fashions of penal rhetoric, which reflected the collapse in the belief of rehabilitation in prisons (and in community disposals) of the 1970s, following the work of people such as Martinson (1974) and Brody (1976). Working within the framework of the Prison Rules (SI, 1964), prisons had been encouraged to assist prisoners to lead "good and useful lives" and move towards self-respect. However, as Morgan (1994: 85) notes, the treatment and training paradigm adopted by the Prison Department suggested an unduly positive role for prisons, one which sentencers might be encouraged to make greater use of. This of course added to the confusion over ideology and purpose. (For a review of the debate concerning humane containment and positive custody see King and Morgan [1980] and the May Committee, [1979].) The present Prison Service *Statement of Purpose* perhaps reflects the more managerialist approach of recent years, when it states: "Her Majesty's Prison Service serves the public by keeping in custody those committed by the courts. Our duty is to look after them with humanity and to help them to lead law-abiding and useful lives in custody and on release.''[1]

The Woolf Report (1991) contained a central conclusion that stability in prisons relies on a proper balance between three elements of regimes: *security* arrangements to prevent escapes, *control* measures to prevent disorder and disruption and procedures for *justice* to ensure all prisoners are treated with humanity and fairness (Player and Jenkins, 1994). This combination was seen to be lacking from most regimes prior to the Strangeways disturbances. A lack of mission can trigger an ideological crisis, producing a moral vacuum that is ripe for filling by a government keen to fulfill its promises of reducing state expenditure whilst increasing resources for law and order agencies (Savage and Nash, 1994; Loveday, 1992). In the case of the prison service, several moves had been undertaken that could be said to have contributed to the declining situation that led up to the Strangeways riots. In 1987 the Government introduced Fresh Start, a fundamental restructuring of the prison service, which will probably be best remembered for its abolition of overtime for prison officers (who had previously often received as much as 30 hours of overtime per week). Fresh Start also ended direct entry into the Governor grade and introduced single-point entry for all prison officers, as in the police service. Fresh Start was more than this, however: it created a functional system of management based on performance targets increasingly set by central government.

The discovery of managerialism helped fill the ideological void at the heart of the prison service as mission statements became closely related to management targets. Part of the Fresh Start agenda was to enhance the role of basic grade prison officers, notably by involving them in educative, training and rehabilitative activities with inmates. However it could be argued that there was an element of cynicism in this. Prison staff are generally not fully trained to take on these tasks; but it soon became clear that prison governors, once they assumed responsibility for their own budgets, were keen to shed the costs of the more expensive imports into the prison, such as teachers and probation officers. Efficiency, effectiveness and economy became more important to the prison service than positive regime activity, which was curtailed as financial imperatives bit more deeply into budgets. Despite reports such as that prepared by Ian Dunbar (1985), which extolled the virtues of the dynamic security measures used in the United States, it was clear that management effectiveness was to be the most important measure of success: ''The signal preoccupation of the prison system in England and Wales since the 1980s therefore, has been with the efficiency of management practices, the distribution of resources and cost-effective delivery of services'' (Sparks, 1996b: 214).

How did all this fit with the Woolf inquiry? Against a background of prisoner discontent, declining staff morale, a tighter squeeze on resources, a challenge to established purpose and a growth in numbers, what would be the new agenda? It was clear from the main recommendations arising from the Woolf report that the problem of prisons was to be viewed in a wider context: as a symptom of malaise within the wider criminal justice system. The report listed 12 key recommendations as follows:

1. Closer cooperation between the different parts of the criminal justice system. For this purpose a national forum and local committees should be established.
2. More visible leadership of the Prison Service by a Director General who is, and is seen to be, the operational head and in day-to-day charge of the service. To achieve this there should be a published compact, or contract given by ministers to the Director General of the Prison Service, who should be responsible for the performance of that contract and publicly answerable for the day-to-day operations of the Prison Service.
3. Increased delegation of responsibility to governors of establishments.
4. An enhanced role for prison officers.
5. A compact, or contract, for each prisoner setting out the prisoner's expectations and responsibilities in the prison in which he or she is held.
6. A national system of Accredited Standards, with which, in time, each prison establishment would be required to comply.
7. A new Prison Rule that no establishment should hold more prisoners than provided for in its certified normal level of accommodation, with provisions for Parliament to be informed of exceptional circumstances that require a material departure from this rule.
8. A public commitment from Ministers setting a timetable to provide access to sanitation (i.e., toilet facilities—many cells still do not have either urinals or commodes) for all inmates at the earliest practical date and not later than February 1996.
9. Better prospects for prisoners to maintain their links with families and the community through more visits and home leaves and through being located in community prisons as near to their homes as possible.
10. A division of prison establishments into small and more manageable and secure units.
11. A separate statement of purpose, separate conditions (from sentenced prisoners) and generally a lower security categorisation for remand prisoners.
12. Improved standards of justice within prisons: the prison administration must provide reasons to a prisoner for any decision that materially and adversely affects him, establish a grievance procedure and disciplinary proceedings that ensure that the governor (i.e., warden) deals with most matters under his present powers, relieve Boards of Visitors of their adjudicatory role and provide for final access to an independent Complaints Adjudicator. (Par. 15.5)

Woolf therefore set a radical agenda and perhaps went much further than the government might have expected. Nonetheless the government, as well as many penal reformers, welcomed the report. The government produced a White Paper, *Custody, Care and Justice* (Home Office, 1991), setting out a timetable for ending "slopping out,"[2] for example, and improving standards. However, the relentless rise in numbers, fuelled by the Home Secretary's tough stance on crime, has pushed the reformist agenda backwards in many respects, particularly in the provision of positive regimes. The setting of improved standards is increasingly seen as the hope of, and one of the primary justifications for, privatisation within the prison service, as indicated by the then Home Secretary Kenneth Clarke in 1992:

> To me this is the final answer to the moral question. It cannot be more moral to lock up prisoners for long hours a day with little chance to associate, limited opportunity for visits and little access to work, education or PE, than to see them unlocked all day with access to a full programme of useful activities, simply because the poor programme is provided by staff directly employed by the state and the better programme by staff employed by a contractor of the state. (Sparks, 1996a, 235)

Prison privatisation then is already proceeding perhaps at a faster pace than in the USA; it is wrapped in positive clothes and seen as the panacea for improved conditions. Yet the Home Secretary, Michael Howard, has turned his back on large parts of the progressive Woolf agenda. In striving to toughen the regimes in prisons he is obviating the need for privatisation, or at least altering the rationale for it. As Sparks (1996b) indicates, it could be argued that privatised prisons can be made to react barometrically to the prevailing penal climate because they are unencumbered by traditional vocational and public service ethics. In other words the privatised corrections industry is reacting not so much to market forces as to prevailing penal ideology, perhaps eventually forcing correctional organisations to take a position on where they stand (Sparks, 1996b: 89).

Towards the end of the millennium it is clear that the debate concerning prisons in England and Wales replicates to a great extent that in the USA. Since Margaret Thatcher first came into power, the Conservative Party has been attracted to "things American," especially in the areas of law and order and welfare policy. Yet for some time the liberal traditions of the Home Office were able to curb what might be viewed as the worst excesses of the government; so for every harsh measure a more liberal safeguard was put in place (Savage and Nash, 1994). However, the tenure of Michael Howard at the Home Office saw an almost complete refutation of research evidence in the assertion that prison works. This has meant fundamental U-turns in policy, which have led to the astonishingly rapid undoing of the work of Howard's predecessors. Howard, a very shrewd politician, imported US policies wholesale and gave them local populist credence. "Prison works" has been an effective slogan in raising the political temperature because it has dragged the official opposition party with it. The Labour Party has been very anxious not to be portrayed as "soft on crime" and has therefore supported the Home Secretary more often than it has opposed him. This has enabled a series of punitive measures to be both proposed and passed almost without opposition in the House of Commons. Indeed the major opposition has been from former Conservative Home Secretaries and the senior judiciary.

As America has done in the "War on Drugs," the Home Secretary has targeted certain crimes for harsher treatment: notably sexual, violent and drug offences. This tradition can be traced back to 1983 when the then Home Secretary, Leon Brittain, announced minimum 20-year life sentences for certain offenders. The tradition continued even within the more liberal 1991 CJA, which allowed for "longer than desert" sentences for violent and sexual offenders from whom the public was deemed to need protection. The latest manifestation of a development dubbed as "punitive bifurcation" (Cavadino and Dignan, 1997) is the Crime (Sentences) Bill, which proposes mandatory minimum penalties for a range of offences. It proposes automatic life sentences for those convicted of second serious violent and sexual crimes, mandatory minimum seven-year sentences for third-time class A drug dealers and minimum three-year sentences for third-time adult domestic burglars. These measures are set alongside a severe restriction on early release (in which the remission of a sentence is reduced from 50% to 20% in most cases and is offered only to cooperative prisoners), all of which is likely to significantly increase the prison population and escalate the overcrowding crisis. Even before the bill has become law, the punitive climate has already taken hold. The number of prisoners has steadily increased since the early 1990s and already exceeds 1996 predictions. At that time, the Home Office estimated that there would be 59,000 prisoners by 2003/4. As of March 1996 this number had already been passed, and every week there are 250 to 300 more prisoners. This growth has already forced the prison service to buy a floating prison ship from New York State at a cost of £4 million. This ship will only accommodate two weeks of prison growth, however, and at the time of writing is the subject of a prison officers' union dispute over safety. It remains debatable of course if the increased use of imprisonment will either reduce crime or indeed be focussed upon the serious offenders it is aimed at.

The US experience is frequently cited as a policy that has reduced crime, although reports suggest that this may not be the case. *The Independent* reported on March 9, 1996 that many more small-time marijuana smokers had been caught up in California's three strikes law than "rapists, murderers and kidnappers combined." Nonetheless, the message coming out of the Home Office is that while offenders are in custody they cannot offend in the community, a startling reversal of the White Paper assertion that prison is "an expensive way of making bad people worse" (Home Office, 1990: par. 2.7). The Home Office Research and Planning Unit calculated in 1993 (personal correspondence) that to reduce the crime rate by 1%, an increase in the prison population of 25% would be necessary. Since 1992, an increase well exceeding this rate has occurred with no significant impact on overall crime rates. It appears that longer sentences, more punitive regimes and more prisoners will be features of the criminal justice system for some years to come. The effect on crime may well turn out to be minimal, but the effect on other law and order measures cannot be underestimated, and it is to this that we now turn.

ALTERNATIVES TO CUSTODY

Prisons have long been a major influence on the shape and philosophy of the criminal justice process in England and Wales. At the present time, they appear to be on course to be the central and dominant component of the penal process over the next few years. It would be easy to say that this is the natural outcome of four successive Conservative governments that have pledged to strengthen the law and order agenda. Yet this assumption would be false and based on naive interpretations of the increasingly important New Right rhetoric. Conservative penal policy has been a complex blend of a tough stance and economic restraint (Savage and Nash, 1995). Throughout the 1980s and into the early 1990s the Treasury, allied to a liberal tradition at the Home Office, was able to mollify the "red meat" pronouncements of Conservative Home Secretaries. The evidence would now suggest that this phase is over and that a new era of prison works and penal austerity has begun.

The history of alternatives to custody in England and Wales is intimately bound up with the history of the probation service. This chapter therefore briefly describes the origins of this service and its landmark developments in an attempt to present its position as the millennium draws near, a position that is increasingly akin to an American-style correctional service rather than to its European counterpart.

Building on early developments in America, (the Massachusetts Act, 1878), the origins of the probation service in England and Wales reflected the concerns of individual citizens who supported the reform rather than punishment of criminals, particularly where alcohol appeared to play a significant part in the offending. This concern represented a wider Victorian concern with the moral degeneration of the urban working class and a positivist belief that people could change. Several key contributors can be seen as influencing the reformist agenda in the 19th century. In 1830 Bentham (1970) had developed his utilitarian philosophy, which called for a balance between deterrence and retribution, a balance necessary so as not to prevent the eventual reintegration of the offender into the society that he had rationally chosen to forsake. Lombroso (1876) developed his thesis of the criminal individual and criminal classes—people born to offend because of certain individual characteristics. Meanwhile, in France some 30 years earlier, Quetelet and Guerry had produced work concluding that crime was the result of social causes (May, 1991: 6). We therefore have a trilogy of crime causation: free will, individual pathology and social causes. It would appear to be difficult to devise a theory of crime causation that fused all three ideas. This did take place, however, when links were made between criminological thinking and political and moral thinking. The result was, in essence, the individualisation of crime (Garland, 1985). This idea has been a central tenet of the probation service since its formation in 1907. It is currently under attack from a government determined to again present crime as an act freely entered into by the criminal and not as a result of social or economic causes. (For an account of probation service history see Jarvis [1972] and McWilliams [1983, 1985, 1986].)

Early, non-statutory work in probation had been carried out by people known as police court missionaries, who were members of the Church of England Temperance Society. They represented the reforming zeal of Victorian society but were not the only ones chosen to work as probation officers following the 1907 Probation of Offenders Act. The choice was left to local magistrates. Nonetheless it is important to note that, nearly 100 years later, there is considerable pressure on the probation service to again work with the independent and voluntary sector, particularly for non-serious offenders. This time though the reason is the government's desire to save money and to break the hold of public sector professionals rather than a commitment to charitable reform.

The early history of the probation service is therefore founded upon a belief in change, or more accurately, treatment. The original ethos of the service was spelt out in an amendment to the 1907 bill:

> To visit or receive reports from the person under supervision at such reasonable intervals as the probation officer may think fit; to see that he observes the conditions of his recognisance; to report to the Court on his behaviour; to advise, assist and befriend him and, when necessary, to endeavour to find him suitable employment. (cited in Jarvis, 1972: 16)

The words "advise, assist and befriend" became one of the hallmarks of probation practice. However, to a great extent, they were a negative association for the probation service of the 1980s. As the individualisation of crime became politically unacceptable, the ethos of probation, which was committed to helping the offender, became unpopular. This was to become one of the battles to be fought by the probation service under successive conservative governments. Their success, or lack of, in those battles will be discussed below.

Probation service history since its inception is one of increasing central control, although for a long while, the guiding principle was of a local service. Several departmental committees in the period before the Second World War examined both the duties of probation officers and the framework in which they operated. For example, a departmental committee in 1920 recommended that more probation officer posts be created and that the central government pay 50% of the cost of the probation service in the belief that increased use of probation would eventually introduce cost savings elsewhere, notably within prisons (an idea revisited with vigour in the 1980s). However, unlike future Thatcher governments, the 1920 report did not envisage any loss in local autonomy. With the 1925 Criminal Justice Act it became mandatory for every criminal court to have a probation officer attached to it; local authorities were responsible for his or her pay. Between 1925 and 1933 the number of people aged 17 and over subject to probation supervision rose from 15,904 to 18,934 (May, 1991: 12), a result probably of an increase in probation officers and a concern with rising crime. Alongside a growing bureaucratisation of the service was a push among probation officers for professional recognition—something which would be harshly challenged 50 years later—notably as the importance of diagnosis increased in professional practice. A good indication of this development was the publication in 1925 of Cyril Burt's book *The Young Delinquent*. Burt argued that it was important to study the offender's characteristics rather than the offence. He recommended that officers study psychology. In 1995 the Home Office produced a report suggesting that probation officers did not need a social casework background and recommending instead on-the-job competency training of such people as recruits from the armed forces (Home Office, 1995). In the years 1934 through 1936 departmental committees reported on the inadequacy of training, the isolated nature of officer's work, the overreliance on part-time staff and the small number of women probation officers. Reorganisation was recommended based on county boundaries, a system eventually introduced in 1948 by the Criminal Justice Act of that year. This act, in repealing all previous probation legislation, established the beginnings of the modern probation bureaucracy and saw the introduction of a 50% government grant. This naturally led to the establishment of a government inspectorate to ensure that the money was efficiently and effectively spent and also had the effect of increasing centralisation of probation practice, although it was not until the 1980s that this really took hold. However, despite an increased specification of the duties of staff, especially principal and senior probation officers, professional independence remained a fundamental feature of probation practice, as Jarvis (1972: 64) noted: "The sturdy independence of the individual officer had long held sway, and was to do so long after the Rules had been issued." It was this independence, indeed the mystery of probation practice, which was to be challenged and effectively lost by the 1990s.

Finally, in this very brief resume of probation service history, it is worth noting the report of the Morrison Committee in 1962, which affirmed that probation orders were to be made *instead of* a sentence. This report also promoted the idea of strong supervision of the order in the face of rising crime figures. At this stage the protection of society and the regulation of behaviour began to receive prominence. The former was to become the standard for probation practice in the 1990s, whilst the latter increasingly began to focus on the management of offenders in the community. In 1972 the present-day probation structure was created, as was the introduction of an 80% Treasury grant, a sum of money that was to increasingly determine the style of probation practice and reduce professional and local autonomy. Perhaps the last period in which social work values were to play a dominant part in probation history was the early 1970s when training was transferred from the Home Office to the Central Council for Education and Training in Social Work (CCETSW), and a requirement was created that all probation officers have a Certificate of Qualification in Social Work (CQSW). This requirement was not destined to last beyond its 25th anniversary.

The probation service in England and Wales had reached a stage in the late 1950s when students came from around the world to examine its probation methods (Hamai et al., 1995: 51). Its professional standing was considerable, and it enjoyed a good relationship with sentencers in the courts. At times it was sufficient for the probation officer simply to recommend the imposition of a probation order for it to be passed, a long way from the detailed supervision plans that have emerged since the 1980s. There remained a belief that an offender's behaviour could be changed and there was, as yet, no significant challenge to professional autonomy. Yet changes were beginning to take place. For example, the Streatfield Committee, reporting in 1961, emphasised the role of the probation officer as a witness for the court, not for the defence or prosecution. The result was a move towards an emphasis on national rather than local policies and a focus on classes of offenders rather than individuals (Newburn, 1995: 89). Another very significant development arose out of the report of the Advisory Council on the Treatment of Offenders (ACTO) in 1963, which recommended a substantial increase in, and reorganisation of, the probation service to include the supervision of people released from custody and the taking over of welfare work within prisons (from 1966). This was ultimately to lead to a significant shift in the caseload of the probation service: for example, in 1951, 82.4% of the caseload was made up of probationers and 9.9% of aftercare clients. By 1981 these figures were 31.9% and 37.6% respectively (Newburn, 1995: 91). The 1975 Criminal Justice Act enabled the probation service to provide training centres and probation and bail hostels and also introduced the Community Service Order, which enabled offenders to make reparation in the community by means of unpaid work supervised by the probation service as an alternative to custody. This order was to become a very significant aspect of the work of the probation service.

Before describing the actual provision of community sentences at the present time and particularly the impact of the 1991 Criminal Justice Act, it is worth summarising the changes that took place in the 1970s: that is, before the fundamental policy and practice shifts of the 1980s and 1990s. As already noted, the probation service was increasingly asked to take on the responsibility of more serious cases, not necessarily through the courts, but through their release from custody. In particular, the task of parole supervision took on a more public protection role (Newburn, 1995: 92).[3] Intellectually there was also a large question mark raised over the nature of probation intervention: in other words, was it a humane approach or another form of state intrusion? This led to both a more radical approach to social work (Walker and Beaumont, 1981) and a questioning of effectiveness, especially in the face of mounting evidence that "nothing worked" (Martinson, 1974; Brody, 1975). The combination of all these factors resulted in an overall decline in the use of probation orders by the courts because courts at all levels allegedly no longer had confidence in the effectiveness of probation and because probation officers were no longer clear about their role.

Margaret Thatcher's first election victory in 1979 had been largely based on the promise of a tough law and order agenda. In promising more police and prison officers and tougher sentencing, the Conservatives managed to paint the Labour government as "soft on crime," as apologists for the criminal. Yet the tough stance on law and order, notably the introduction of "short, sharp, shock" sentences for young offenders, and the extension of the tariff for certain life sentence prisoners, masked a considered effort to increase the use of community penalties, or alternatives to custody as they were then known. We then saw what has since become known as a process of "bifurcation" (Bottoms, 1977, 1980), whereby an outwardly punitive approach is adopted towards certain classes of offenders (usually violent, sex and drug offenders), whilst sentencers are encouraged to avoid the use of custody for non-serious offenders. To do this of course, whilst appearing to be tough on law and order issues, it was necessary to recast the community penalties in a more punitive light, one which emphasised discipline and control. In other words, the overall punitive approach has an influence on all penalties, therefore pushing even non-custodial penalties up-tariff. The apotheosis of this process was to become the 1991 Criminal Justice Act.

The Green and White papers that prefaced the 1991 CJA spelt out the future shape of community penalties. The titles themselves begin to reflect government thinking, *Punishment in the Community* (1988) and *Crime, Justice and Protecting the Public* (1990). The government was keen to expand the use of community penalties for non-serious offenders but did not wish to appear to be letting-off offenders. This meant that community penalties, a new term, were to be redefined in terms of punishment in the community, a deprivation of liberty. The amount of deprivation, the punishment element of the sentence, was to be relative to the seriousness of the crime; in other words, a just desserts philosophy was to be enshrined in law. To accompany this shift in emphasis it was necessary to present the probation service as a more disciplined, controlling (and controlled—see the Statement of National Objectives for Probation, Home Office, 1984) organisation, one in which the courts would have confidence. It is clear that the overall intention of the 1991 CJA was to reduce both the use of custody and the actual numbers in custody (the prison population was reduced by several thousand in the months immediately following the implementation of the 1991 CJA in October 1992). The probation service was therefore faced with a carrot and stick situation. The carrot was the offer of being placed centre stage in the government's law and order programme with the promise of expansion and greater funding. For a social work-based service under a Conservative administration this was almost manna from heaven. The stick however meant, to many practitioners, the forsaking of traditional values and loss of professional autonomy, notably with the introduction of national standards, which now govern virtually every aspect of probation service duties.

The 1991 CJA introduced an attempt to structure sentencing whilst continuing to allow judicial discretion in sentencing—something now much more under threat with the proposed introduction of mandatory minimum penalties. It created a banded structure of sentences, related to offence seriousness, which placed community penalties just below the custody threshold. Community sentences were to be imposed when the offence was "serious enough," whilst custody was only to be imposed when the offence was "so serious" that only custody would do. Definitions of these criteria remained vague, however, and it was not clear if it was possible any longer to pass a sentence as an alternative to custody. In effect it was not, because if the crime matched the criteria, then a custodial sentence had to be passed. This was of course a serious matter for probation officers, who during the 1980s had been exhorted by the Home Office to tackle the problem of providing custodial alternatives for young male offenders predominantly charged with burglary offences. Similarly an argument had raged over the suspended sentence of imprisonment; for how could a prison sentence be suspended if its imposition was merited by the seriousness of the crime? Again, this is a literal interpretation of the legislation, but it indicates how the economics of the situation, along with judicial preference, made this a difficult matter for the legislators. In the years preceding the 1991 CJA, some 44,000 suspended sentences had been passed annually. Their abolition would not only have significantly increased the prison population but also would have heavily interfered with judicial discretion. The sentence therefore remained on the statute book with the proviso that its imposition should be accompanied by some form of additional reparation, such as a compensation order, so that the offender was not seen to be getting away with his crime.

The government had therefore managed to introduce a Criminal Justice Act—described in *The Times* (21 August 1990) as one of the most enlightened acts of the century—which had the explicit aim of reducing the prison population. It did this by not only toughening up the conditions of community penalties and reducing the discretion of the probation service, but interestingly by redefining custody in New Right terms. Prison was seen to negate personal responsibility for the crime, to punish family members left behind and remove the opportunity for reparation. Prison was defined as "nannying," in similar terms to those used in the attack on the welfare state (Home Office, 1990: 6). Hence a Conservative Home Secretary was able to convince the wavering party faithful that serious offenders would be punished by even longer prison sentences, whilst less serious offenders would be made to face up to their responsibilities and not be such a drain on the public purse.

Prior to the 1991 CJA the courts could choose from a range of community penalties. Probation Orders could be from six months to three years, with or without a range of additional conditions. Crucially the offender had to consent to the order. Community Service Orders imposed work in the community ranging from 40 to 240 hours to be completed in 12 months. This order in particular was seen as an alternative to custody. The 1991 Act toughened the conditions of probation orders, making the order a sentence in its own right that was no longer imposed instead of a sentence. This enabled it to be combined with other penalties, something which was not possible when it was not defined as a sentence. In particular, this was epitomised by the creation of a new Combination Order, where the court was able to combine a probation order with a Community Service Order. This overturned one of the long held distinctions in probation practice that an offender in need should receive the assistance of a probation order, whilst one not in need should work in the community. This new order represented the ultimate community sanction at the time, containing elements of treatment and punishment. The government also has a curfew order on the books that will allow a curfew of up to 12 hours to be imposed for a maximum of six months. However, at the present time a supervising agency has not accepted responsibility for this order. The punitive nature of community (probation-led) disposals had, however, been in evidence before the 1991 CJA. Experiments with tracking offenders, closely monitoring offenders' movements, (using ancillary probation staff and volunteers) had been developed in the 1980s. Similar schemes known as ''intensive probation'' (a more frequent form of contact aimed at high-risk offenders) had been tried but were not found to be any more effective in terms of reducing recidivism than ordinary supervision (Mair et al., 1994). The government was not the only mover in the raising of the punitive stakes. In 1988 the Association of Chief Officers of Probation (ACOP) released a document entitled *More Demanding than Prison*, stating its case that community penalties were a viable alternative to custody. In aligning itself, to a certain extent, with the new government agenda, it could be argued that the managers of the service have gone some considerable way to contributing to the change in probation values that have caused such dismay in the rank and file in recent years.

The upwards punitive drift has not, however, abated. The increased focus on imprisonment (and the punitive nature of that disposal) has had a knock-on (consequential) effect on community disposals. The National Standards for probation service have been revised twice already. Each time, there has been a renewed emphasis on tightening up breach procedures for community penalties. Probation orders increasingly include restrictive conditions, and probation officers are more frequently overseeing conditions such as urine analysis for substance abusers. This appears to move the service closer to its American community corrections counterpart. However, there is a certain amount of rehabilitative light at the end of the tunnel. The probation service in England and Wales has adopted the approach of ''what works'' (Gendreau et al., 1995; Gendreau, 1996) developing cognitive/behavioural group therapy work based on thorough risk assessment and a targeted approach to criminogenic factors. This approach has been approved by the Home Office, although the cynic might say that this is not so much because of a belief in rehabilitation but because it reduces probation officer discretion and makes staff more accountable to programmes of work. Sentencers and managers can be more confident about what staff are doing.

CONCLUSION

Towards the end of the millennium the probation service stands at the crossroads. It survived nearly 20 years of Conservative government but in doing so shifted its philosophy and organisation enormously. Each change increased the ratchet of control and the transformation into a community correctional service appears almost complete. The protection of the public has emerged as a crucial objective for the service, and the management of risk has become its day-to-day rationale. The quest for what works may retain elements of the old probation tradition, but a move towards Cohen's punitive city (1979) appears closer than ever. The probation service in England and Wales could be on the brink of dismemberment. It is already obliged by the Home Office to spend 5% of its annual budget on partnership work with the voluntary and independent sector. Its work in bail hostels is an increasingly attractive target for the private security industry. Prison governors are considering using non-probation staff to run traditionally probation-led groups inside of prisons as a cost-effective option. The National Association for the Care and Resettlement of Offenders (NACRO)—an independent organisation—has made no secret of its desire to take on the post-release supervision of short-term prisoners. The reluctance of probation staff to take on responsibility for electronic tagging may mean that this area of work, linked with bail and potentially supervision orders, will move to another agency. The probation service has a long and impressive record of working with serious and high-risk offenders in the community (Shaw 1996), yet the government appears to be keen on passing this work out to people without social work training, whose task is seen to be the management of offenders in the community, rather than the seeking of positive change in their behaviour. In both the probation and prison services the achievement of short-term managerial targets appears to be the immediate future rather than any attempt to work on the more imponderable but potentially more beneficial long-term changes in offending behaviour.

NOTES

1. This "mission statement" is to be found on the gate of every prison service establishment.

2. The absence of in-cell toilet facilities has meant that, in many prisons, prisoners locked up overnight are required to use buckets, which must be carried to a disposal point each morning.

3. It should be noted that in England and Wales, parole supervision refers to prisoners released early under license to a probation officer. Supervision refers to community sentences.

CHAPTER 8

Crime Statistics

KEN PEASE

INTRODUCTION

When Noel Coward was regaled with the theatrical cliche ''The show must go on,'' he responded, ''Why''? This is also a good answer when one hears the statement that statistics of crime are of great value. It is not clear from the meagre range of uses to which such statistics are typically put what their real value might be. To address the point satisfactorily, we probably have to look at the substance of the statistics somewhat as if they were artefacts of an unknown civilisation, the characteristics of which civilisation we have to infer from those objects. This is somewhat pompous, but we do need some way of distancing ourselves from something that has become so familiar as to be invisible in its characteristics. To limit the scope of the enquiry, attention is restricted in this chapter to statistics from England and Wales. After a look at routine statistics from a distance, crime rates and the difficulties that attach to their calculation are discussed. After that, the role of victimisation surveys in understanding crime and its perception will be discussed, with particular attention to the question of the measure of crime concentration. Finally, an approach is advocated in which there is a concerted attempt to apply the hard-won and massively underutilised data on crime for purposes to which it is relevant. It is hoped that the reader will leave the chapter with a somewhat changed view about how to look upon statistical data on crime, and how such data, with all their imperfections, may do useful service in understanding the world.

CRIME STATISTICS CONSIDERED AS ARTEFACTS

In what follows, there is a tension between the characteristics of the product and inferences about the producers. It should be said at the outset that the writer has very high regard for the statistical and criminological expertise of those who compile crime statistics in the United Kingdom. To say that their expertise is shoehorned into a restrictive format that reflects a world view far less sophisticated than their own cannot be interpreted as a criticism of them. In fact, many trends of the last two decades have revealed the sophistication of the compilers. First, the research and statistics arms of the Home Office have been combined into a single Research and Statistics Directorate (RSD). One of the subtexts of the change is that statistics are not finished products, but the raw material of imaginative and checkable inferences. This is reflected in the RSD *Mission Statement* (HMSO, 1994), which reads:

> The Research and Statistics Directorate is an integral part of the Home Office, serving Ministers and the department, its services, Parliament and the public through research, development and statistics. Information and knowledge from these sources informs policy development and the management of programmes: their dissemination improves wider public understanding of matters of Home Office concern. This view of RSD as an improvement-oriented service does not release it from the shackles of the kinds of information which it must by law collect, but it does show that its purpose is to guide policy and practice towards avenues which (at least) are not at odds with the data. (HMSO, 1994: 2)

A second sign of the sophistication of the producers is the appearance of an occasional digest, *Information on the Criminal Justice System*, which locates national crime and criminal justice data in appropriate contexts. Much use will be made of the data from this digest later in the chapter, and the digest should be required reading for those seriously interested in crime counting. All that said, the writer does strongly believe that a much greater preparedness to speculate and hypothesise in the work of the RSD would immeasurably enhance its usefulness. To urge this when the statistics are prepared within one of the great Departments of State is perhaps naive, but in terms of value for money gained from RSD, this seems the single most necessary change.

The statistical products that are regularly or frequently produced are of three kinds. The first is entitled *Criminal Statistics England and Wales Year X*. This one-volume text is published every year. There are no gaps in the series. Many copies of this publication exist, and copies are reliably found in large libraries and police force headquarters. Later volumes in the series come in a distinctive yellow-brown cover.

The second kind of statistical product is much rarer. Also to be found in yellow-brown covers, these are volumes supplementary to the *Criminal Statistics*, and are titled *Criminal Statistics England and Wales: Supplementary Tables Year X Volume X*. Of these, volume 1 deals with proceedings in magistrates' courts, volume 2 covers proceedings in the Crown Court, volume 3 bears the snappy title *Recorded offences, firearms offences and court proceedings by police force area, cautions* and volume 4 is *Proceedings in magistrates courts—*

data for individual Petty Sessional Divisions. Copies of these volumes are so rare that it is clear that not many people care to have their knowledge of criminal statistics supplemented in the ways offered, if indeed they know about the possibility of such supplementation.

The third kind of statistical product consists of ad hoc reports on the statistics of matters bearing directly or indirectly upon crime, such as the issuing of firearms licences, the number of prisoners on life licences, and the incidence of fires started deliberately. These ad hoc reports are much shorter than the other statistical sources, of a different cover colour and are distributed free. Although their contents are often illuminating, this illumination has to be provided by the reader, since in common with the other publications, they are free of interpretive commentary. Many of these reports form issues in the *Home Office Statistical Bulletin* series.

The first attribute of crime statistics as artefacts is that they are periodic (with no gaps) and the result of immense skill and effort. *Criminal Statistics England and Wales* in particular is beautifully produced. It obviously matters greatly to someone that these volumes be prepared, and they have been compiled wonderfully well. The distinctions incorporated, changes in counting rules and the like are meticulously documented. Whatever their purpose, the care taken to get them right is such that their accuracy is paramount. Whatever criticism the historian or future criminologist might make of their content, the professionalism of those who translated the mandated content into print is admirable beyond question. This is no less true of the rarer supplementary volumes, despite their rarity. In terms of effort expended in compilation per probable reader, the supplementary statistics are perhaps unique.

The second attribute of crime statistics is the centrality of the police in their pages. This is especially true of the commonest volume in the series, *Criminal Statistics*. Indeed, the legislative requirement to produce statistics is driven by requirements on the police to prepare returns for the Home Office. Before even the contents page of *Criminal Statistics*, we read an explanatory note: "This report on the statistics relating to crime and criminal proceedings in England and Wales for the year X includes the Abstracts of Police Returns which are laid before Parliament in accordance with section 54 of the Police Act 1964" (HMSO, 1994: 2).

The numbers in the first third (after the introductory chapter) of a typical recent volume represent notifiable offences recorded by the police. They are not statistics of offences known to the people committing or suffering them, nor to the Town Hall or Customs and Excise, nor even those known to the police, but those *recorded* by the police. Police recording is the turnstile through which an event gains admittance to *Criminal Statistics*. Furthermore, the tabulations of crime by area are by *police force* area, and the inclusion of increases and decreases in recorded crime by force area adds just the hint of competition between forces. The prominent table that looks at crime clearance rates by force area adds more than a hint of competition.

The third noteworthy attribute of crime statistics is their seamless joining of crime counting and offender processing. The title of the central volume, *Criminal Statistics* rather than merely *Crime Statistics*, gives notice of this. In many ways the structure of *Criminal Statistics* mirrors the marginalisation of the crime victim as clearly as does the criminal court process itself. The image depicted by *Criminal Statistics* is one in which the sequelae of crime concern what (if anything) happens to the offender, not what happens to the victim or to the physical context that made victimisation occur. At least two sets of lives may be changed by an offence: those of the perpetrator and his or her connections, and those of the victim and his or her connections. There is nothing inexorable about the choice as crime statistics of data that document the first set of consequences and neglect the second, but that is how the process emerged. It could have been otherwise. Imagine a history in which the victim was so central that the volume of statistics had been entitled *Victim Statistics*, which in due course had to be supplemented by surveys of offenders. In fact, precisely the opposite happened. It would be interesting (but outside the scope of this chapter) to work through what would have been the consequences of such a history for the practice of crime control. On the basis that "what gets counted, counts," the choice of offender processing as the "natural" continuation of crime counting does matter.

The fourth point about *Criminal Statistics* that strikes the reader as a reflection of the society that produced it is the categorisation of offences. In this case, of course, the statistics largely reflect the distinctions made by criminal law. Table 8.1 sets out the categories of notifiable sexual offences included in *Criminal Statistics 1995*, their numbers and the percentage cleared. The sexual offence is useful in this context in that it reveals the gender asymmetry in what is recorded as a notifiable offence. It also helps make the point that some offences (like indecency between males) have particularly high clearance rates because coming to know about them (and choosing to act) directly entails their detection.

It could take the whole of this chapter to untangle the world view that underpins these statistics. The specific offence of rape of a male was enacted by the Criminal Justice and Public Order Act of 1994. Male victims of forced buggery thus got reclassified as rape victims. If the offence of rape is the same for men and women victims, why should they be reported separately, rather than in total, as is the case for incest and gross indecency with a child? What kind of magic happens on the 13th and 16th birthdays of young women to move an offence across recording categories? Why do males not appear as victims of unlawful sexual intercourse? At least the last question can be answered; as stated by Smith:

> It is not an offence for a woman to induce or permit a boy under the age of sixteen to have sexual intercourse with her. If she does so and there is no evidence that she did anything more than lie passively, no offence is committed. If, however, before, during or after the sexual intercourse, she does to the boy any act which would be an indecent

assault if it were done without his consent—such as touching his penis—then she is guilty of an indecent assault although he does consent to or encourage the act in question. (Smith, 1996: 488)

The point here is that crime statistics reflect the occasional reality-free dottiness of the criminal law that defines the offences the statistics are obliged to count.

A related point concerning crime counts is the necessity for a healthy scepticism about how many events relate to a single known crime. For example, in one large non-Metropolitan force (personal communication, Inspector Reg Pengelly) in 1995 there were 1,589 offences of handling stolen goods (dishonest handling) recorded, compared with 38,798 for burglary and 96,511 for theft. The clearance rate for handling was close to 100%. Yet logic dictates that, whenever there is theft or burglary to generate cash (for example to feed a drug habit), there is a handling offence for each such theft. The disproportion in the number of recorded theft and handling offences has to be a result of the police's relative prioritisation of the crimes. Interestingly, it seemed from closer inspection that where the handling offence was recorded, this was because it is an offence to which people were more prepared to plead guilty, and that was easier to prove than theft or burglary. There is a dual point to this. First, the figures are clearly a result of police practice. However, the practice is instructive in showing that police are less concerned with the disruption of markets for stolen goods than informed opinion suggests might be productive. These data are not useful in the obvious way, but they turn out to be useful in making a point of practical importance nonetheless.

Fifth, the unit of count is the event rather than any person involved. This serves to mask the extent to which crime clusters around individual people and places, often in ways that suggest chronic offending by the same people against the same people and places. This point will be elaborated later as being central to any recording system that purports to reflect the reality of citizen experience.

Finally, one of the remarkable things is the slightness of the extent to which crime statistics permeate the criminological literature. The argument that crime statistics are necessary to feed the criminological enterprise is based on very shaky ground, when one scans criminology books and journals for evidence of scholars and practitioners drawing sustenance from the statistics. Apart from the annual feeding frenzy of journalists on the day of publication of the statistics, neither is there any consistent or constructive use of criminal statistics by the media. Indeed, it is astonishing how political parties and pressure groups manage to transmit as news occasional analyses of long known crime statistics. Even more depressing, times believed to be crime waves occur when crime becomes a political issue in elections. The statistics seem irrelevant. Column inches seem to be used as evidence of a crime wave in progress (Donziger, 1996).

In short, we may reach the following conclusions about crime statistics as artefacts:

Table 8.1
Notifiable Sexual Offences Known to the Police and Cleared Up, 1995

Offence	Number	% Cleared
Buggery	818	94
Indecent assault on a male	3,150	86
Indecency between males	727	97
Rape of a female	4,986	75
Rape of a male	150	61
Indecent assault on a female	16,876	70
Unlawful sexual intercourse with a girl under 13	178	90
Incest	1,260	94
Procuration	185	105[1]
Abduction	207	93
Bigamy	364	41
Gross indecency with a child	86	93
Total	30,274	76

1. This apparent impossibility occurs because offences recorded in one year may be cleared in a later year.

1. Since they are the product of regular and massive effort, they are either highly prized by those who mandate them, or woven into the processes of statutory obligation, professional judgement or resource allocation so tightly that their discontinuation or interruption is unthinkable. If not so woven, they are a talisman against unknown dire consequences and cannot be interfered with.
2. Each edition of *England and Wales Criminal Statistics* combines, in the same volume, crime counts with police action and subsequent offender processing. By doing so, it places the police and criminal justice agencies at the hub of crime control by a means no more sophisticated than the connection made between sex and motoring by draping a lightly clad young woman over the front of new cars at motor shows.
3. Their units of count are typically unhelpful for the purposes of crime control.
4. They do not permeate criminological discourse, to the extent to which one would expect, given the effort necessary to generate them.

CONSIDERING THE CRIME RATE

At the centre of periodic crime counts lies the notion of the crime rate. On the day when the annual statistics of crime are published, media concern is centred upon this as a moral barometer and as a stick with which to beat the government. A rate comprises a variable expressed in relation to another variable. At its most crude, the crime rate is taken to be crime per time; that is, in 1995 the crime rate was 5.1 million crimes per unit of time (in this case the year). While this seems perfectly good enough for the tabloid press, it is obvious with a moment's thought that one year is not like the next in terms of the factors that make for crime. Most basically, the number of people and businesses to which crime may occur varies over time. This leads *Criminal Statistics: England and Wales* to go on to count crime in relation to population (usually as crimes per 100,000 population). The year was an obviously inadequate denominator. How much better is population? The number of contacts that might end in crime rises faster than the population, so population is a poor substitute for possibly criminogenic contacts. You can't commit a violent or sexual offence while alone, so the factors that lead people to meet and interact with each other are important determinants of rates of crime. These factors include urbanisation, the provision of communal transport and the concentration of commerce. Further, the range and portability of stealable goods has increased enormously over time. The point is succinctly made by Marcus Felson:

> Count television sets, monitor their portability, check their location. Examine travel patterns away from home; numbers of persons moving about with family friends or strangers; adolescent activities with peers and parents; automobilization of youth; shopping patterns, parking patterns and so forth. Check household composition, housing types and patterns of occupancy of buildings and of ties among occupants. Examine when crime fails and when it succeeds, as well as its control. Look at hourly patterns of activity and where people are on the map. Check parental position vis-a-vis their own children and patterns of recognition among neighbours. Like physics and physiology, criminogenesis derives from a movement of physically bounded and identifiable entities about the physical world—movements that can be tracked according to map, clock and calendar. (Felson, 1986: 127)

Felson's point is amplified in Shover's (1996) historical analysis of crime methods.

Given the relevance of those factors, all to be incorporated in the denominator of a crime rate, the search for the right all-purpose rate is clearly bound to fail. That said, there has been a surprising consistency over time in the year-to-year increases in police-recorded crime. This can be illustrated by Figures 8.1 and 8.2, both taken from Barclay (1995).

Figure 8.1 depicts crimes recorded by the police between 1876 and 1994 and shows a giddying set of increases since the mid-1950s. What does it mean? If every year, there is a proportional increase in the range of crime opportunities, would we not expect a *proportional* rather than an absolute increase in recorded crime every year? Figure 8.2 shows that since 1918, the increase in recorded crime has been extremely consistent, at about 5% per year. This suggests (but does *not* prove) that thinking of crime as a result of a complex mixture of social

Figure 8.1
Crimes Recorded by the Police

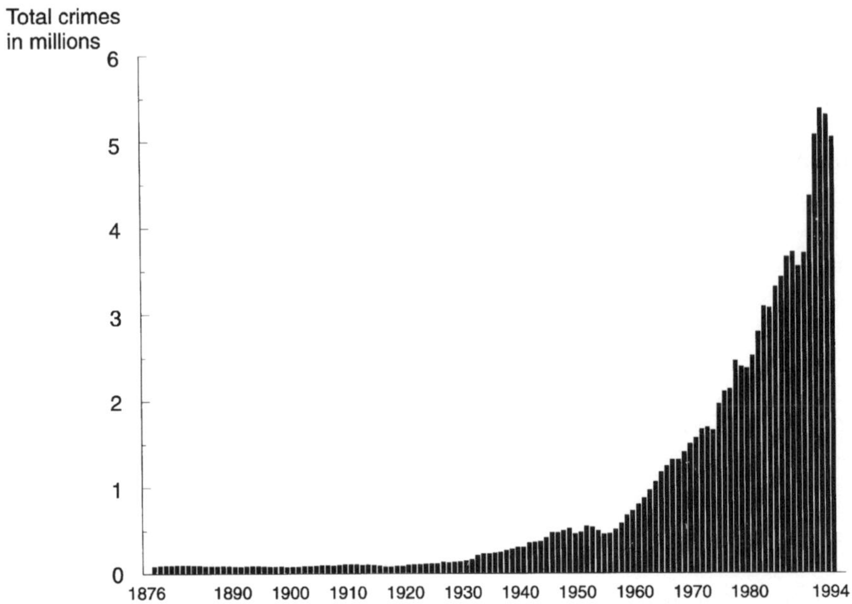

Source: Extracted from Barclay (1995) with permission.

forces whose rate of change is quite stable may be more sensible than interpreting the crime rate as an index of increasing wickedness.

Incidentally, the fluctuations of the data points relative to the regression line in Figure 8.2 may well be a result of economic changes, which at least in England and Wales, determine rates of change of property and personal crimes in differing ways as the economic cycle proceeds, with crimes of violence increasing in tandem with beer consumption at times of economic growth, and crimes against property increasing at times of recession (Council of Europe, 1994). The reason why this relationship is much closer in England and Wales than it is elsewhere in Western Europe is a matter of great interest, easily resolved by English xenophobes by an assertion that English police statistics are the most reliable in Europe!

VICTIMISATION SURVEYS

While much of the substance of crime statistics has remained recognisable over time, the sources of knowledge about crime in all its manifestations have changed enormously. Maguire (1993) asserts, "A Rumplestiltskin-like criminologist, waking up after, say, a 35-year sleep ready to resume (he would almost certainly be male) the task of 'explaining crime' would find himself confronted with a situation so foreign that he would have difficulty in finding a theoretical

Figure 8.2
Growth in Recorded Crime[1, 2]

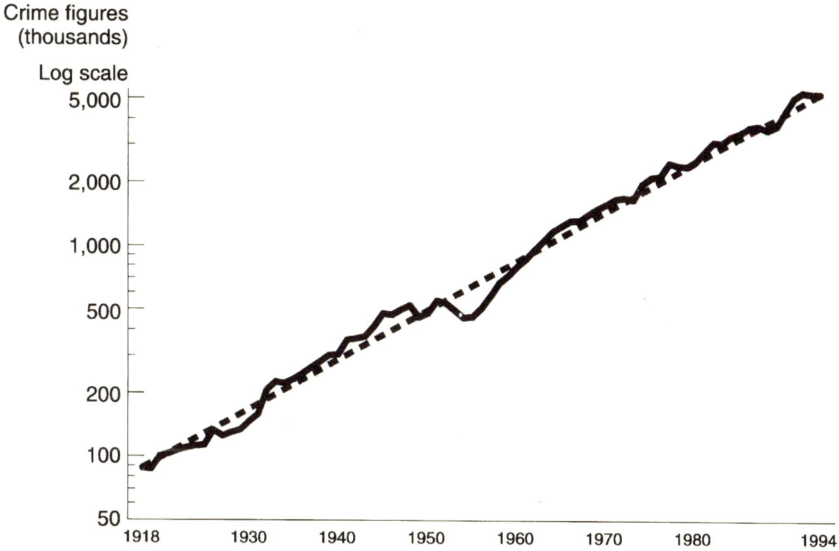

1. The regression line is based on data from 1918 to 1994.
2. Excluding criminal damage of less than £20.
Source: Extracted from Barclay (1995) with permission.

perspective in his toolbag with which to make sense of what he saw'' (Maguire, 1993: 278). Assuming that Mike Maguire has mistaken Rumplestiltskin (who was a child stealer) for Rip van Winkle (who liked to sleep in), the point is a good one. The greatest change in our understanding and measurement of crime during the last 20 years has come from the introduction of victimisation surveys. In these surveys, a representative sample of the population is asked about its experiences of, and attitudes towards, crime. The national survey for England and Wales is conducted every two years and is known as the *British Crime Survey* (BCS). Other Western countries also now carry out periodic victimisation surveys. The US operation, predictably, is the largest. It is known as the *National Crime Victimisation Survey* (NCVS). Victimisation survey results feature heavily in both official commentaries on crime, and some secondary analysis of such surveys are to be found in the criminology literature. Victim surveys, it is probably fair to say, are taking from police recorded crime the mantle of the basic crime count.

The advance that the victimisation survey is typically held to represent over statistics of crimes recorded by the police is that it includes the ''dark figure'' of unrecorded crime, which police data do not. Figure 8.3 represents trends in crime shown in crimes recorded by police, in crimes captured by the BCS and in crimes captured by BCS where the respondent says the incident was reported

Figure 8.3
Trends in Crime,[1] 1981–1993

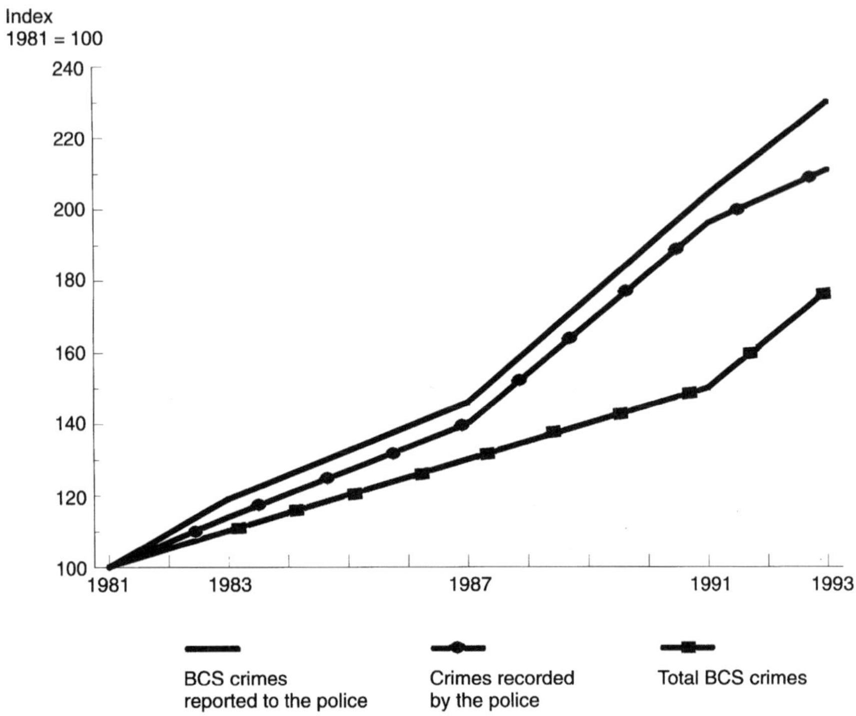

1. Based on a comparable sub-set of offences.
Source: Extracted from Barclay (1995) with permission.

to the police. Trends in crime recorded by the police and crimes said by the victim to have been reported to the police track each other quite closely. Total BCS crimes have risen more slowly than the other two variables. Thus trends in recorded crime in England and Wales, at least, are quite similar when looked at in terms of police statistics and victim reports. If generating more accurate crime trends were the only reason for conducting victimisation surveys, their value would not be secure. But there are other, more subtle, differences between victimisation surveys and police crime statistics. Not all of these differences favour the victimisation survey. Of the benign effects of victim surveys, two are noteworthy:

1. Statistics of crimes known to the police were seen, particularly by criminologists with a Marxist theoretical background, as representing a flawed and self-serving account of events. In focussing upon the manifestation in crime data of the purposes of the capitalist state, they underplayed or wholly neglected the real suffering of crime vic-

tims. Two related developments changed this: the emergence of feminism as a social movement, which brought with it a recognition of the chronic victimisation of many women by men; and the victimisation survey. Statements of crime impact from the victim's mouth were powerful antidotes to a concentration on the flaws of recorded crime data. See Zedner (1994, 1997) for an account of the victim movement that incorporates the role of victimisation surveys.

2. The units of count of victimisation surveys are victimised people and victimised households. The capacity of statistics of recorded crime to destroy the real life linkages between events was not mirrored in the victimisation survey, which to some extent could be told as a story of an emerging relationship between perpetrator and victim. Sadly, the habits of thought that criminologists brought to bear upon conventional crime statistics have limited the analysis of victimisation surveys in this way, but favoured forms of analysis are now changing in the direction of seeing chronic victimisation as typically a relationship between the same perpetrator and the chronic victim, rather than as a series of unrelated events having in common only their direction at a single victim.

As for the malign effects of conventional victim surveys, two will be selected for mention:

1. Conventional victimisation surveys, both national and local, exclude certain categories of victim, notably businesses, children and those resident in prison or residential care homes. These are likely to be heavily victimised groups. They also exclude victims of fraud and sexual offences who do not realise they are being victimised.
2. Victimisation surveys ask questions other than those that deal with victimisation experiences. Economies of scale make it prudent to do this. Once one is in someone's home, and particularly if they are not recent victims, it is better to get the information one can rather than complete the interview in a very short time.

The non-victimisation questions are referred to here as "filler" questions. Early local surveys (e.g., Jones et al., 1986), consistent with the preoccupations of their local authority sponsors, included questions about police accountability among their filler items. Nationally, questions about crime fear were popular filler items. The consequence of this was that some issues were publicised as important, for no better reason than that they were the filler items of choice. This can be illustrated by the contrast between crime anger and crime fear.[1] There is now an enormous criminological literature on crime fear (for a national analysis, see Maxfield, 1984), to the point at which the crime problem is frequently depicted as representing dual problems of crime victimisation and crime fear. There is no corresponding literature on crime anger. Is this because, when people are asked about crime, they express fear more often than anger? It is not. When crime victims are asked about their emotional response, anger is the most frequent. A recent local analysis showing this (Mawby and Walklate, 1997) is presented in modified form as Table 8.2. It shows anger to be a far more

Table 8.2
Percentage of Burglary Victims and Other Adults in Household Suffering Emotional Reactions of Kinds Listed (multiple responses permitted)

Place	**Plymouth**		**Salford**	
Emotion	*Self*	*Other Adult*	*Self*	*Other Adult*
Anger	78	61	77	61
Shock	56	46	56	42
Fear	31	24	41	30
Sleeplessness	43	27	30	18
Tears	22	16	21	17

Source: Adapted from Mawby and Walklate (1997: 280).

frequent response to burglary victimisation than fear, and these responses have the same patterns as those in the *British Crime Survey*.

Table 8.2 refers to the emotional response of victims rather than the emotional response of anticipating possible victimisation. What are the national data about that from the *British Crime Survey*? The answer is that there are none, because the question is not asked. In other words, the criminological literature on crime fear is very much present, and the criminological literature on crime anger is absent, not because of anything that victims or other citizens report, but as a result of the filler questions that criminologists ask. The agenda differs with the scope of filler questions and is reflected in them. It would be interesting (but dangerous) to conduct a victimisation survey that allows the expression of hatred, vengeance and beliefs about the circumstances under which individual freedoms must be eroded in the cause of crime control. The agenda that such an enterprise would set would be no less valid than those currently cited. It is instructive to think about this point in the context of the current vogue for Zero Tolerance policing. This vogue is said by North American criminologists to be more marked in the UK. It may be possible to link this to the greater distancing of the victim movement in the UK from anger. In the USA, Mothers Against Drunk Driving (MADD) and similar victim organisations wear their anger more prominently than the victim movement here. It may be that failing to draw the teeth of victim anger by allowing its frank expression has led us to a preference for hard-line policing that we could have avoided.

UNPACKING THE CRIME RATE

Crime counts expressed as rates in the conventional way are not particularly meaningful, and perhaps not particularly helpful for everyday life or tactics of crime control. How does knowing that recorded crime per head in Devon and Cornwall in 1995 stood at around half the level of crime in Humberside in the same year help one live one's life, even assuming that factors other than population do not drive crime rates (although they do) and that recorded crime is an adequate proxy for crime experienced?[2]

There are three basic ways of counting victimisation experience. The first takes as its basic count the proportion of those available to be victimised who are victimised. This index is known as prevalence. The second measure (incidence) concerns the number of victimisations per person available to be victimised. So if, in a population of ten people, one person is victimised twice and no one else is, the prevalence of victimisation is .1 (one person in ten) and the incidence is .2 (two victimisations in a population of ten people).

It has long been recognised by those familiar with the problem that these measures are important and different, although it is a distinction that is typically unclear (or unconsidered) in media reporting of crime experience. Sparks (1981) stresses:

> Both of these measures are important; each answers a different kind of question. Measures of incidence might be important, for example, in estimating demands for police services or aid to victims; prevalence measures are needed for the estimation of risk. At the moment, the latter are rarely reported, which is rather like counting up the number of measle spots in a given year, rather than the number of persons who have had the measles. (Sparks, 1981: 19)

However, there is a third measure of crime experience that even Sparks does not mention. This is the number of victimisations per victim (crime concentration). In the population of ten previously mentioned, this measure would be 2 (2 victimisations against a single victim). To continue the measles example, the measure would be the number of measles spots per measles sufferer. Crime concentration offers a better handle on crime experience than either of the other two measures in terms of crime control. If levels of concentration are high generally, or high in particular contexts, then crime control resources can be deployed accordingly.

From the five annual volumes of statistics in yellow-brown covers, one can learn many things. However, one can learn nothing about the central question of how victimisation is distributed amongst victims. There is thus no suggestion about the real differences in one's likelihood of being repeatedly victimised (and hence the precautions one would be prudent to take). The police statistics that contribute to the returns to the Home Office on which the basic yellow-brown volume is based were clearly not set up to allow the important questions about crime concentration to be addressed.

A little time must be taken to illustrate the degree of concentration typically found in victimisation surveys. The example is modified from Farrell (1995). In a fast-moving research area, the Farrell review is the best available, although now somewhat dated. In summary, Farrell examines, using data from the 1992 BCS, the proportion of respondents suffering crime and the proportion of incidents captured that each group accounts for. Thus, the data show that 60% of people suffered no offence, and (surprise, surprise) this group accounted for no incidents. The data show that 20% of people suffered just one incident, accounting for 19% of all incidents captured, and that the 9% of people who suffered two incidents accounted for 17% of all incidents captured. The 5% of people who suffered three incidents each accounted for 12% of the total incidents captured. The 2% of people suffering four incidents each accounted for 9% of all incidents captured, and the 4% of people suffering five or more incidents accounted for 44% of all incidents. Thus victimisation seems heavily concentrated on a small proportion of citizens.

One of the surprises from this way of looking at the data concerns the link between area differences in rate of victimisation and the extent of victim concentration. If one takes all BCS sampling points, ranks them in terms of crime incidence, then divides them into deciles, from the 10% of areas with the lowest rates of crime to the 10% of areas with the highest rates of crime, it is clear that victim concentration is the primary determinant of what constitutes a high-crime area. This is represented in Figures 8.4 and 8.5, which are pictorial representations of the data of Trickett et al. (1992).

Figures 8.4 and 8.5 plot the prevalence, incidence and concentration of the deciles for property and personal crime respectively. Thus, for example, looking at Figure 8.4, in the tenth decile (highest crime), the prevalence rate is .31; thus, some 31% of households suffer some property crime. The incidence is 1.1; that is, each household in the area suffers 1.1 such crimes. The concentration is 3.6; that is, those victimised suffer an average of 3.6 such crimes each. The practical implication of this concerns the extent to which crime could be reduced simply by eliminating repeats against the same target. The theoretical point is that this changes how we think about what constitutes a high-crime area. This linkage between crime concentration and crime hot spots has been taken forward excitingly by Alex Hirschfield and his colleagues at Liverpool University (Johnson et al., 1997).

Looking at concentration rates revolutionises ways of thinking about crime; it shows that sequences against the same person are frequent and allows the crime problem to be reconfigured as one of quasi-relationships rather than independent events. Of course this is the way we were already accustomed to think of crimes like domestic violence, but not of other volume crimes. While the data here are national, Hope (1994) applies the same approach to problems on one council estate, which proves equally illuminating. He refers to the dynamic of change revealed by the patterns of prevalence and concentration considered together as "crime flux" (developing this notion from Barr and Pease [1990]). It is crime flux that we need to understand.

The impression of chronic victimisation as a continuing link between offender and victim is strengthened by another kind of analysis of the BCS. If more than one crime of the same type has been suffered, the respondent is asked, "Were any of these very similar incidents, where the same thing was done under the

Figure 8.4
Property Crime Ratios

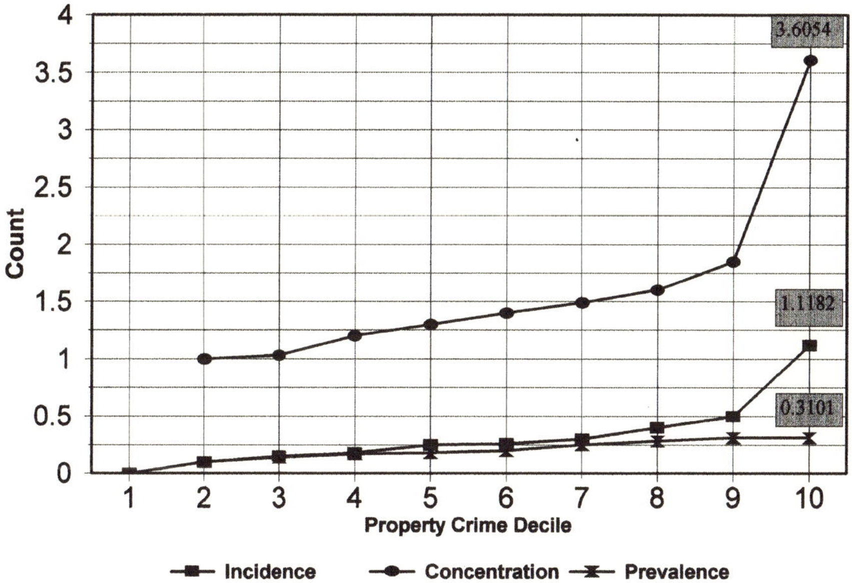

Source: Adapted from Farrell, 1995.

same circumstances and probably by the same people?'' Table 8.3 shows, by crime type, the proportion of all crimes that formed series, and the proportion of repeated crimes that formed series. Thus, for example, 53% of all assaults were part of a series of very similar events, which were probably committed by the same person (and assaults are crimes where there would be least doubt about the perpetrator's identity). Where someone had been assaulted more than once, the proportion of all the events that formed part of a series (rather than being different events by different people) was 74%. For assault, threat and criminal damage in particular, crime concentration is very marked.

RECLAIMING THE USES

Although there are many limitations to crime statistics, perhaps the most remarkable thing about them is how little they are used to inform topics of policy interest. With some imagination and a little lateral thinking, arguably any of the tables in any of the volumes could be thought of in ways that inform policy. They would seldom be conclusive, but some uses could be made of them. In this final section before reaching brief conclusions, this will be demonstrated. One instance, tragically topical at the time of writing because of the Dunblane massacre of schoolchildren with legally held guns is the question of how the

Figure 8.5
Personal Crime Ratios

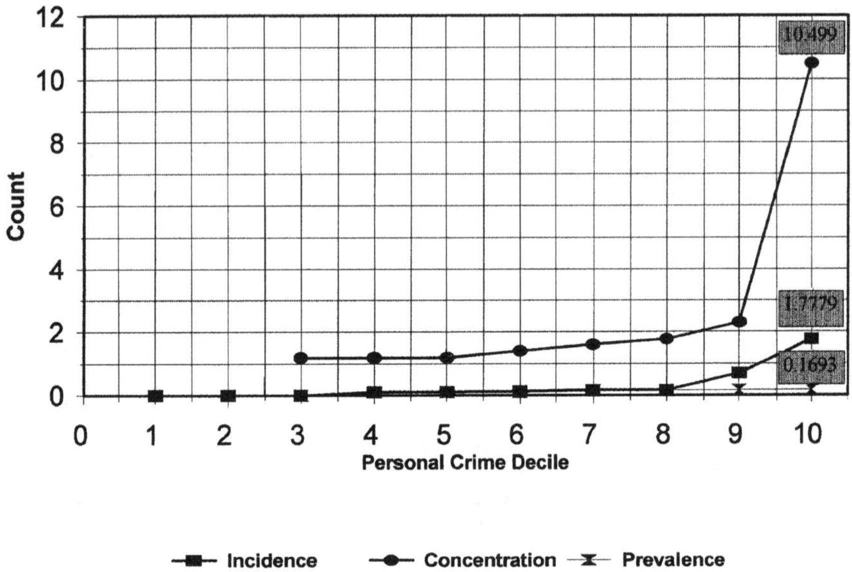

Source: Adapted from BCS, 1992.

issue and renewal of firearms certificates has changed over time. All the data in what follows is taken from *Home Office Statistical Bulletin 11/96*, dated May 21, 1996. The writer knows virtually nothing about firearms, and the point of this exercise is not to reveal any definitive truths about firearms regulation, but what the trends might suggest. To the writer's knowledge, this kind of analysis has not hitherto been carried out.

Figure 8.6 shows the number of firearms certificates on issue on December 31 of each year between 1968 and 1995. While certificates do not bear a one-to-one relationship with weapons (there being some three weapons held per certificate), the certificate is the appropriate unit of count for most enforcement questions.

Looking specifically at the period beginning in 1983, for which more detailed information exists, we see a decline of over 11% in the number of firearm certificates on issue. Why has this taken place? To clarify what is happening, Figure 8.7 shows the number of new firearms certificates granted and renewed. It will be seen that the grant of new firearms licences has remained fairly constant, but the number of renewals per year has declined, so that in 1995, there were some 5,000 fewer renewals than in 1983. The fact that the decline in renewals is much less than the decline in certificates on issue is simply explained. The licence is for three years, so the decline in renewals over three

Table 8.3
Series Crime as a Proportion of Repeated Crime and of All Crime, BCS, 1992

Crime Type	Number of Crimes	Series/ Repeats (%)	Series/ Total (%)
Vehicle theft	402	57	11
Theft from vehicle	1,582	70	30
Damage to vehicle	2,138	74	37
Bicycle theft	395	54	16
Burglary	598	76	21
Break-in with damage	66	50	20
Attempted burglary	667	79	34
Theft from dwelling	121	75	25
Theft from outside dwelling	1,244	84	44
Damage to outside dwelling	1,086	94	58
Theft from person	504	77	20
Attempted theft from person	238	84	35
Other theft	1,308	71	29
Damage to personal property	446	81	43
Assault	1,923	74	53
Threat	2,749	89	74

Source: Adapted from Chenery et al. (1995).

years has a cumulative effect on certificates on issue. The same is true of new certificates, so that the number of certificates on issue at the end of a three-year period should be the sum of renewals and new certificates over the previous three years combined. In fact the number on issue is always somewhat less than this, presumably because of people relinquishing valid licences before their expiry.

Thus, the reduction in the number of firearms licences is wholly explained by the reduction in the number of firearms certificates renewed, and not at all by a decline in the requests for new licences. That these two indices of popular interest in owning firearms should look so different is intriguing, and one's first (cynical) judgement is that firearms have increasingly continued to be held despite the holder's failure to renew the licence. This alternative should perhaps be checked out. There are recording safeguards against this happening, but it would be nice to have the reassurance of a check on the weapons holdings of those who have recently relinquished a licence (or even merely the threat of this, to see if rates of renewal increased in response to that threat of exposure).

Having hypothesised a possible breakdown in the controls surrounding firearms licences, is there any other evidence of a decline in enforcement? Figure

Figure 8.6
Number of Firearms Licences Issued, 1968–1995

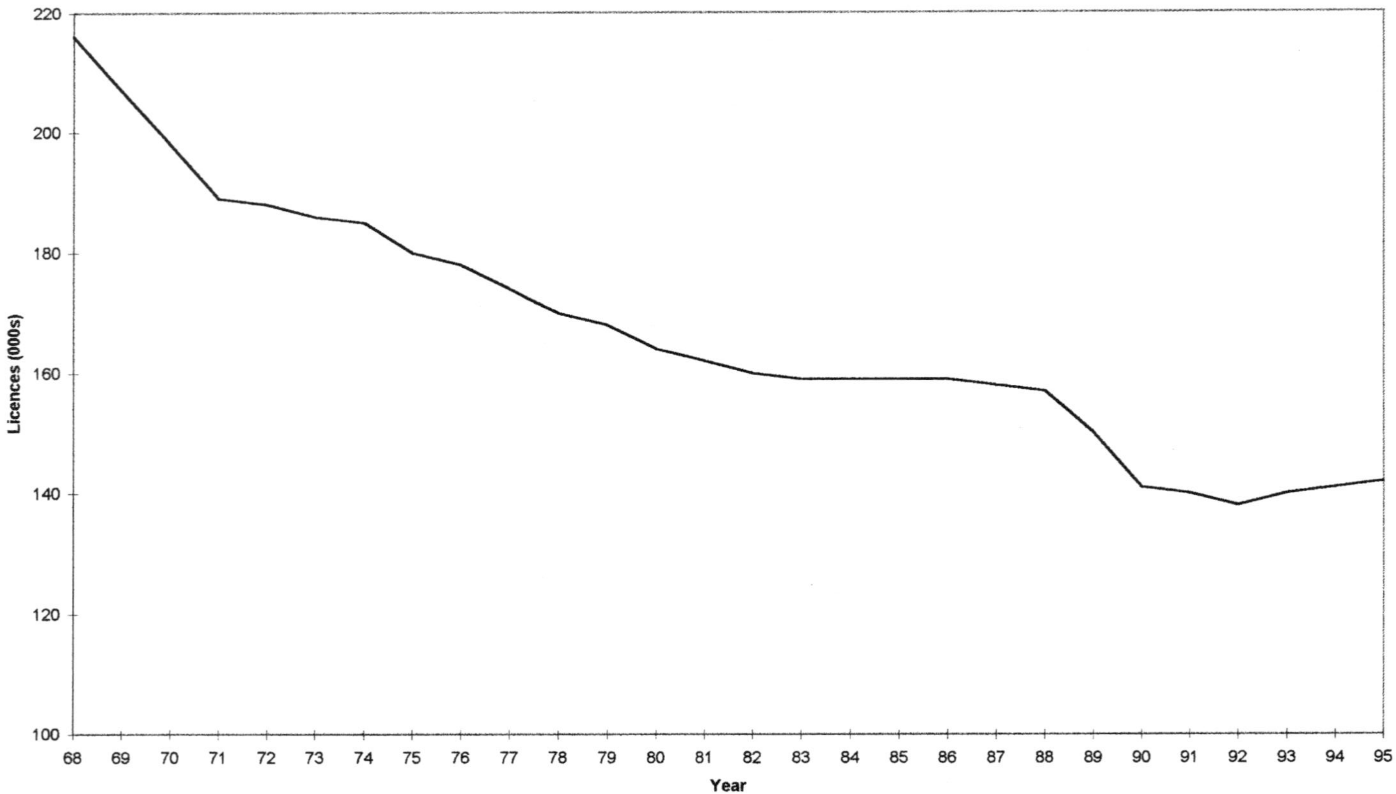

Figure 8.7
New and Renewed Licences, 1983–1995

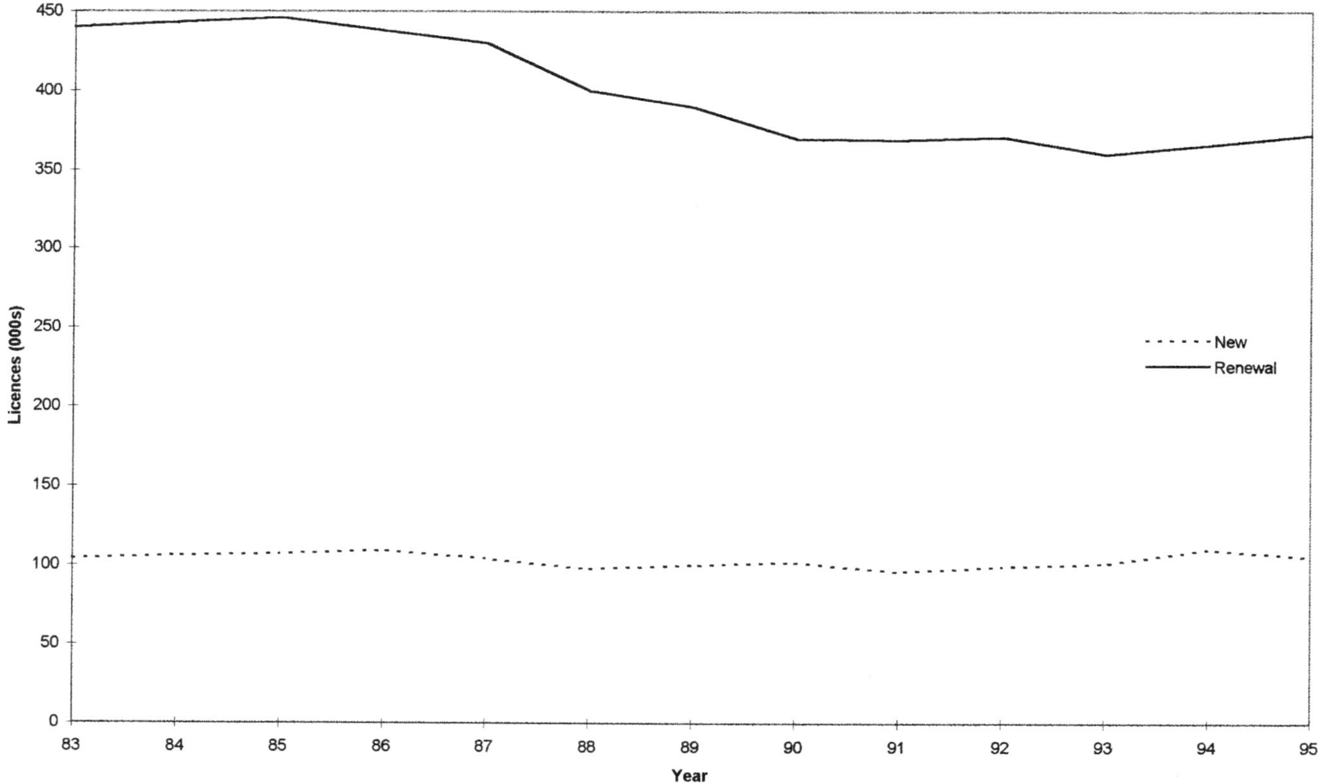

8.8 shows the rate of refusal of new certificates and renewals. Because rates of refusal are so low, for ease of exposition they have been multiplied by ten. Two conclusions may be drawn from Figure 8.8. The first is that the rate of refusal of new certificates is always much higher than the rate of refusal of renewals. It seems to be far more difficult to obtain a certificate than to renew one. This is interesting in that Thomas Hamilton, the killer of the Dunblane children, had held his weapons legally for some years. The second observation is that the rate of refusal has declined markedly over time, with a blip of refusals of renewals in 1988/89. It is tempting to think that the increase in refusals of renewal may be ascribed to the Hungerford Massacre in 1988.[3]

The hypothesis of diminishing rigour in firearms regulation remains tenable, is indeed strengthened, by the examination of changing rates of refusal of new or renewed certificates. The next question concerns levels of refusal by police force area. Do forces vary in this respect? The results of an analysis of this question for 1999 is contained in the Appendix, but the methods used and selected results are briefly described here. Total applications (whether for a new licence or a renewal) were calculated and taken as the denominator in the calculation. Refusals of new licences or licence renewals were summed, multiplied by ten (for ease of expression) and used as the numerator. The rate thus calculated can be taken as an index of stringency of enforcement of firearms licencing. It will be seen that force variation is enormous, from Hertfordshire, which never declined a firearms certificate in 1995, to West Yorkshire, which turned down 2 in every 100 applications. It is not possible to link rates of use of firearms in crime by force area using the published statistics, but it would surely be worthwhile to take the analysis forward to see what level of public protection, if any, was afforded by the variation in rates of refusal.

CONCLUSION

Despite all the caution that is undoubtedly necessary when dealing with social products like crime statistics, an essentially optimistic view is justified. Crime statistics are interesting in their own right, and as reflections of a world view and the variations in power among those whose sins are tabulated. Looking at older volumes of statistics shows how much that world view has changed. The advent of the victimisation survey has added a range of ways of looking at the data, with their own attendant dangers. Recognition of the extent of victim concentration is of central importance in this. Third, a challenge exists in retrieving added value from a wealth of data that remain virtually unanalysed. The modest exercise using firearms licence data for one year probably merits fuller treatment, and a similar exercise could have been undertaken with much more data whose meaning currently remains effectively hidden, despite its routine tabulation.

Figure 8.8
Rates of Refusal of New and Renewed Licences, 1983–1995

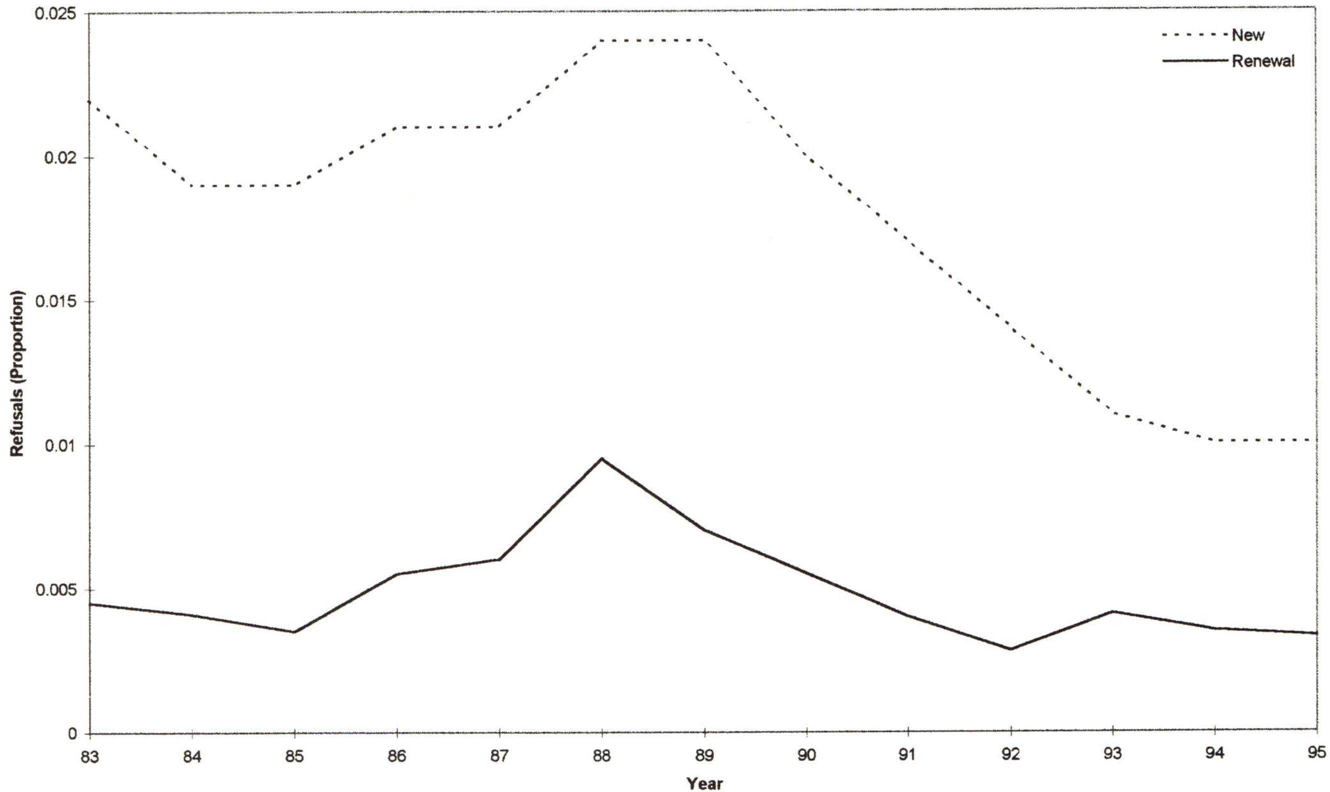

APPENDIX: REFUSAL OF FIREARMS RATE (*10): FORCE VARIATION 1995

Force	Refusal Rate	Force	Refusal Rate
Hertfordshire	.00	Nottinghamshire	.03
Lincolnshire	.00	South Wales	.03
City of London	.00	Lancashire	.04
Northamptonshire	.00	Thames Valley	.04
South Yorkhire	.00	North Wales	.05
Sussex	.00	Dorset	.05
Wiltshire	.00	West Midlands	.05
Gwent	.00	Gtr. Manchester	.06
Dyfed-Powys	.01	Avon & Somerset	.06
Cumbria	.01	North Yorkshire	.07
Northumbria	.01	Metropolitan	.07
Essex	.02	Leicestershire	.07
Merseyside	.02	Humberside	.09
Gloucestershire	.02	Staffordshire	.09
Surrey	.02	Norfolk	.10
Derbyshire	.02	Kent	.10
Suffolk	.02	Hampshire	.11
Cheshire	.02	Warwickshire	.13
Durham	.02	Bedfordshire	.17
Cambridgeshire	.03	West Mercia	.19
Devon & Cornwall	.03	West Yorkshire	.20
Cleveland	.03		

NOTES

1. The author is grateful to Jason Ditton for alerting him to this point, which is very important and should have been self-evident but was so only to Jason.

2. In what follows, the author is particularly indebted to his former colleague, Dr. Tim Hope, whose exposition of the issues concerned at the annual meeting of the American Society of Criminology in Miami in November 1994 influenced the content of this section.

3. In 1988, following a rampage in Hungerford, Berkshire in which Michael Ryan killed 16 people, the government introduced new legislation, the Firearms Act 1988, which substantially altered the types of weapons people were authorised to possess.

CHAPTER 9

Developments in Radical Criminology in England and Wales

NIGEL BREARLEY

INTRODUCTION

The history of the development of radical criminology in England and Wales has, as one might anticipate of critical endeavours, been somewhat chequered and riven with contention. Initial developments have been portrayed as a somewhat heroic struggle for academic recognition in the face of an entrenched and, arguably, philistine establishment followed by a period of exciting and rapid emergence, virtual domination of the academy and then a fragmentation and retreat from the defining heights of the field in competition with other emergent and competing paradigms. As with all histories of thought, the truth is far too multifaceted to be neatly summarised in a sentence. This chapter will endeavour to explore the development and current state of radical criminology with reference to both the interior and exterior histories of the paradigm(s), concluding with comment on current circumstances that impact on the development and prospects of contemporary scholarship and research. In these endeavours students are fortunate to find that, as with many areas of critical thought, there has been a strong reflexive tradition within radical criminology and the sociology of deviance that enables a fair analysis to be made from the writings of a number of prominent contributors and detractors (Wiles, 1976; Cohen, 1981; Rock, 1988a, 1988b; Young, 1988; Tierney, 1996).

Young has provided us with a useful dichotomy for examining the main factors that have shaped the emergence of a radical paradigm in criminology. Broadly, Young argues that significant influences may be identified in both the *exterior* and *interior* history of the perspectives that, separately and combined, have shaped the current state of affairs (Young, 1988: 116–170).

For our purposes, *exterior histories* are those that identify the macro, political, economic and cultural circumstances that have impacted on the interior histories. The *interior history* consists of the theoretical orientations, working practices and cultural space within the academy and related professional and intellectual areas. Young deploys these terms to describe the paradigm shift that occurred in British criminology in the 1960s and 1970s. In this chapter the two histories will be interlaced and the development of radical criminology in England and Wales described in three stages: emergence, consolidation and fragmentation.

EMERGENCE

Post-War Reconstruction and the Social Democratic Poverty Project

Until the 1950s British criminology had largely been a project of government. This is to say, it had been concerned with the identification, legal processing and appropriate disposal of malefactors so as to apparently maximise public tranquillity. As a result, the study of crime and deviance had been concentrated amongst legal commentators, criminal justice practitioners and some schools of medicine. There were few significant institutional locations in seats of higher learning and hence no criminological *academy* to speak of (Garland, 1985, 1988, 1994; Morris, 1988; Martin, 1988).

The experience of significantly increased levels of state control of the economy and public services during the Second World War and the election of a social democratic Labour Party administration in 1945 led to a mild expansion of criminology as a project of socially interventionist government in the post-war period. This is not to say that the nature of the criminological project changed significantly other than in the sense that the government saw that it had a duty to support research, development and investment in the public sector to abolish need in order to secure a minimum basis of welfare for the population. Alongside this welfarist project was a limited commitment to enhance public security. It was anticipated that crime would rise for awhile after the war as a function of significant social disruption, but that this problem would be reduced as social welfare initiatives were developed and economic fortunes picked up (Taylor, 1981).

Among those who had anticipated the rise in the incidence of "normal" crime in the post-war period was Hermann Mannheim, who with two other European emigres, Leon Radzinowicz and Max Grunhut, did much to partly shake British academic criminology out of its myopic overconcentration on medical and psychological matters (Morris, 1988: 156). These early post-war pioneers and their students contributed a number of innovations, particularly in quantitative research. They also established the legitimacy of the study of criminology in the small university sector and in government circles.

By the late 1950s a small criminological constituency was emerging with a base in academia and in government service. This development of a critical mass of thinkers, commentators, teachers and researchers permitted the sharing of ideas within an academy that was able to read further than its own initial parochial and applied concerns. Influences from the United States, such as Cohen's *Delinquent Boys* (1955), did much to stimulate interest in sociological, sub-cultural groups. Barbara Wootton reviewed contemporary criminological thought and attempted to dent the pretensions of psychoanalysts and psychiatrists in their efforts to dominate criminology through a concentration on predicting and treating delinquency. In her highly influential book, Wootton argued for the need for much more empirical work focussing on *social* factors in the generation of criminal behaviour (Wootton, 1959).

Another influence from the United States was the use of the area study as pioneered especially in Chicago in the 1920s and 1930s. There had been area studies in England conducted since the 19th century, but Terence Morris located his study of the London suburb of Croydon within the framework of the Chicago School. Morris made sociological observations concerning delinquency and public housing allocation policy—asserting a new focus on sociological influences on high-volume "routine" rather than "pathological" crime (Morris, 1957). Changes in the exterior history of criminology were soon to lead to a significant development from these small beginnings.

The Academy Takes Off

The British economy and society took a long time to recover from the ravages of the Second World War. This, combined with a protracted retreat from the Empire, produced a period of national dissatisfaction with the time taken for the benefits of post-war optimism to come to fruition. These nagging dissatisfactions rumbled throughout the Conservative administration of 1951–1964 and took the form of labour unrest, protests concerning the Cold War and the nuclear deterrent. The humiliating Suez debacle and a number of scandals in public life added to the concerns. The public sentiment held that Britain had experienced "thirteen wasted years," and eventually led to the coming to power of another Labour government promising a new, modern, "classless" Britain. This new government project under the premiership of Harold Wilson was inspired by the occasional jealous glance at the impressive consumerism of the post-war United States and the modernising and democraticising zeal of Presidents Kennedy and Johnson. The essence of the project was an emphasis on a careful brokering of the relationship between capital and labour and significant investment in education, science and technology whilst enhancing the welfare net established by the 1945 Labour administration.

The result was a burst of social and cultural change. Levels of household consumption rose and the "cult of youth" reached a celebratory peak with "Swinging London," the Beatles and spectacular developments in the arts and sciences. Many of the individuals who pioneered these developments to a limited extent challenged and broke traditional class barriers, becoming icons of Wilson's democratising and modernising project. Following the bleak heritage of the "Hungry thirties," the Second World War and the somewhat disappointing fifties, it appeared that Britain was finally becoming *modern*.

Among the ambitious modernising developments attempted during the period of this administration, 1964–70, was a significant expansion of higher education. The 1960s saw the emergence of bright, new, modern universities built of glass and concrete on green-field sites on the edges of provincial towns. The polytechnic institutions, art colleges and colleges of education also expanded in size and numbers, and the new educational estate provided rich ground for the expansion of the study of new subjects. In the social sciences these developments led to a significant expansion of the academy—a development that was to open up the scope of critical debate concerning the intellectual heritage behind many of the welfare-inspired institutions that shaped the social terrain.

Subject matter for this renewed social science academy abounded. Post-war welfarism had been broadly accepted by both of Britain's main political parties, and it was widely anticipated that such developments would eventually lead to an optimum social balance between the interests of capital and labour leading to prosperity under social democratic capitalism. During the 1964–70 Wilson government there was a good deal of reference to "the national interest," notably to legitimate demands for wage restraint and caution in expanding public spending. This impacted on the enhanced wage ambitions of labour and on welfare professionals seeking state funds to implement new and innovative policies aimed at ameliorating hardship and need. The British economy was not strong, however, and the demands for funds to meet the ambitions of modernisation and to realign or equalise incomes led to more industrial relations problems and a loss of faith in government ability to proceed with the modernising social democratic project.

Radicalising the Academy

The probing inquiries of the academy and interested professionals revealed many areas of unmet need in terms of poverty and disadvantage. The existing institutional arrangements to meet these needs frequently tended to disempower recipients of welfare benefits in the interests of keeping costs within boundaries acceptable to the dictates of the Treasury and the government. There was also a concern that whilst absolute poverty remained a problem, there was a more general problem in British society—*relative deprivation*. These criticisms suggested that social disorders were a product of an awareness of unfairness and a lack of genuine opening up of opportunity, social mobility and equalisation of wealth rather than of poverty *per se* (Runciman, 1966). Hence criticism took on a more *socialist* as opposed to *social democratic* edge. Many academic and professional enquirers began to fundamentally question the potential for existing social and economic arrangements to make a civilising difference to British society (Taylor, 1981).

American Imports, Delinquent Solutions and Labels

In terms of the interior history of criminology, there had already been some innovative work emerging as a response to this crisis. Much of this development was inspired by ideas imported from the United States, which had a far larger, and in many ways more developed, social science academy. The strain theory of Robert Merton, the sub-cultural approaches of Albert Cohen (1955) and Walter Miller (1958), their more directly sociologically located revision in the work of Cloward and Ohlin (1960) and Sykes and Matza (1957) combined with the Chicago ecology tradition, especially as adopted by Morris (1957) inspired Downes (1966) in his distinctive appreciation of delinquency among London's East End youths. Downes's work utilised ethnographic methods of data collection giving a new, potentially *appreciative* edge to the study of delinquency in Britain. The voice of the subjects of social control was being reported to provide an accurate portrayal of the social perspective of offenders and norm-breakers as opposed to the motivations imputed to them by psychologists, psychiatrists, police officers and welfare professionals. Downes's work represents an interim piece in the emergence of radical criminology in the 1960s. It is, however, pivotal in its taking on of a range of critical theoretical approaches being pioneered in the United States. Downes admitted that the exciting mature work of David Matza (1964) was unavailable to him at the time of completing his work and that the introduction of the idea of the *drift* into delinquency and the hardening of a delinquent self-identity through the labelling process might have altered his appreciation (Downes, 1966: ix). Others were to take that opportunity.

Perhaps the most influential of the academic imports from the United States at this time was, however, Howard Becker's *Outsiders*, which appeared as the manifesto for labelling theory and introduced the British criminological audience to symbolic interactionism (1963). The concept of social reaction was only vaguely appreciated outside of the United States, and even there works such as Lemert's (1951) were peripheral to the structural functionalist approaches that monopolised Anglo-American sociology. In this context, the impact of Becker's work cannot be underestimated in the first phase of the emergence of radical criminology in Britain. Combined with the influence of sub-cultural theorists, *Outsiders* provided a perspective from which both rule making and rule breaking might be appreciated. Crime, or indeed any other form of socially defined deviance, was held not to be a quality inherent to any behaviour or person but a product of society's reaction to certain types of rule breaking. It also served to explain how intervention, be it by social control agencies or welfare professionals, into the lives of individuals and groups may serve to confirm a deviant self-image and harden a commitment to behaviours deemed socially unacceptable.

The approach also promoted the view that a social problem consists not only of a fixed and given condition but includes the perception (and its definition by certain people) that the condition poses a threat that is against their interests and that something should be done about it. Allied to Becker's influential work were two appreciations of the application of the approach in historical contexts—Kai Erikson's study of witchcraft allegations and labelling in 17th century New England (1966) and Gusfield's study of the development of alcohol prohibition (1963). Although the origins of these works could also be traced to the altogether more mainstream structural functionalism of contemporary American sociology, they nonetheless asserted the necessity for serious commentators on deviance to pay attention to the labelling process and the role of moral entrepreneurs—groups who seek to have social or legal change enacted and enforced in line with their own distinctive interests and perspective on the world. It is for this reason, the diverse sociological pedigree of labelling approaches, that they tend to be termed labelling *perspectives*, rather than labelling *theory*.

Becker and other adherents to labelling perspectives provided critical thinkers with a new militancy. In 1967 Becker's article, "Whose Side Are We On?" insisted that it was a necessary task of the sociologist to take the side of the underdog in society. This was because, as a rule, superordinate groups (with vested interests) and the agents of social control tended to dominate public images of deviants. Such works articulated the intellectual and practical necessity of taking the perspective of the deviant actor seriously, of appreciating the circumstances and motivations that shape and harden rule and norm breaking behaviour. The adoption of such approaches served to question the accounts of delinquency and deviance provided by experts, be they law enforcement agents, social workers, teachers, psychiatrists or psychologists. It is no coincidence therefore that symbolic interactionism and labelling perspectives achieved a popularity at a time when welfarism—an approach that carefully diagnosed social disorders in terms of expert professional repertoires and rationed resources to meet needs—was coming under criticism and strain.

In this context those academics and practitioners who were critical of how established professional perspectives and practice could often be seen to override the interests of those labelled deviant and to provide coercive and inadequate solutions to their personal and social requirements came to unify around radicalising perspectives. The very term "criminology" fell into discredit amongst these commentators during the later part of the 1960s as it was felt that the intellectual requirements of symbolic interactionism, labelling perspectives, ethnomethodology and phenomenology meant that crime should only be viewed as a particular and shifting form of socially defined deviance. Whilst there were disparate theoretical interests among this group, they came to see themselves as representatives of "new deviancy theory." Most adherents to the cause therefore came to identify themselves as "sociologists of deviance" rather than as "criminologists." The attendance of many of these "young Turks" of criminology at conferences and psychologically orientated professional and academic organisations led to an accelerated disillusionment with the control and welfarist emphasis of the proceedings.

Hence, in July 1968 many of the sociologists of deviance developed their own sub-cultural solution and organised and attended the first of the National Deviancy Conferences (NDC) at the University of York (Cohen, 1981: 233). The range of theorising and subject matter that was addressed in the early days of the NDC was startling for its breadth and originality. The role of the police in amplifying deviance, police-public interaction, the social construction of definitions of suicide, changes in the organisation of thieving, the social meaning of soccer hooliganism, blackmail and industrial sabotage were the topics of the papers contained in the first published book of proceedings (Cohen, 1971). Later compilations addressed theoretical concerns in social reaction theories as well as substantive issues (Taylor and Taylor, 1973; Rock and McIntosh, 1974; National Deviancy Conference, 1980).

A number of important works were also completed or in preparation at this time. These included the phenomenonlogically oriented textbook by Phillipson (1971); the work of Box (1971), which drew on a number of influential critical endeavours and explored the possible implications of a radical incorporation of control theory; Cohen and Taylor's subversive study of long-term imprisonment within a maximum security institution (1972); and Young's (1971) study of drug use in London. Cohen's (1972) work on the "mods and rockers" youth and culture conflict phenomenon led to the popularisation of the term *moral panic* to describe circumstances in which a social problem comes to be identified, often by the mass media, and is then sustained and amplified by the interest and activities of other cultural and state agents and commentators.

Many of the deliberations at the NDC focussed on applying various interpretations of labelling approaches. Others examined the problems associated with the micro- and mid-range perspectives that were the staple fare of the early meetings and sought to draw together some of the concerns of contributors in order to develop a more totalising theoretical position. A major concern with labelling perspectives is that they had often been found to be lacking in their ability to explain how the powerful came to be powerful and how their power came to be rooted in the contemporary social structure. Hence labelling theory was castigated by some for its lack of attention to issues of structure, power and history.

The allegation that the symbolic interactionist based strands of labelling theory in particular neglected the importance of the impact of the systematic interrelationships among institutions, organisations and social classes; large-scale social change; and other structural phenomena was to a large extent acknowledged by adherents to the position. For the most part, defenders of symbolic interactionist approaches would argue that they were *social psychologists* rather than *sociologists* and that, whilst they had a duty to be aware of structural influences on their field of study, such factors need not be explained and accounted for in as much detail as might be required of a sociologist. The same argument and counterargument read equally as well for the allegation that labelling perspectives neglect an understanding of history as a process out of which labelling may occur at different times and places over different matters.

Thio argued that labelling perspectives were not entirely radical because they tended to incline sociologists toward concentrating on the deviance of the powerless rather than the powerful (1973: 8). Similarly, Liazos suggested that labelling approaches tended towards an emphasis on "nuts, sluts and perverts" at the expense of examining "covert institutionalised violence" (1972: 11). This neglect of the role of raising a critical view of the nature and impact of social power led to many radical criminologists in England attempting to refocus their activities around an appreciation of the political economy of crime.

A further criticism that emerged around this time was that labelling theories tended to see the human actor as a passive recipient of labels who is totally at the mercy of official labellers. Many NDC participants, as well as American critics such as Alvin Gouldner (1968: 38), saw *their* deviants as acting distinctly more purposefully than that. Hence a number of the participants adopted a more freely willed model of man as a basis for their studies, arguing that many deviants, far from being passive actors, are decision makers whose rule breaking has authenticity and meaning. Some of these criticisms are undoubtedly fair as observations on the limitations of labelling perspectives, but they also tend to focus on a very narrow view of the range of approaches that come under that broad title. A defence against these allegations is contained in Plummer (1979), who observes of the toppling of labelling perspectives as the mainstay of the sociology of deviance: "In just ten years, labelling has moved from being the radical critic of established orthodoxies to being the harbinger of new orthodoxies to be criticised (Plummer, 1979: 85). Becker, in a contribution to the proceedings of the NDC, also acknowledged that labelling theory and new deviancy theory had initially been very liberating perspectives, but they left unattended the basic problem of the *aetiology*—the ultimate causes—of deviance (Becker, 1974).

The Bigger Picture—The New Criminology

The task of the next stage of the development of radical criminology therefore was to retain the critical qualities of labelling theory whilst seeking to extend the critique of the criminal justice system, and other agents of social control, within an appreciation of the underlying capitalist economic order.

The exterior history of the field was offering increasing material for reference and study. In common with many Western countries, Britain was continuing to experience a period of economic crisis and national self-doubt and uncertainty. Industrial relations problems and monetary crisis had led to the election of a new Conservative Party administration under Ted Heath. Government efforts to exercise firmer control of labour wage demands and industrial disputes led to increased levels of industrial conflict, and at one stage the country experienced electrical power cuts, and industry was restricted to working a three-day week to conserve energy. Youth culture was increasingly coming to be labelled as a source of concern, especially when radical elements took part in protests against the Vietnam War, attended major open air music festivals and embarked on a range of counter-cultural pursuits. A very small group took part in politically motivated bombings under the title of The Angry Brigade. The emergence of a Civil Rights Movement in Northern Ireland in the late 1960s rapidly led to an intensification of cultural factionalism and local terrorism, which spilled over into a series of bombing campaigns in Britain. The status of British blacks and immigrant communities also came to be highly politicised, and race relations became a mounting subject of social conflict.

The impact of the 1973 Oil Crisis, spiralling inflation and industrial unrest led to the eventual fall of the Conservative Heath Government in 1974 and the coming to power of a Labour administration. Efforts to control wage inflation led to further conflict with the trade unions, despite attempts to strike industrial relations deals and to develop and enforce price and income policies. A number of prominent strikes led to conflict between police and pickets. In the mid-1970s, there were outbreaks of riotous street conflict between the police and black youth, these were often triangular conflicts between protestors of the extreme right wing political groups, left wing anti-racist counterdemonstrators and the police. Black youth also became increasingly marginalised, politically, socially and economically, as levels of unemployment rose.

In this context a group of the new deviancy theorists moved from the middle-range sub-culture and interactionist labelling perspectives to one more heavily influenced by Marxism. At the same time, however, Marxism itself was going through something of a revival and revision as a critical theory.

Others had written on the relationship between crime and social structure. The entire field of Conflict Theory, which had enjoyed some influence in the United States with writers such as Vold (1958), Turk (1969), Chambliss and Seidman (1971) and Quinney (1969, 1970a and 1970b), had received little attention in Britain, although the basic approach resonated with the writings of the Anglophile international academic Ralph Dahrendorf (1959). It should also be noted that Chambliss and Quinney, in particular, subsequently developed their work along more distinctly Marxist lines.

Given that many of the new deviancy writings had accepted class conflict as the backdrop to the labelling process, it was only a matter of time before a criminology emerged that could both accommodate the free willed social actors of new deviancy theory and locate them in the context of structure, power and history. The seminal text in this tradition was Taylor, Walton and Young's *The New Criminology* (1973). This work was an impressive summary and critique of previous criminological ideas and provided indicators that the authors considered would give rise to a crime-free society. The book was founded on the following ideas:

- Crime is a two-sided affair—the cause of criminalisable behaviour and the identification of the power to criminalise.
- Capitalism is crime producing (criminogenic) as crime is a product of material and social inequalities that are inherent to the logic of capitalism.
- Whilst the positivist and correctionalist concerns of traditional criminology aimed to eliminate individual and social pathology, *The New Criminology* held that the only way to eliminate crime is to abolish inequality and thus the power and need to criminalise—as crime would disappear, so would the power and need to stigmatise and criminalise people or groups.

The New Criminology argued that crime is grounded in the material conditions of capitalism. To these authors this was a much more satisfactory explanation than merely attributing crime to poverty as many liberal sociologists had done. The new criminologists considered that poverty, both in absolute and relative terms, was a product of the same iniquitous social relations that gave rise to crime. Therefore, to base ideas concerning the causes of crime on poverty is an inadequate explanation that effectively disguises the complex forces that do cause inequalities, poverty and crime.

Drawing on labelling perspectives, the new criminologists considered the power to criminalise, make laws, prosecute offenders, or particular groups that are perceived as offenders, to be a function of the state—which also happened to be a focus of a great deal of contemporary Marxist debate with regards to the nature and function of the state within society. The state was also seen to vary in form during different historical periods, and the techniques that it employs to maintain social discipline, ultimately in the interest of the powerful, also varies.

Innovative as it was, *The New Criminology* was subjected to some immediate criticisms. The work was very generalised and schematic in its prescription for a crime-free, socialist, "good" society. From the standpoint of the 1990s the concluding chapter in particular appears absurdly utopian. The work also failed to provide an adequate definition of crime and deviance: were the authors assuming common causes for burglary, rape and white collar offending? How did they appreciate the social and individual harm that can be the outcome of crime? Victims were conspicuous by their absence.

As with labelling perspectives, there was an unfortunate interpretation that could be read into the text that saw the deviant as a romantic figure engaged in proto-revolutionary behaviour—a claim resisted by Taylor and Walton although they appear to have had in mind the righteous struggles of political activists and counter cultural figures rather than the common, or garden variety, burglar or street robber (Taylor and Walton, 1975: 235–36). It can be argued that since the publication of *The New Criminology*, very little has been achieved to produce a truly social view of deviance. In their subsequent edited work, Taylor, Walton and Young (1975) attended to particular rather than global concerns and moved away from the "grand theory" of the original programme.

The retreat from grand theorising was encouraged by the rapidly emerging diverse accounts of criminal activity by sociologists and social historians. Thompson (1975) and Hay, Linebaugh, and Thompson (1975) demonstrated that criminal behaviour has never been a homogenous concept and that the state is much more multifaceted and operates in a more complex manner than implied by Taylor, Walton and Young. According to the historians, the Rule of Law cannot simply be conceptualised as an external coercive force repressing the working class; it could possibly offer protection from certain abuses of power and intra-class offending.

Marxist scholars such as Hirst (1975) were sharply critical of the potential for labelling perspectives and Marxism to be wedded in one theory; the two were held to be theoretically incompatible. Hirst saw *The New Criminology* as ultimately a work on labelling perspectives with elements of Marxism grafted on almost for effect (Hirst, 1975: 243).

Changes in Marxist scholarship and the translation and enhanced availability of the works of diverse and innovative modern Marxists during the 1970s left the first wave of New Criminologists somewhat stranded intellectually. The state had previously been understood as a monolithic representation of the political form of economic class domination. In the 1970s, however, the focus of Marxist theorising altered to appreciate the idea of the state as a more complex site of class struggle, and the roles of culture, ideology and hegemony in liberating and constraining human action received enhanced attention.

Policing the Crisis and the Emergence of Feminist Perspectives

Many of the complex new issues in Marxist theorising, along with the influences from new deviancy theory, were addressed by revisionists of the New Criminology, a large group of whom worked at Birmingham Centre for Contemporary Cultural Studies (BCCCS) under the directorship of Professor Stuart Hall. This group was particularly active in the 1970s, building on sub-cultural and labelling approaches and developing them within an increasingly sophisticated Marxist framework that benefitted from the general expansion of scholarship in the field. The BCCCS produced numerous working papers and a number of important and influential books, including *Resistance through Rituals* (Hall and Jefferson, 1976), which analysed the social history of numerous youth sub-cultures within a largely Marxist framework that saw youth culture and the particular selection of style and artefacts as sub-cultural solutions to the problems faced by youth in capitalist economies in crisis. The *magnum opus* of the group was, however, *Policing the Crisis* (Hall et al., 1978), which addressed the substantive issue of the ''moral panic'' surrounding street robbery in Britain in the 1970s. The role of the police and the media in amplifying the problem and the identification of street robbery as a problem of black youth and black communities were welded into an analysis of the crisis in British capitalism under which circumstances conspired to identify race, youth and crime as a metaphor for disorder. This justified greater levels of repression by state agencies, which further added to the amplification of crime as a social problem.

The radical development of sub-cultural theory was also enriched by contributions from Parker (1975), who examined the life experiences of young men in Liverpool who episodically committed offences as a temporary solution to harsh material circumstances and by collections on youth cultures such as that of Mungham and Pearson (1976). Pryce (1979) studied Afro-Caribbean youth in the St. Pauls area of Bristol and found that, in the context of being a generation or more away from immigrant status, certain sub-cultural solutions to racism, unemployment, low status or menial work and poor material circumstances were forms of crime that gave a feeling of mastery and autonomy over their lives.

It was also during this period that one of the most glaring omissions in the development of criminology became especially apparent—the role and experience of women in both the commission of crime and, importantly, as victims of crime. What would now be recognised as the women's movement in Britain had only slowly emerged in the very late 1960s with the development of the women's liberation movement and the fitful provision of women's refuges and rape crisis centres. Criminology and the sociology of deviance were, however, relatively slow in appreciating the importance of these developments, and the first identifiable feminist work in the field was Smart's *Women, Crime and Criminology* (1977). Smart argued that the task of feminist criminology was to find "alternative modes of conceptualising the social world" (Smart, 1977: 180). This has certainly been achieved, but not in one unifying theoretical project. There have since emerged numerous feminist perspectives although all might be seen as being "in essence, anti-positivistic and critical of stereotypical images of women, and the question of women is central. They also share an interest in using methodologies which are sympathetic to these concerns (Hanmar and Saunders, 1984, cited in Gelsthorpe and Morris, 1988: 227).

A good deal of early work from feminist perspectives concentrated on exposing discriminatory practices and seeking out and identifying the sexism in the criminal justice system (Carlen, 1983, 1985; Edwards, 1984). Other work focussed on women's victimisation, particularly by the crimes of domestic violence and sexual assault, challenging many stereotypical assumptions about women who are victimised (Smart, 1977; Hanmar, 1978). During this period of the development of radical criminology, the emphasis was very much on critiques of this nature, and there was little effort to merge feminist perspectives with mainstream criminology even within radical circles. Yet the absence of a gender appreciation within criminology was startling once revealed and the mysteries of patriarchy exposed. Eileen Leonard cited Barbara Wootton to starkly reinforce this point:

> It is surely, to say the least, very odd that half the population should apparently be immune to the criminogenic factors which have led to the downfall of so significant a

> proportion of the other half. Equally odd it is, too, that although the criminological experience of different countries varies considerably, nevertheless the sex differentiation remains. (Wootton, cited in Leonard, 1982: xi)

A substantial critique is not however a theory, and it was some time before theoretical themes consolidated (Gelsthorpe and Morris, 1988: 230). The main theoretical thrust that emerged in the 1980s was rejection of the study merely of women who break laws and norms in favour of a concentration on those who break the law and norms, those who conform and the *relationship* between them in order to clarify the concept of "normal" society and reveal the covert controls that persuade women into conformity (Gelsthorpe and Morris, 1988: 230).

In terms of the impact of feminist thought and research on the work of mainstream (or *malestream*) criminology, there remained little integration. Frances Heidensohn termed the limited accommodation of feminist writing the "lean-to" approach (1987: 23). Many male criminologists learned to use non-sexist language; some amended second editions of books to include a page or two referring to women's experience. Despite a growing diversity in feminist work to incorporate race and gender issues, which generated an equivalent study of masculinities, not a vast amount has changed (Gelsthorpe and Morris, 1990). Textbooks usually have a chapter on the growing volume of feminist work, somewhat ghettoising this important field. Lecture programmes, likewise, usually have a discreet class or two, if not a whole but separate course. Feminist thought and research then and, to a large extent, still today appear peripheral to criminology—even, despite some token and some genuine efforts at integration and inclusion, to radical criminology (Gelsthorpe and Morris, 1990: 232).

The range of feminist perspectives has multiplied, and substantial diversity has emerged. This includes liberal, radical, socialist and black feminisms, as well as radical, socialist and bourgeois versions. The general claim that the experience of women had remained opaque in criminological visions and that the focus of criminology had been on men and male crime and deviance is perhaps less true than 15 years ago. The entire discussion of women's position in society and the nature and form of patriarchy, however, served to further open up the potential scope of criminology and the sociology of deviance. New concerns emerged about the nature and distribution of power, which connected, albeit often only vaguely, with the concerns of radical criminology. In more recent years, this ever broadening debate about gender and crime has drawn on a greatly expanded range of sociological and social psychological thought. It has opened up a wider debate, which now seeks to explore the social context of the production of, and distinctions between, both feminisms and femininitities and masculinity and masculinities as perspectives on the nature of gender distinctions and the manner in which they are reproduced socially and politically (Tierney, 1996: 267).

CONSOLIDATION

Criminology Ends Here

By the mid-1970s, the criminological academy had come to be substantially occupied by a cohort of personalities, especially sociologists, who had been recruited to cater to the boom in higher education. This process consolidated the influence of radical criminology in higher education. The bulk of these academics were adherents to various strands of new deviancy theory and the new criminologies. Rock, in his study of academic careers in British criminology, termed this cohort "the fortunate generation" (Rock, 1988a: 191; 1994: 133). The author is reminded of a remark made by his undergraduate tutor in the late 1970s concerning the Birmingham Centre's *Policing the Crisis* that "criminology ends here!" Such optimism was indicative of the depth of influence that radical approaches had on the academy by that point. However, research based on radical perspectives had remained largely unfunded by major funding institutions, who were largely concerned with supporting less critical, generally positivist, applied studies. Some work was supported by charitable organisations and monies gleaned from internal university funds, but the bulk was unsubsidised. There was considerable rancour over the level of funding to "official," mainly positivist and correctionalist groups and individuals, and this served to fuel the rhetorical resentment that appeared in radical texts.

The fortunate days of the fortunate generation were, however, coming to a close for reasons that demand a return to the exterior history of the subject.

The Callaghan Labour Party administration had by 1979 failed to balance welfarism, reformism, industrial relations and inflation. The level of unemployment rose. There were numerous hard hitting strikes culminating in the Winter of Discontent of 1978–1979. Racial tensions were mounting, and serious disorders between police and black youths broke out at the Afro-Caribbean cultural celebration, the Notting Hill Carnival, in 1976 and 1977. Extreme right wing political parties, such as the National Front, gained limited yet increased support for their racist policies and staged provocative marches, often through areas of significant black residence.

The pervading sense of national insecurity and an enduring moral panic over general issues of social order, including race and crime as identified by Hall et al. (1978), led to a sharp break in the post-war British political culture. The broad bipartisan approach to domestic politics crashed with the election of the Thatcher administration in 1979. The period of commitment to economic planning and welfare consensus was abolished almost overnight. Thatcherism was a mixture of faith in the dynamism of the free market and old fashioned Conservatism. It harkened back to a mythical past that trumpeted the success of Victorian values in producing entrepreneurship and wealth whilst conveniently neglecting the negative aspects of that history—the poverty, brutality, corruption and sectional repression.

Among the early challenges was a radical effort to create a "leaner, fitter economy." This led to spiralling levels of unemployment, as uncompetitive industrial and commercial concerns closed down. The lack of hope for a future of meaningful employment spread progressively over a substantial proportion of the younger generation, and many sought sub-cultural solutions to these problems. Critical commentators in the 1970s had criticised the use of the term "sub-culture," as it suggested that there was a definite mainstream culture against which it could be compared. Yet by the early 1980s many parts of the country were so economically depressed that there existed entire communities with little investment in mainstream culture. It was the youthful aspects of these cultures that were most visible on the streets and hence the most vulnerable to police attention and labelling as crime levels rose and the spiral of deviancy amplification developed as described by Hall et al. (1978). These developments were further identified in the context of a crisis in capitalism giving rise to the development of an increasingly authoritarian state in Hall (1980).

In Bristol in 1980 serious rioting broke out following the raid on a black-owned cafe in the depressed St. Pauls district. The police were the focus of the resistance by young black people to the bleak quality of their circumstances and the challenges to their sub-cultural solutions by the forces of law and order. In 1981 serious and much more widespread rioting occurred all over Britain but notably in Brixton (South London), Liverpool and Manchester, as well as in much smaller and traditionally peaceable communities. In Brixton the riots were initially sparked by a large-scale street-level operation to stop and search people to apprehend burglary and robbery suspects, whilst in other places youthful resentment concerning police street-level activity provided the background for flashpoints to occur, or copycatting to take place.

The Scarman Report (1981, 1986) into the disorders, whilst by no means as comprehensive as the inquiry into American urban disorders of the 1960s (National Advisory Commission on Civil Disorders, 1968), highlighted the social origins of the riots. Attempts to make British policing more socially sensitive and better equipped to deal with riots in the future were underway before the ink was dry on Lord Scarman's report. There was however much to learn and develop and a policing culture to change (Cowell et al., 1982; Benyon, 1984). Before the reform process was fully underway, however, in 1985 further explosive rioting occurred in Brixton and also in Tottenham (North London) and Handsworth in Birmingham. Again it was police operations that provided the spark to the tinder of economic and political marginalisation and racial tension.

Further outbreaks of public disorder occurred during industrial relations disputes as the Conservative Government confronted workers whose jobs were threatened as a result of its stringent economic policies. The 1984–1985 Miners' Strike was the most notable of these as it brought about the national coordination and mobilisation of the traditionally locally based and locally accountable British police services.

FRAGMENTATION

We Told You So!

Just at the time when radical criminologists and sociologists of deviance could have pointed to their accumulated work and taunted, "We told you this sort of thing would happen," developments militated against them. Participation in higher education continued to rise, but with government efforts to reduce public spending, investment became patchy. Staff in the social sciences were faced with growing teaching and administrative loads, and Conservative education ministers emphasised the funding of applied research aimed at applications in business and technology. In this context unsubsidised radical commentary and research became more difficult to carry out, and new academic positions became more difficult to come by. As Rock documented, virtually no criminologists were recruited into British higher education in the early 1980s and only a handful in succeeding years (Rock, 1988a, 1994).

New Challenges and a Falling-Out

The riots of the 1980s did, however, confirm to radical criminologists that their theoretical explorations and small-scale fieldwork activities not only produced results "in the laboratory" but that social problems were confirmed to be largely as they had explained them. The precise nature of a desirable programme of change, however, led to further schisms within the radical paradigm. The concerns of new deviancy theory and the concentration on deviance rather than crime came to be seen in a more pragmatic perspective, and the emergence of competing paradigms from the political right and official discourses gave rise to further diversity among the new criminologists, notably in a distinction between New Left Realists and Critical Criminologists.

Right Realism

Conservative criminology received a considerable boost with the writings of James Q. Wilson in the United States, notably with the publication, popularity and political influence of his work *Thinking About Crime* (1975, 1983). Broad in scope and written for a popular audience, Wilson's work attacked social democratic welfarism and its influence on crime rates and crime control policy. Wilson's "right realism" demanded "tough but fair" action by agents of social control to enable the "respectable" elements of society to regain control of neighbourhoods. Wilson's work represents a rather traditional conservatism with an emphasis on recapturing a lost past of prosperity gained from honest endeavour. His work, *On Character* (1991), is in many ways resonant of the return to Victorian values demands of the Thatcher administration. In his collaboration with Richard Herrnstein, the reliance of this approach on positivist interpretations of the nature and causes of criminality is strongly asserted (Wilson and Herrnstein, 1985). (For a debate on varieties of right wing perspectives on crime see Tame [1991].)

The New Administrative Criminology

In terms of official state-subsidised criminology, a further alternative paradigm had emerged. Whilst the Home Office and Cambridge Institute of Criminology continued to carry out administrative and individual positivist inspired research, by the late 1970s a new pragmatic strand of administrative criminology was emerging. This New Administrative Criminology initially had little to say about the aetiology of crime. The primary focus of the work was to discover what might be done to prevent crime and to develop projects to demonstrate the effectiveness of any given initiative. The influences on this perspective included the American architect/anthropologist/criminologist, Oscar Newman, who had developed the concept of "defensible space" (1972). This approach suggested that good property design could encourage a sense of territoriality among residents, provide opportunities for surveillance and facilitate the exercise of informal social control over space, which would work against crime. These ideas were extensively tested in the United States and attracted substantial funding for trials and demonstration projects, which were able to show some success in reducing crime as well as enhancing neighbourliness and a sense of safety.

Defensible space was but one idea that contributed to the development of the concept of "crime as opportunity"—a crime prevention orientated theory that held that most crime was opportunistic in nature and could be prevented by adjustments to the construction or management of facilities ("target hardening") in order to make crime against them more difficult to commit, or to enhance the likelihood of the offender being apprehended—an approach termed "situational crime prevention" (Mayhew et al., 1976; Clarke and Mayhew, 1980). To support the development of situational crime prevention, the British Home Office embarked on a large-scale victim survey, to be repeated approximately every two years, inspired by the *American National Crime Survey*. The purpose of mounting the *British Crime Survey*, an expensive research project, was both to provide an alternative measure of the volume and distribution of crime from that generated from police recorded statistics and to provide information concerning the areas, groups and individuals in society whose fear and experience of crime could be reduced by the implementation of crime prevention measures.

The development of Situational Crime Prevention gave a whole new lease of life to officially sponsored criminology in Britain, which had been dogged by allegations that "nothing works" in the field of crime reduction (Bright, 1991). The approach was pragmatic and attractive to policy makers and commentators in the 1970s and 1980s because, being equivocal about the aetiology of crime, it could appear to be politically neutral and hence avoid awkward engagement with the punitive and populist policy demands of the Conservative administrations.

Left Realism

The challenges from New Right Realism, as exemplified by the works of James Q. Wilson, and the pragmatism of the New Administrative Criminology, as well as the work of Elliot Currie in the United States (1985), inspired new directions in radical criminology. Both New Right Realism and the New Administrative Criminology, combined with feminist theorising and research, had led to an enhanced role for victims as significant components of the basic criminological equation. Radical criminologies, like virtually all previous criminologies, had previously been distinctly offender centred. The rise in recorded and victim survey-measured crime in the Thatcher years, as well as the social disorganisation and chaos that was revealed as a result of the riots, led to calls requiring that something had to be done about law and order by adherents to left of centre politics. Jock Young had commented on the dangers of romanticizing the deviant and neglecting the social harm that could be caused by crime soon after the publication of *The New Criminology* and subsequently (Young, 1975). By 1984, academics had attempted to develop a radical criminology that was theoretically informed by the concerns of the radical left yet able to engage at an empirical level with official criminologists and commentators of the right. The initial result was *What Is to Be Done about Law and Order?* (Lea and Young, 1984). This work sparked off a rancorous debate in the field of radical criminology. The work appeared to challenge the inequality/labelling/deviancy amplification focus of most radical criminology and acknowledge that black youth probably did proportionally commit more conventionally defined crime. That the main victims of this crime were generally also the less powerful in society introduced concern for the victims of offending into the radical paradigm. The acceptance of marginalised, especially black youths, as disproportionately involved in conventional crime was qualified by recourse to standard radical sub-cultural theory noting that this disproportionate representation was merely a rational response, or solution, however ''magical'' (to use the term deployed by the Birmingham Centre commentators), to racism and severe social, economic and political marginalisation. The remedies to this aetiological account were held to be the tasks of any future socialist or revised social democratic government and should include enhanced democratic accountability of police to the needs of local communities.

The New Left Realists also saw the opportunity to develop the ideas of social and situational crime prevention within their more politically committed framework, emphasising the need to improve police efficiency and sensitivity and target high-crime areas to implement programmes to reduce the fear and experience of crime. Left Realists also took on the idea of crime surveys, adjusted from the standard Home Office format to reflect their political priorities, to produce empirical work to support and inform their commentaries and theorising (Kinsey, 1985; Kinsey, Lea and Young, 1986; Jones et al., 1986).

Subsequently, Young renewed his attack on what he termed the Left Idealists in radical criminology (although they preferred to retain the title of Critical Criminologists). The main focus of the contention was that Young et al. emphasised street crime as a real problem that needed to be acknowledged and addressed if government, the police and other social control agencies were to be brought to book for their failure to protect victims of crime, especially in inner-city areas. The Critical Criminologists, adherents to the initial radical criminology project that emphasised the lack of attention to the crimes of the powerful and the deviancy amplifying tendencies of the mass media and agents of social control, saw such deviations from the faith as heresy (Scraton, 1987). In many ways this debate was resonant of the combative period of the 1970s and the rising assertiveness of the radicals over other types of criminologists (Young, 1991; Scraton and Chadwick, 1991). Important questions were, however, raised concerning the aetiological crisis in Western criminology: about the causes of criminal and harm inducing behaviour. Young's answer appeared to call for a revitalisation of a politically informed subcultural theory and an improved integration of the lessons of radical and feminist perspectives, all relocated in a radical, policy-oriented model (Young, 1986, 1991, 1994; Matthews and Young, 1992). In this way challenges from writers such as James Q. Wilson that the left had ignored street crime, or had expected other social policies to ameliorate it and had failed, could be countered. Also, by learning the possible advantages of developing both situational and social crime prevention measures and incorporating them into social democratic policies and by engaging in empirical work to assess police effectiveness in terms of public satisfaction and safety, the New Left Realists have demonstrated a commitment to policy relevance that may serve them well in terms of "doing something about law and order."

In recent years the ideas of the New Left Realists have come to some degree of *rapproachment* with the crime control policies promoted by the Labour Party administration that was elected at the time of writing. There are concerns that the incoming administration is particularly worried about appearing to be soft on crime—an allegation frequently slung at Labour governments—and that the Home Secretary is likely to carry forward many of the repressive ideas of the Conservatives. Nevertheless there are promising plans for the enhancement of official emphasis on crime prevention and a commitment to do something about the appallingly high levels of imprisonment, which at one point appeared to have become a former Conservative Home Secretary's performance indicator.

Despite the shift towards pragmatism marked by New Left Realism in British criminology, there remains a substantial constituency of critical criminologists and sociologists of deviance who continue to support the view that criminology is an inappropriate term for the study of law making and breaking and norm creation and violation (Cohen, 1988, 1994). The impact of the work of the

French historian of ideas, Michel Foucault, in the late 1970s did much to re-conceptualise the ways in which social power operates. This led to the exploration of knowledge/power relations and to the examination of techniques of power and control across a broad historical backcloth (Foucault, 1977; Stenson and Cowell, 1991). Indirectly the work of Foucault, combined with a variety of feminist perspectives that stressed the importance of subjective appreciations and experiences of deviance, opened the door to a fascination with the implications of the concept of post-modernity and post-modern thought. These ideas have captured the imaginations of many erstwhile radical criminologists and new deviancy theorists, although the full implications of this potential alternative paradigm (or non-paradigm) shift remain tentative and are outside the scope of this chapter. A useful collection of writings, a number of which explore the anti-criminology sociological perspective and explore the implications of post-modern thought and the impact of post-modernity on criminology, can be found in Nelken (1994).

CONCLUSION

We have examined the emergence of a radical paradigm in British criminology, first by examining the background of its development in criticisms of the social democratic post-war poverty project, criticism of which developed from the American-inspired work of the early subculturalists and new deviancy theorists. Second, we have explored the political radicalisation of these perspectives and the steady accommodation of a variety of Marxist perspectives during a period of national economic, political and cultural crisis, noting how the academy came to be substantially influenced, if not dominated, by a variety of radical criminologies and sociologies of deviance. Finally we noted a fragmentation of the paradigm in the face of challenges from competing perspectives from the political right and from administrative criminology.

This fragmentation is perhaps in some ways overstated as there have always been internal tensions within the broad church of radical criminology. It is perhaps true to say, however, that the radical paradigm has reached the status of a general orthodoxy in the social scientific study of crime and has, at least within the academy, achieved the status of normal science, the bickering largely being about how ideas from other perspectives are detached from their distinctive theoretical bases and integrated into the paradigm.

It is sometimes surprising to reflect on how many ideas and concepts from radical perspectives on crime have entered into conventional understanding. The idea of a moral panic is no longer a specialised sociological term and can be found in broadsheet newspapers and in the deliberations of police officers and policy makers and shapers. The idea that a person can be labelled, and that this may have an impact on their future actions, is not uncommon and is a major consideration in juvenile justice policy and decision making. The radical critique of official crime statistics as an inadequate measure of the volume of crime actually taking place is now well recognised by all who show an intelligent interest in such matters. These are but a few examples of how academic debate, research and commentary in the field of radical criminology has impacted on the world outside of the academy.

In 1988, Rock commented:

> The fortunate generation remains the major executor of the British tradition. And there appears to have been a consequent fall in the rate of intellectual innovation. Theoretical revolution no longer follows theoretical revolution in a dizzy procession. Instead sociologists of deviance seem still to be investigating the ramifications of the ideas which were introduced in the 1960s: they have become the normal scientists of ethnography, interactionism, feminism . . . and Marxism. (Rock, 1988a: 192)

This being the case, it is to be wondered what the future will bring for the radical paradigm in criminology. The new entrants to criminology, whilst many are sympathetic to radical concerns, often find themselves chasing research grants from major funding bodies and teaching, researching and writing in fields that are outside of this paradigm. This is to a large extent a product of the introduction of a performance culture into British higher education that does not favour, or particularly encourage, unsubsidised activity. In this climate it is possible to find even some of the radicals of the fortunate generation carrying out research for government departments to maintain or enhance the image of their departments and themselves within the university and to earn funds that might eventually subsidise their preferred endeavours. Radical criminology still shapes a great deal of the teaching in British universities, but it remains unclear precisely how research and development can be continued in the absence of time, funds and the support of higher education institutions for critical activity. The loss of the tradition will be a loss to scholarship. As Colin Sumner noted:

> Criminology cannot be limited to policy orientated studies and must retain its integrity as an area of independent, critical inquiry of interest to scholars from a variety of disciplinary backgrounds. A criminology that wants to remain dynamic and worthy of its complex subject matter must therefore constantly renew theoretical debate, explore current issues, and develop new methods of research. To allow itself to be limited by the often narrowly political interests of government departments or the funding agencies' need for parochial "relevance," especially in an age when "realism" is so often defined by short-run philosophies, is to promote its own destruction as an intellectual enterprise. (Sumner, 1990: xi)

CHAPTER 10

The Politics of Criminal Justice Policy

STEPHEN P. SAVAGE

INTRODUCTION

Within a matter of days after taking office in May 1997, the new Labour Government announced that alongside new policies on education and the welfare state, criminal justice reform was to be an early priority for the new administration. This development acted as further evidence of a trend that has been in evidence since the late 1970s: the *politicisation of criminal justice*. For much of the post-war period, criminal justice, or "law and order," was a subject of relative political neutrality across British political parties (Downes and Morgan, 1994). While differences between the parties certainly were apparent, these tended to be around differences of emphasis and degree rather than fundamental principles. Only over the issue of capital punishment were significant divisions apparent, and even these were narrowing around a veritable consensus. It was Margaret Thatcher's election to the leadership of the Conservative Party (then in opposition) that signalled the first real departure from this arrangement. As the Labour Government struggled with nationwide industrial unrest, Thatcher began a campaign that was to reap benefits in the run-up to the 1979 General Election. This campaign was based on the image of an increasingly lawless Britain under the Labour Government, lawless both in terms of rising crime but also in terms of public disorder, political protest and labour unrest. Thatcher's statement on the eve of the General Election that "the demand in the country will be for two things: less tax and more law and order" (Savage, 1990) was prophetic in a number of ways. The election of a Conservative Government that had made law and order a central platform of its agenda for Britain was an indication that crime, policing and criminal justice had become politically charged issues. It has been that way ever since. The result has been an explosion of central government inspired initiatives in the criminal justice field; indeed, there have been more Acts of Parliament on policing and criminal justice issues since 1980 than in the *whole* post-war period prior to that.

The aim of this chapter is to trace the variety of ways in which the politicisation of criminal justice has been expressed in criminal justice policy since 1979. It will focus in particular on the extent to which criminal justice policy has at various points been politically-led rather than research-led and as such has been characterised by policy shifts and even on some occasions by policy reversals. The effect of this has been an unstable climate in which rationality in policy making has all too often had to take second stage to political exigency and short-termism. In this context, coherent management and delivery of criminal justice services have been extremely difficult to attain.

This discussion will begin with a general overview of sources of influence over criminal justice policy in England and Wales. It will then proceed to outline a number of phases in criminal justice policy from 1979 to the present, phases that have reflected shifting priorities coincidental with changes in the political cycle. It will conclude with some brief comments about the lessons that can be learnt from an overview of the undulations characterising criminal justice policy in Britain in recent years.

SOURCES OF INFLUENCE OVER CRIMINAL JUSTICE POLICY

Criminal justice policy is shaped by a wide variety of factors and processes. Some of these operate at a level outside of government itself—professional and occupational bodies such as the Law Society and Bar Council, the Association of Chief Police Officers, the Police Federation, the National Association of Probation Officers and the Magistrates' Association. The effectiveness of such groupings in influencing or shaping criminal justice policy varies across the bodies concerned, and over time (Savage, Charman and Cope, 1997). The extent to which such pressure groups enjoy the attention of government depends on the political climate at the time. For example, and as we shall see later, police representative groups appeared to have disproportionate influence over criminal justice policy in the final years of Conservative government in the mid-1990s (Savage, Charman and Cope, 1997). Previously the legal professions were an important source of influence over the directions taken in criminal justice policy. Overall, however, the key determinants of criminal justice policy lie within central government itself. It is the sources of influence at the governmental level, and in relation to that at party political level, that warrant most consideration.

A very apparent feature of government policy under the Conservatives since 1979 has been the extent to which public policy as a whole has been shaped by *political ideology*. The disruption of the "post-war consensus" associated with the "conviction" politics of Margaret Thatcher entailed the ideologisation of public policy across the board. Public policy came increasingly to bear the hallmarks of the New Right (Savage, Atkinson and Robins, 1994). Criminal justice policy was no exception. For example, the Criminal Justice Act of 1991 incorporated a number of measures to engage parents of juvenile offenders in court hearings and the penal process, such as the parental fines system in which the offender's parents could be required to pay the fine meted out as punishment for the crime. This reflects the ideological commitment of the right to notions of parental responsibility and blame, and more generally the emphasis on family values. What is more, law and order operates as a core element of Conservative ideology in its own right (Brake and Hale, 1992); criminal justice policy holds an inherent ideological attraction for Conservative politicians.

A second source of influence over criminal justice policy has been *financial*. While in general expenditure levels on policing, criminal justice and the penal system have been far more generous than in other areas of public policy, given the privileged status granted to this sector under the Thatcher administrations, financial considerations have figured in the formation of criminal justice policy. For example, the pursuit of "punishment in the community" during the 1980s was closely tied to a strategy of reducing the financial burden of imprisonment, as has been the movement towards the privatisation of the prison service. Given that expenditure on justice and law as a percentage of general government expenditure had increased from 4% to 6% between 1981 and 1991 (HMSO, 1993: 177), this has become an issue of growing concern to both Conservative and Labour governments.

Thirdly, criminal justice policy has been *politically driven*. Often in response to particular widely publicised incidents of crime, the British government has sought to take political advantage by means of immediate reforms of specific areas of the criminal justice system. For example, in response to public disquiet over sentences passed in a number of high-profile rape cases, the Criminal Justice Act of 1988 made it possible for the Attorney General to refer cases to the Court of Appeal where an over lenient sentence was suspected. More fundamentally, as we shall see later, the "law and order ticket" was mobilised by the Conservatives in the early to mid-1990s to placate political opponents from within its own ranks. Given the status of law and order as an issue of public concern, the role of criminal justice policy as a weapon in the armoury of political expediency is difficult to resist. The British Labour Party's engagement with the law and order question when in opposition demonstrates that political motives are equally as important outside of Conservative quarters. When he was Shadow Home Secretary, Tony Blair appeared to hit the right populist note with his 1993 slogan "tough on crime; tough on the causes of crime". Instead of following the tradition of effectively conceding that law and order was Conservative political property, this stance signalled a determination to compete head-to-head with the Conservatives on one of their most cherished territories. As we shall see later, there was and is much to play for in this respect.

A fourth motive force behind criminal justice policy is more ambiguous—it relates to the extent to which policy is *knowledge driven*. The British Home

Office employs an army of researchers and commissions numerous research undertakings. It has at its disposal an enviable supply of research material on the effectiveness of many aspects of the police, criminal justice and penal systems. Reassuringly, on some occasions the knowledge made available by Home Office research departments has influenced law and order policy. Perhaps the best example of this is the strategy of "situational crime prevention." Home Office research has for some time shown that crime can be controlled through environmentally-based measures, such as improved security of premises and improved design of buildings to eradicate concealed entrances (Hough and Mayhew, 1982). In terms of cost-effectiveness, investment in reducing opportunities for crime has been shown to be a wise one in terms of specific projects such as "target hardening." The government's commitment of resources to crime prevention initiatives, starting in the mid-1980s with campaigns such as "Crime Concern," was to an extent an acceptance of the relevance of the knowledge base generated by the Home Office's own in-house research (it was also, of course, related to opportunities to involve the business community in the crime control process). Although there is no evidence that situational measures were pursued to an extent sufficient to impact on recorded or unrecorded crime (which continued to rise throughout this period), the acceptance of at least its potential was revealing. In the field of criminal justice another source of knowledge-based influence has come in the form of commissions of inquiry. Since 1979 the major examples of this have been the Royal Commission on Criminal Procedure (1981), the Scarman Report (1981), the Woolf Report (1991) and the Royal Commission on Criminal Justice (1993). Although governments do not have to accept the research on which such inquiries are based, and are not bound by the recommendations for reform presented, inevitably such documents carry significant weight in the formation of policy. Royal Commissions may indeed become once again providers of frameworks for policy making. It was clear that they were not valued by Thatcher when she was Prime Minister, but since her departure they have been employed again. The Labour Government is likely to be particularly sympathetic to the role Royal Commissions can fulfill in informing the policy process.

The relationships between these four factors determining criminal justice policy—ideology, finance, politics and knowledge—are complex and uneven. They may be complementary and mutually supportive. For example (as we shall elaborate later), the shift to punishment in the community in the mid-1980s would seem to have been financially driven but was presented for public consumption in the ideological clothes of notions such as "just deserts." They may, however, be contradictory and mutually exclusive. An example of this is the establishment of the so-called short sharp shock sentences (shorter sentences for young offenders in toughened-up detention centres) in the Criminal Justice Act of 1982. This measure was politically driven—based on a pre-election commitment—but ran against the Home Office's own research findings on the effectiveness of such sentences (Gelsthorpe and Morris, 1994). Knowledge, at least for a period, had to take second stage to politics. More generally, a point we shall elaborate later, the policy objectives underpinning criminal justice reforms, however driven, are constantly confronting the financial constraints of limited public expenditure.

Related to the complexities of interplay between the motive forces of criminal justice policy is the evidence that, at various times since the Conservatives took office in 1979, policy in this area has found itself pulling in different, even opposite, directions. Alongside primary agendas for law and order have been secondary agendas, often less obvious, and in some cases running counter to the dominant, more rhetorical, agenda. This has been referred to as "bifurcation" or "twin tracking" (Hudson, 1987), a process whereby criminal justice policy pursues parallel, and potentially conflicting, objectives (and possibly satisfies both punitive and liberal sides at one and the same time). For example, the Criminal Justice Act of 1991 embodied bifurcation by emphasising the reduction of the use of custody for persistent property offenders, whilst at the same time increasing the length of custodial sentences for sexual and violent crimes—a trend replicated in many jurisdictions in Europe and in the USA (Hudson, 1993), and considered by some to be a long-term general tendency within Western penology (Melossi and Pavarini, 1981).

The main point to make in this context is that the often contradictory motive forces behind British criminal justice policy, which have generated equally contradictory combinations of primary and secondary law and order agendas, have also created a series of watersheds in policy reform in this area under the Conservatives since 1979. More specifically, it is argued that it is now possible to identify *four* major phases of criminal justice policy since 1979, the fourth of which, at the time of writing, is still emergent. While such attempts to periodise policy changes are always at risk of oversimplification, the policy shifts in question are sufficiently dramatic to warrant such a classification (Savage and Nash, 1994).

Phase One: Establishing the Law and Order Agenda

The first phase of Conservative criminal justice policy in many ways predates the Conservative Party's assumption of office in 1979 and relates to the strategy of establishing law and order as a pillar of the party's electoral appeal. As Margaret Thatcher stated in the run-up to the General Election, "The demand in the country will be for two things: less tax and more law and order." Rising crime and disorder—including industrial unrest—were presented as a threat to the fabric of the nation (Downes and Morgan, 1994). The solution rested in a range of measures that were to toughen up the state's capacity to control and reduce crime. The party's natural ideological association with law and order was to be employed in a more explicit way than before in pursuit of its political ambitions. The party's success in the 1979 General Election was in part evidence that this strategy paid dividends.

Two features of the criminal justice process acted as the forward troops in this campaign (Savage, 1990). Soon after taking office the Thatcher Administration announced substantial increases in expenditure on the police service. Commitments were made to maintain expenditure on the police at levels over and above those in other areas of the public sector. A scheduled rise in the number of officers, resources for improved equipment, and, above all, major increases in police salaries, were to form the basis of this commitment. A pledge was also made to increase police powers where necessary in order to combat crime effectively. Whilst one can question the extent to which such commitments were delivered in practice (Savage, 1990), there was clearly evidence that the Conservatives were throwing their weight behind the police service as the front line in the war on crime.

The second area of criminal justice that was featured in this agenda was policy regarding young offenders. Pre- and post-election rhetoric focussed on the problems of juvenile crime and the need for a tougher stance in penalising youth crime. In the Queen's Speech in 1979, a commitment was made "to publish proposals for strengthening the law relating to juvenile and young offenders." The government's 1980 White Paper, *Young Offenders*, stressed the role of deterrence as a function of criminal justice and presented plans for the "short sharp shock" of brief detention centre orders in toughened-up penal establishments, to be subsequently embodied in legislation by the Criminal Justice Act of 1982. The government also drew up plans for a major programme of prison building to free the courts from the pressures of prison overcrowding. A comprehensive package, involving measures for the police service, the courts and the penal system, could thus be presented as the Conservatives' response to the problem of crime.

There was, however, a secondary agenda at work during this phase, less public (depending on the audience) and to an extent working in opposite directions (Gelsthorpe and Morris, 1994: 967). Furthermore, as the 1980's progressed this secondary agenda became ever more influential in directing criminal justice policy. As regards young offenders, alongside the apparent strategy to get tough with juvenile offenders, the government, through the Criminal Justice Act of 1982 and various Home Office circulars, sought means to divert large numbers of juveniles from the criminal justice and custodial systems. For example, the Act required the courts, where a custodial sentence was being passed, to state publicly the reasons why—in the light of criteria spelling out that non-custodial measures should be tried out first. Non-custodial sentences such as community service were extended, and police cautioning of juveniles encouraged—in many respects a continuation of juvenile policy of previous administrations. The government was thus pursuing a twin-track policy: increasing the severity of punishments for some offenders, yet extending and encouraging non-custodial and diversionary measures for others. Despite the deterrent rhetoric, there was growing concern in Home Office circles over both the financial cost and lack of effectiveness of custodial penalties (Gelsthorpe and Morris, 1994). As we shall see, these concerns were to become increasingly influential as the decade wore on.

Another feature of the secondary agenda during this phase applied to the police service. Despite the government's initial commitment to ''real'' increases in expenditure on the police (i.e., increases over and above the rate of inflation), as early as 1983 the Home Office began to impose an efficiency and effectiveness drive on the service, under the rubric of the Financial Management Initiative. Circular 114/1983, a Home Office document sent to all police forces encouraging forces to pursue the ''3 E's'' (economy, effectiveness and efficiency) was released as the first wave in what was to become a flood of centrally inspired measures to reform police management and police resource allocation (Leishman and Savage, 1993). Although Margaret Thatcher was still prepared to announce in 1985 that ''Never, ever, have you heard me say that we will economize on law and order,'' the foundations for doing precisely that had already been laid some years previously. The police service was clearly in the firing line, even if the bullet took some time to arrive.

Therefore, the first phase of Conservative criminal justice policy was typified by a primary agenda that was *politically* and *ideologically* driven. This stressed, at least in its rhetoric, more severe and extensive custodial penalties, and a strengthened police service backed up by increased resources. However, alongside that primary agenda existed a secondary agenda, more influenced by *financial* concerns, which in that respect drew opportunistically upon the *knowledge base* established within the Home Office on such matters as the lack of effectiveness of custodial penalties. If the political expediency of establishing a law and order agenda had already born fruit, the concern for reduced public expenditure on law and order, once secondary, had begun to gain primacy as the mid-1980s were reached. A second phase in criminal justice policy had begun to take shape.

Phase Two: The Age of Reason?

In a quiet but concerted way, a sea change in law and order policy took place during the mid-1980s. It was not necessarily a question of a totally new range of policies suddenly emerging, but rather essentially one of existing, but low-key, policies coming to the fore, and of previously high profile strategies slipping into the background. It also involved the greater influence of financial considerations on the one hand, and rationality in policy-making (that is, decisions supported by a research base) on the other.

One reflection of this, as intimated earlier, was the rise of crime prevention as a front-line strategy in crime reduction (see Pease, 1994). Criminological research, much of it based within the Home Office, had presented a convincing case that a cost-effective means of controlling crime was through reducing opportunities for crime (Clarke and Mayhew, 1980). Target-hardening through improved physical security is one obvious example of this. Better design of buildings and estates, to reduce hidden entrances and increase opportunities for observation of vulnerable areas, is another. Such information had been in the possession of the Home Office since the 1970s. However, it was not until the mid-1980s that the research and its implications began to make a significant impact on government policy. The launch of "Crime Concern" in 1987, a major initiative bringing together central and local government, the police, the voluntary agencies and a range of private sector bodies, was the high point of this development; crime prevention and opportunity-reduction were its main pillars. The message went out that, while the police would have to continue to be seen as the key agency in crime control, much could be done through self-help and crime prevention campaigns managed outside of the police service. It was one element of what Douglas Hurd, when Home Secretary, referred to as "active citizenship." Thus the notion of partnership, between law-enforcement and criminal justice agencies on the one hand, and a range of other public and private and independent agencies on the other, began to colour policy and practice in crime control.

More radical, however, were the policy shifts taking place over sentencing and the penal system. In a striking rebuttal of earlier Conservative priorities on crime control, the Home Office, in a handbook for sentencers written in 1986, stated that: "The research evidence . . . suggests that within the realistic range of choice, imposing particular sentences, or particularly severe sentences, has a very limited effect on crime" (HMSO, 1986).

The 1988 Green Paper, *Punishment, Custody and the Community*, continued in this vein, almost dismissing the effectiveness of deterrent sentencing out of hand, but going even further by attacking custody-based punishments, especially for young offenders: "Even a short period of custody is quite likely to confirm them as criminals, particularly if they acquire new criminal skills from more sophisticated offenders" (HMSO, 1988: 34).

Such a distancing process from the erstwhile principle of custody-based deterrence opened the way for a positive endorsement of punishments in the community. While a commitment was maintained to imprison those who were a danger to the community, and for extending the penalties for those thus defined, a range of new forms of non-custodial penalties and a reworking of some established disposals (such as the curfew order) were presented, together with sentencing guidelines, to restrict the scope for the courts to pass custodial sentences. Furthermore, the philosophy that sentences should be proportionate to the offence and not based on the offender (previous convictions should not, according to this view, be key elements in passing sentences) was introduced, constituting another nail in the coffin of deterrent sentencing (at least for a short period of time, as we shall see later).

The thrust behind these shifts would appear to have been two-fold. On the one hand, community-based punishments such as community service orders and supervision orders, had proven to be far less costly forms of punishing offenders than custodial penalties. The added attraction of the proposed disposals was the prospect of passing on some responsibilities of supervision to the private and even voluntary sectors. On the other hand, research had demonstrated the lack of effectiveness of imprisonment in terms of deterrence and reconviction rates; prison was both expensive and in most cases ineffective. Faced with the probability of an ever-rising, or at least very large, custodial population, considerations of cost-effectiveness appeared to have won the day. The Criminal Justice Act of 1991 put these measures into statute. In effect, the act almost constituted a "new consensus" on criminal justice (Gelsthorpe and Morris, 1994: 980), however brief its life span. It embodied measures for a radical shift to community-based penalties not unlike those advocated by both opposition parties. Ironically, under the wing of the "anti-consensus" ideology of Thatcherism, Home Office policy had taken a decidedly centrist step.

As we have argued, financial considerations would seem to have played a key part in this development. One should also acknowledge the role of key individuals in facilitating the shift. At centre stage was Douglas Hurd as Home Secretary. Hurd was one of the few left-of-centre (or "wet") ministers to survive throughout the Thatcher era, and the fact that a range of progressive policies emerged from the Home Office from the mid- to late-1980s had much to do with his stewardship at the Home Department. A crucial role was also played by senior civil servants such as David Faulkner, who was Deputy Secretary at the Home Office from 1982 to 1992, initially in charge of research and statistics, and latterly in charge of criminal justice policy. As was subsequently made clear, Faulkner helped to steer a strategy for criminal justice reform that was, in his own words, "largely driven by consultation with professionals, academics and representatives of informed opinion" (*The Guardian*, 16 April 1994). Faulkner's own heated attack on later Home Office reversals of this policy approach bore witness to the identity of the period of the mid- to late-1980s as one characterised by receptiveness to research-informed policy.

However, while financial and knowledge-based considerations were increasingly the driving forces behind the Phase Two agenda for criminal justice, problems of a political and ideological nature were becoming apparent. Not least, the Home Secretary was faced with selling the package to the Conservative Party at large. Were these not, after all, the policies advocated by the opposition parties? What was Conservative about punishment in the community and the attack on imprisonment? This dilemma appears to have been addressed through ideological foot-work—by bringing in the classically conservative principle of "just deserts."

Although the policy agenda set out in the 1988 Green Paper was broadly replicated in the 1990 White Paper, *Crime, Justice and Protecting the Public*, the framework within which that policy was *presented* had been transformed. By the time of publication of the White Paper, retribution and just deserts were now the ideological clothing for the new emphasis on community-based penalties—the new language of *punishment* in the community held sway. Community sentences were to be graded "to reflect the concept of graduated restrictions on liberty, which are related to the seriousness of offending. This is consistent with the just deserts principle'' (HMSO, 1990: 19).

To avoid any confusion that community-based penalties might be associated with liberal notions of the treatment or welfare of the offender, labels which were too easily identifiable with the ''softly, softly'' of the 1970s, the White Paper presented them in terms of retribution, as measures that were essentially about *restrictions of liberty*. A further ideological twist was made in relation to custodial punishments, which were now to be seen as encouraging a culture of dependence among inmates. Suddenly the idea that custody might *remove* personal responsibility (''nannying'' the prisoner) had been discovered. Classically right wing notions of just deserts and dependency culture were thus marshalled to deliver the message in favour of a major shift from imprisonment to community sentences. If not the motive force behind such a policy shift, they were at least offered as palliatives to those who would find such measures hard to swallow.

What such contortions revealed, however, were underlying tensions both within New Right thought as a whole, and New Right criminology in particular (Tame, 1991). The more general tension, even contradiction, is between the neo-liberalist and neo-conservative foundations of New Right philosophy (Atkinson and Savage, 1994; Green, 1987). Neo-liberalism emphasises a minimalist role for the state, one which restricts the state as far as is possible to such functions as defence and law and order, all else is to be left to the exigencies of the free market. Neo-conservativism, on the other hand, advocates a strong state in certain respects, most particularly those connected with the need to maintain order, loyalty and respect for authority (Gamble, 1988: 54). Whilst attempts have been made to marry the two tendencies within the radical right, most notably in the British case by means of the ideology of Thatcherism (Savage and Robins, 1990), conflict between them would seem inevitable. The most evident tension was over public expenditure. There was an almost unavoidable contradiction in Thatcher's 1979 pledge of *both* ''less tax'' and ''more law and order.'' As the neo-liberal demand for reductions in public expenditure encroached ever more into the inner workings of the public sector, so the anomaly of an open cheque-book for law and order became more apparent. As the 1980s progressed, the conflict between, on the one hand, a deterrent and retributivist penal strategy, traditionally inclined towards the extended use of (expensive) custodial measures, and on the other, the concern to limit public expenditure, was addressed in terms of an ideological game plan. Deterrence was effectively abandoned, and retribution was redefined as an objective best realised in a *non*-custodial setting. The question was whether this financially motivated shift in public policy towards punishment in the community could be sold to the electorate, but perhaps more importantly to the Tory faithful.

Ultimately, the irony of a well-entrenched Conservative government, which had originally ridden in on a tough law and order platform, turning to such apparently progressive policies, was difficult to sustain. No sooner had the Criminal Justice Act of 1991 been enacted than tensions were beginning to tell. Means-tested fines or ''unit-fines,'' one of the ''rationalist'' reforms contained in the act, were incurring the ridicule of the media and the wrath of magistrates. Disorder involving juveniles on a number of provincial housing estates in 1991 and 1992, and spectacular media coverage of a series of joy-riding incidents, stimulated a renewed panic about youth crime. Perhaps above all, the brutal killing in Liverpool of a two-year-old boy, James Bulger, in the spring of 1993, set aflame widespread public anger and concern about crime amongst British youth. Public statements of concern emanating from the judiciary over having hands tied in sentencing were also increasingly in evidence. Coming against the backcloth of a relentless rise in officially recorded crime, political pressures were mounting on the Conservative government to respond. Such a response was indeed forthcoming, but it was arguably driven more by the internal politics of the Conservative Party than by public disquiet about crime. Nevertheless, a third phase in criminal justice policy was emergent.

Phase Three: Regaining the High Ground

The growing public and media disquiet over crime and disorder during the early years of the Conservatives' fourth term of office, following the 1992 General Election, was made all the more politically acute when the Labour Party began to gain ground on law and order. The ''new realism'' that had featured increasingly in Labour's general policy agenda was beginning to take effect on the party's stance on criminal justice policy, just as it had earlier on nuclear defence (on which the Labour Party had reversed its former stance). As has been mentioned, Tony Blair's slogan of ''tough on crime; tough on the causes of crime,'' was seemingly well received. Simultaneously, public support for the Conservatives on the law and order issue was beginning to show a quite dramatic downward trend. For example, whereas opinion polls as late as April 1992 were showing that 41% of those polled expressed belief that the Conservative Party ''had the best policies on crime,'' by March 1993 that figure had dropped to 19% (*The Guardian*, 21 March 1994). The alarm bells were ringing.

The wider political context was one, furthermore, which left the Conservatives vulnerable. The 1992 General Election left them with only a small majority in Parliament; that majority was soon to be reduced further after a number of by-election disasters, when former safe seats were lost to the opposition. Alongside that were the deep divisions over Europe, threatening the obedience of Conservative back-benchers in the House, and therefore the capacity of the Major government to command an effective majority in Parliament. Of paramount importance was the need to maintain party unity, above all to placate those hostile to further integration with the European Union. Crime, coupled with the related issue of single-parenthood, was to function as a key player in the strategy to resolve that difficulty. The aim seemed to be to win back the high ground on law and order, together with the political benefits, internal and external to the party, that would accrue. The fact that the Euro-sceptics in the Conservative Party were also in almost every case to the far right on issues of law and order made that strategy particularly attractive. In this respect, it was ironically previous Conservative policy on criminal justice that was a primary target of that strategy.

In the debate in Parliament that followed the Queen's Speech of November 1993, which outlined forthcoming legislation, the Prime Minister John Major stated that criminal justice reform would be the centrepiece of the forthcoming Parliamentary session. Coming in the wake of the Conservative Party Conference, at which the Home Secretary Michael Howard announced, to the delight of the assembled, a major law and order package to tackle crime, the scene was set for yet another agenda for British criminal justice policy under the Conservatives. However, despite the attempt to present that agenda as a reversal of the trend of the last 30 years, those close to the workings of criminal justice knew that what it reversed above all were the Conservative's own reforms, particularly those of the late-1980s and early-1990s. At the very time when the impact of those reforms was first beginning to show through, in sentencing patterns and more belatedly in the size of the prison population, the government had outlined measures that would seem to have undermined many of the objectives behind such developments.

In the highly charged atmosphere of the 1993 Conservative Party Conference the Home Secretary announced a wide range of measures to reform criminal justice policy. Seeking to appeal simultaneously both to the rank and file and to the "angry silent majority," Howard listed no less than 27 measures to tackle crime. They covered virtually every aspect of the criminal justice process, from the rights of suspects to an expansion of the prison system. They included restrictions on squatting, on anti-hunting campaigns, and even on certain musical events ("raves"). One of the most controversial measures was the abolition of the right to silence, against the recommendations of the 1993 Royal Commission on Criminal Justice: judges would now be able to comment negatively on a suspect's decision to remain silent. This was a measure sought particularly by the police service, with whom Howard was in dispute elsewhere over reforms of discipline procedures, police management and conditions of employment and the structure of the police authorities. More indicative than the abolition to the right to silence, however, was the tone of Howard's comments on the role of imprisonment:

> We shall no longer judge the success of our system of justice by a fall in our prison population. . . . Let us be clear. Prison works. It makes sure that we are protected from murderers, muggers and rapists, and it makes many who are tempted to commit crime think twice. (Speech made to Conservative Party Annual Conference, October 1993)

The abandonment of the view put forward in the 1990 White Paper, and the research evidence it acknowledged, could hardly be more stark. Deterrence through custody was back in the limelight. A new commitment was made to the expansion of custodial punishment. The plans included another round of prison building, new secure training centres (boot camps) for 12 to 14-year-old persistent offenders, all to be built by the private sector, and measures to double the maximum sentence in young offender institutions to two years. A range of new policies designed to end repeat offending by those on bail, including the ending of the presumption in favour of bail, were also presented. In the following week Howard announced steps to curb the use of police cautions and increase the likelihood that offenders, particularly burglars, would be subject to criminal prosecution (*The Guardian*, 16 October 1993).

Although Howard also set out criminal justice policies more broadly acceptable to the opposition parties, such as greater support for victims of crime—without any real increase in funding (indeed the grant to the Criminal Injuries Compensation Board was to be cut)—it was clear that the get tough stance on crime, particularly juvenile crime, was to be the new primary agenda. The fact that his proposals met with the warm approval of representatives of the police service spoke volumes, particularly in the light of its concurrent battles with the Home Secretary over police reform. The Chairman of the Police Federation, representing police rank and file, referred to the plans as "first class," and senior police officers welcomed the measures, especially those relating to offenders on bail. Alternatively, Liberty, the civil liberties group, dubbed the Howard proposals as a "hangers' and floggers' charter," a label no doubt pleasing to the Home Secretary in his strategy to strengthen the image of the Conservatives as the party of law and order.

The timing and tone of the new plans for criminal justice were evidence that political considerations were driving the policy agenda. Margaret Thatcher's endorsement of the Prime Minister's position in a television interview shortly after the Party Conference was symbolic in this respect. The approach taken by ministers of appealing to the rank and file with a range of speeches attacking benefit claimants, single parents and other favoured targets of the populist right, clearly met with the approval of the former Prime Minister—an indication that it was also well received by the far right of the Conservative Party in general. The strategy was a thinly disguised attempt to placate potentially dangerous critics of the Major premiership, particularly those hostile to the government's stance on Europe. A cornerstone of this strategy was the law and order trump card. Criminal justice policy was to be used as a weapon in the fight to win the hearts and minds of those sectors of the party whose hostility the Prime Minister could not afford. Thatcher's endorsement seemed to indicate that the gamble, at least temporarily, had paid off.

Political factors, therefore, would seem to have played a crucial role in the establishment of a new third agenda for criminal justice under the Conservatives, the essence of which was subsequently set out in the Criminal Justice and Public Order Act of 1994. Winning back the high ground on law and order was to be a means of gaining political support internal, and possibly external, to the party.

The vulnerability of criminal justice policy to political forces is not, of course, a status unique to Britain. With reference to criminal justice policy across Europe, Hudson has referred to ''An era of reactive innovation, with penal policy responding to the demands of public/political panics about rising levels of predatory crime and to fiscal constraints imposed by recession'' (Hudson, 1993: 31).

This more widespread tendency notwithstanding, a feature of the British context is the *short-termism* of the political strategy in question, and the contradictory trends this has generated. As a consequence, the British government had committed itself to a range of policies that could well reverse the overall direction of criminal justice, away from that set only a few years previously by the Conservatives themselves. As Faulkner has stated, comparing the new agenda with that preceding it: ''Within a period of less than 12 months, much of the programme has been politically discredited and seems to have been largely abandoned'' (*Guardian*, 16 April 1994). Of course, concerns of political expediency have always been a component of government's approaches to criminal justice policy: that is, an inevitable concomitant of the relationship between policy and politics. What distinguished the new Conservative agenda, however, was the degree of reversal of its own former agenda this has entailed, the nakedness of the motives underpinning the shift, and the dramatic effect this was to have on the management of criminal justice in Britain. What was also acute was the growing tension between the two ideologies of conservatism referred to earlier: the retributivist/deterrent approach to law and order on the one hand, and a reductionist approach to the state on the other. The new agenda for criminal justice will inevitably be faced with financial pressures. There was little doubt that plans such as those to restrict police cautions, reduce bail and extend custodial regimes and penalties for juvenile offenders would lead to substantial increases in the law and order budget. Further privatisation of sectors of the criminal justice and penal process was unlikely to contain such increases in more than marginal ways. The paradox for the government was the coexistence of an expansionary approach to criminal justice on the one hand with the financial imperative to reduce the burden of public expenditure on the other. The contradiction between the law and order and minimal state components of New Right thought referred to above was again apparent. Just as the pressures to reduce the costs of the penal system were key factors in encouraging the shift towards community-based penalties in the mid-1980s, so similar downward pressures were beginning to tell as the full implications of the new deterrent agenda started to become apparent.

We now know, of course, that ''winning back the high ground'' on law and order was not a successful campaign. The Conservatives' crushing defeat in the 1997 General Election means that they do not have to come to terms with the full financial impact of their deterrent strategy. The election of a Labour Government has guaranteed the emergence of a fourth phase in criminal justice policy.

Phase Four: Back to Rationalism in Criminal Justice Policy?

During his period as Shadow Home Secretary, Jack Straw deliberately cultivated a stance on law and order policy that would appeal to a wide audience, including those who had traditionally voted Conservative. This was to make him an object of attack from the old left and many on the civil libertarian wing for selling out to populism and for accepting the right wing agenda for criminal justice. It was his statements about antisocial behaviour and his attacks on winos and squeegee merchants that bore the brunt of this attack:

> In conjunction with tackling the underlying causes of crime, the community has a right to expect more responsible and less anti-social behavior from its citizens. That means less intimidation, bullying and loutish behaviour on the streets and in our towns and city centres. (Straw, 1995: 18)

Such comments were not welcome to those already concerned with the extremities of Howard's policies, who saw in Straw's approach even further challenges to civil liberties and a continuing neglect of the social causes of crime. However, Labour's emerging position on law and order was far more complex than many had argued. To begin with, while Straw offered a boisterous *rhetoric* on law and order, when it came to specific *policies*, the picture was less clear, as in other policy areas, deliberately so. Secondly, concerns over antisocial behaviour were in fact in line with the growing emphasis on *communitarian* principles in New Labour's agenda for Britain. This was to be made clear in Straw's first speech to Parliament as Home Secretary, when he rounded on the Conservatives' role in undermining community bonds:

> For the past 18 years Britain had a Government who preached the values of self-interest above everything else. It should therefore come as no surprise that some people then chose to ignore their responsibilities to other people. Where there is "no such thing as society," there can be no shared standards of behaviour. Where there is a steady erosion of community, of shared values, links between individuals collapse and people become more fearful and distrustful of others. It's "Get what you can, don't worry about anyone else"—the instincts of those who commit crime. (*Hansard*, 19 May 1997)

This is an altogether different interpretation of the basis of crime professed under Howard, one which points to *social* solutions to crime and not simply solutions directed at the individual offender. Without abandoning the "no excuse for crime" principle, thus accepting a legitimate role for an element of retribution in penal policy, the early message was a clear shift in approach to crime reduction in favour of socially-based strategies: whilst criminal behaviour can never be excused, social and economic factors such as deprivation and unemployment are bound to create conditions in which people can more easily be tempted into crime" (Straw, 1995: 8).

What was to emerge was another twin-track approach to criminal justice, but one weighted more in favour of social interventionism and less on deterrence. The *Crime and Disorder Bill* announced in Parliament after the General Election introduced both tough and tender measures. On the one hand, it set out plans to restrict the use of police cautions (formal warnings issued by the police as an alternative to charging), created new sentencing powers for juveniles including "parental responsibility orders" requiring parents to attend guidance sessions and abolished the presumption that children aged 10 to 13 are incapable of telling right from wrong (the defence would now have to prove incapability). It also created the community safety order to restrain antisocial behaviour and made allowance for curfew orders for children. On the other hand, the new legislation introduced by Labour was to be targeted at *social crime prevention.* It was announced that local authorities would have placed upon them a statutory responsibility to work with the police to form partnerships to help prevent crime. This plan reflected the findings of the 1991 Morgan Report, *Safer communities: the local delivery of crime prevention through the partnership approach.* (Home Office, 1991) the recommendations of which the Conservative Government chose largely to ignore. The focus of the Morgan Report was the notion of "community safety," which went well beyond physical or situational crime prevention to embrace socially-based strategies to deal with unemployment and community and youth work. Essentially, this framework for coping with crime reflected the views of the majority of academic criminologists that only socially directed measures to reduce crime would succeed in the long term. In addition to this wider policy, the new government also introduced plans to confront racially-motivated violence more directly, establish new reparation orders requiring offenders to work for the victim or the local community and reform the Crown Prosecution Service to make it more responsive to local priorities.

On balance the new agenda was weighted very much more in favour of community- and socially-oriented approaches to crime than previous approaches, above all those of the Howard regime. It sought to go much further in this regard than the policies that emerged under what has been labelled here "Phase Two." In this respect it is reasonable to argue that rationalism, policy informed by research and analysis, was now placed in the ascendency as a source of policy formation and policy influence. The findings of mainstream academic criminologists, once dismissed as "socialist" and "apologists of criminals" were emerging back into the daylight. There is much of encouragement in this, although subsequent developments, most probably of a political or financial nature, may well serve to undermine the initial strategy in the longer term. However, for all the cynicism directed at Straw's earlier rhetoric on law and order, there was enough of substance in the legislation that followed to warrant the identification of a fourth phase in criminal justice policy in Britain, one much more open to debate and informed judgement.

CONCLUSION

Whilst an examination of the extent to which criminal justice policy in England and Wales has undergone transformation, reversal and upheaval is itself of intrinsic interest and significance, it also highlights some broader questions about the status of criminal justice and the policy process. Crime is one of the issues of greatest concern and the cause of much anxiety to the public at large. Indeed, the 1996 *International Crime Victimisation Survey* found that England and Wales had the worst crime record in the industrialised world, with one in three people having been the victim of crime in the past year. It also found that, in part as a consequence of this, people in England and Wales suffered the highest rates of feelings of insecurity and fear of crime (ICVS, 1997). It is hardly surprising therefore that crime is a politically loaded area attached to the highest of stakes. This has meant that periodically criminal justice policy, perhaps more than most other fields of public policy, has found itself prey to political considerations, which can outweigh all others at certain points in time, including those steeped in sound and reliable research. This has caused considerable damage to the organisation, management and delivery of criminal justice services by creating an unstable and inconsistent environment, one only made worse by the ever growing resource constraints endemic to the public sector, even one as relatively protected as the law and order sector.

It may be that the subjection of criminal justice policy to the political market place will remain an inevitable feature of the scenery. However, a means of avoiding this, or at least limiting it, could be the establishment of a standing equivalent of the Royal Commission, a body that could be charged with undertaking a regular review of the role, function and effectiveness of criminal justice. In its deliberations it could draw upon research both from within and outside of the Home Office and allow full and equal representation from, and consultation with, the various bodies associated with the delivery of criminal justice—the police, legal professions, prosecutors, court officers, the probation service, the judiciary and the prison service. In recent years we have witnessed the emergence of criminal justice forums at local and regional levels to coordinate criminal justice processes. The creation of an equivalent body at the national level to inform and influence criminal justice *policy* might be a means by which greater coherence and rationalism could be enshrined.

APPENDIX 1

Films, Videos and Television Programmes

FRANK LEISHMAN

Being at the very centre of popular culture, crime and law enforcement are staples of both cinema and television. Media-constructed images may, as Reiner (1994) put it, *refract* rather than reflect reality. Nevertheless, the depictions of criminal justice activities on film and video play an increasingly important role in shaping public perceptions of the issues and dynamics of the justice process in action. For students in law and criminology programmes, selected and critical viewing of crime and police drama can be a useful aid to study and understanding. This short section offers some pointers as to videos and movies worth a look in this connection.

In relation to policing, Reiner (1994) flags dominant moments in the dialectical progression of styles and stereotypes. Because the police are arguably the gatekeepers of the entire criminal justice process, policing dramas provide a unique vantage point from which to gauge wider concerns and moods about law, power and justice that were prevalent at the time of their making. The seminal British film, *The Blue Lamp* (1949, Ealing Studios), mentioned by Brearley (this volume) introduced the enduring archetypical English bobby, George Dixon (Jack Warner), who embodied decency, common sense and symbolic reassurance. Though murdered midway through the film, Dixon was subsequently resurrected and enjoyed a 20-year reincarnation on British television.

The consensual community cop image of Dixon was pretty much turned on its head during the 1970s with the emergence of *The Sweeney*,[1] a ''screeching tyres show,'' which centred around characters in Scotland Yard's elite Flying Squad. *The Sweeney* captures the sense of urgency about law and order and its emergence as a political issue in the run-up to the 1979 General Election, as discussed in Savage's chapter. A long-running television series, it spawned two feature films, the first of which, *Sweeney!* (1976, EMI/Euston Films), is much the better. A full videography and excellent contextual analysis of the show is to be found in Donald (1985).

As Reiner (1994) observes, the synthesis of the two seeming polar opposite views of English policing and society arrived in the 1980s with Thames Television's *The Bill*,[2] still a popular thrice-weekly half-hour British TV show, many episodes of which are obtainable on video. *The Bill* focuses on street-level policing in a busy London district, and various episodes thus touch upon aspects alluded to by Holdaway, Johnston and McKenzie in their chapters in this book. The assistance of a Metropolitan Police ''liaison unit'' staffed by officers from Scotland Yard, ensures that topical issues and concerns are injected into the story lines, which often follow officers into the courtroom situation. Kingsley's (1994) tenth anniversary guide to the programme includes a comprehensive guide to the characters and locations and useful synopses of past episodes.

Picking up on some of the themes mentioned in earlier contributions to this volume, a quartet of stylish modern movies suggest themselves. *Dance With a Stranger* (1985, Goldcrest/NFFC/First Picture Co.) deals with the case of Ruth Ellis, the last woman to be hanged in Britain and captures some of the seedy atmosphere of 1950s London clubland. *The Long Good Friday* (1980, Black Lion/Calendar) and *The Krays* (1990, Rank/Parkfield) give gory glimpses of London gangland activities, the latter dealing with the criminal careers of the real-life Kray twins with whose cooperation it was made. On the moral panic front, the movie inspired by a rock album by The Who, *Quadrophenia* (1979, Brent-Walker/Polytel), deals with the confrontation between Mods and Rockers in 1960s Brighton and contains a memorable courtroom sequence featuring the rock star Sting as a charismatic Mod leader.

On the subject of prisons, perhaps the most controversial and grittiest British movie on this theme is *Scum* (1979, GTO/Berwick Street Films), a film which began life as a TV play but was subsequently banned by the BBC. However, one of the most popular and ironic TV treatments of imprisonment in England was the BBC situation comedy programme, *Porridge*,[3] which generated a feature film of the same name in 1979 (Black Lion/Witzend). This and other media materials on the British prison are examined in an engaging chapter by Mason (1995), which usefully amplifies themes introduced by Nash in Chapter 7.

Some of the most perceptive and commercially successful films on law, power and justice in England have, not surprisingly, been inspired by the troubles in Northern Ireland, in particular by the activities of the IRA, which Tupman discusses in Chapter 3. Worthy of particular mention here are *Hidden Agenda* (1990, Enterprise/Hemdale) and *In the Name of the Father* (1993, Universal/Hell's Kitchen/Gabriel Byrne), both of which were inspired by real-life events. The former is a powerful political drama concerning the investigation by a senior mainland British police officer into allegations of a ''shoot-to-kill'' policy of members of the Royal Ulster Constabulary, while the latter deals indignantly with one of the most notorious English miscarriage of justice cases, the Guildford pub bombings. *In the Name of the Father* was widely criticised, however, for taking liberties with the truth of the case and also for its inaccurate portrayal of English courtroom procedures, which, interestingly, are distinctly Americanised.

NOTES

1. The title *The Sweeney* results from the application of Cockney rhyming-slang. Sweeney Todd (the demon barber of Fleet Street, London) equals Flying Squad. In the proper application of rhyming slang, only the first word of the rhyme is used.

2. ''The Bill'' is a slang nickname for the police, almost exclusively referring to London Metropolitan Police officers. It is a shortening of the phrase ''Old Bill'' and, although the derivation of it is not clear, it may be associated with a World War I newspaper cartoon character (Old Bill), famous for advising a fellow soldier trapped in the mud-filled trenches of a battlefield in France, ''Go and find yer own 'ole!''

3. ''Doing porridge'' is a vernacular expression to describe a term of imprisonment. It stems from the practice, now long abandoned, that most, if not all, prison meals were some form of porridge oats.

APPENDIX 2

Recommended Readings

IAN K. MCKENZIE

This short section outlines a few of the key books on the nature of policing and the criminal justice system in the UK. The list is far from exhaustive and, as with all such lists, will omit texts that others may consider should have been included and will include those some may think should be omitted. To those who are offended the author apologises.

Holdaway, S. (1983). *Inside the British police: A force at work.* Oxford: Blackwell. Simon Holdaway, a sociologist, joined the British Police. During the period of his service he conducted covert participant observer research into aspects of police culture and police activity. This is the report of his research.

Leishman, F., Savage, S. P., and Loveday, B. (Eds.) (1994). *Core issues in policing.* London: Longman. This book examines key issues from accountability, through police interviewing techniques, to the police use of force and deadly force. It includes chapters written by academics and by practitioners. It has become the recommended text for a number of police/criminal justice courses in the UK.

Lustgarten, L. (1986). *The governance of police.* London: Sweet and Maxwell. There is some degree of complexity about the nature of police accountability in England and Wales. This volume examines the legal and historical background to the debate and proposes how the policy/operations divide referred to in this book might be addressed.

Maguire, M., Morgan, R., and Reiner, R. (Eds.) (1994). *The Oxford handbook of criminology.* Oxford: Oxford University Press. Containing a wide selection of individual chapters dealing with everything from crime causation, through victimology, to sentencing (and much else besides), this book is essential reading for those seeking a broad overview of criminal justice and criminological policy, practice and theory.

McConville, M., Sanders, A., Bridges, L., and Leng, R. (1994). *Standing accused.* Oxford: Oxford University Press. This book does for lawyers what *The case for the prosecution* (see below) does for the police. It is based on empirical research and is essentially deconstructive. That is, it is critical of the role played by lawyers in the criminal justice system and of the manner in which this role is performed.

McConville, M., Sanders, A., and Leng, R. (1991). *The case for the prosecution*. London: Routledge. This book, based upon the results of empirical research, examines the process through which, according to the authors, a criminal case against an accused is "constructed" by the prosecution (including but not limited to the police) in such a way that the anticipated outcome (prosecution and conviction) is more likely to be achieved. It is controversial and contentious but well worth reading.

Reiner, R. (1995). *The politics of the police*. Hemel Hempstead: Harvester Wheatsheaf. Considered by many the "Bible" of police studies in England and Wales, this book contains chapters on police accountability, police organisation, the history and development of organised policing and representations of police officers and policing in films and television programmes. It is written with verve and considerable style. It is highly recommended.

Stephens, M., and Becker, S. (Eds.) (1994). *Police force, police service*. London: Macmillian. This book examines the balance between the role of police officers in the UK as, on the one hand, law enforcement officers and, on the other hand, as carers. The book examines such issues as the policing of (and by) women, the policing of minority ethnic groups and the role of the police in the management of other sensitive issues.

References

ACOP. (1988). *More demanding than prison*. Wakefield: Association of Chief Officers of Probation.

ACPO. (1995). *International, national and inter-force crime: Interim report*. London: Association of Chief Police Officers.

Advisory Council on the Penal System. (1968). *The regime for long-term prisoners in conditions of maximum security*. London: HMSO.

Anderson, M. (1989). *Policing the world: Interpol and the politics of International Co-operation*. Oxford: Clarendon Press.

Angell, I. (1996). Conference Paper delivered at Centre for Computer Security Research Conference, London School of Economics, June 1996.

Arblaster, A. (1977). Terrorism: Myths, meanings and morals. *Political Studies*, XXV (3), 413–424.

Ashworth, A. (1994). *The criminal process*. Oxford: Oxford University Press.

Ashworth, A. (1996). Crime, community and creeping consequentialism. *Criminal Law Review*, 220.

Atkinson, R., and Savage, S. (1994). The conservatives and public policy. In S. Savage, R. Atkinson, and L. Robins (Eds.), *Public policy in Britain*. London: Macmillan.

Baldwin-Edwards, M., and Hebenton, B. (1994). Will SIS be Europe's ''Big Brother''? In M. Anderson and M. den Boer (Eds.), *Policing across national boundaries*. London: Pinter.

Baldwin, J. (1985). *Pre-trial criminal justice*. Oxford: Blackwell.

Baldwin, J., and McConville, M. (1977). *Negotiated justice*. Oxford: Martin Robertson.

Banton, M. (1964). *The policeman in the community*. New York: Basic Books.

Banton, M. (1967). *Race relations*. London: Tavistock.

Barclay, G. (Ed.) (1995). *Information on the criminal justice system in England and Wales: Digest 3*. London: Home Office.

Barr, R., and Pease, K. (1990). Crime placement, displacement and deflection. In M. Tonry and N. Morris (Eds.), *Crime and justice 12*. Chicago: University of Chicago Press.

Baun, A. (1987). An interesting development within Interpol: The Technical Committee on Cooperation in Europe. *International Criminal Police Review* (405) (March–April), 24–25.

Bayley, D.H. (1977). The limits of police reform. In D.H. Bayley (Ed.), *Police and society*. London: Sage.

Bayley, D.H. (1977). *Police and society*. London: Sage.

Beatty, D.M. (Ed.) (1994). *Human rights and judicial review: A comparative perspective*. Dordrecht: M. Nijhoff.

Becker, H.S. (1963). *Outsiders: studies in the sociology of deviance*. New York: Free Press.

Becker, H.S. (1967). Whose side are we on? *Social Problems*, 14(3), 239–247.

Becker, H.S. (1974). Labelling theory reconsidered. In P. Rock and M. McIntosh (Eds.), *Deviance and social control*. London: Tavistock.

Bennetto, J. (1994). Police seek wider use of armed patrols. *The Independent*, 8 July 1994.

Bentham, J. (1970). *An introduction to the principles of morals and legislation*. London: Methuen.

Benyon, J. (Ed.) (1984). *Scarman and after*. Oxford: Pergamon Press.

Benyon, J. (1986). *A tale of failure: Race and policing*. University of Warwick: Centre for Research in Ethnic Relations.

Beresford, P.C.F.M. (1979). *The official IRA and republican clubs in Northern Ireland 1968–74, and their relations with other political and paramilitary groups*. Unpublished Ph.D. Thesis, University of Exeter.

Bishop, P., and Mallie, E. (1988). *The provisional IRA*. London: Corgi.

Black Flag, Journal of the Anarchist Black Cross. Issues from 1973–1975.

Blom-Cooper, L., and Drabble, R. (1982). Police perceptions of crime: Brixton and the operational response. *British Journal of Criminology*, 22(1), 184–187.

Bonger, W. (1936). *Introduction to criminology*. London: Methuen.

Bonnifacio, P. (1991). *The psychological effects of police work: A psychodynamic approach*. New York: Plenum Press.

Bossard, A. (1990). *Transnational crime and criminal law*. Chicago: Office of International Criminal Justice.

Boston Globe. (1996). Zero-tolerance policing in Houston: No crime is too small. http://www.2.nando.net/newsroom/ntn/nation/010296/nation488_7.html.

Bottoms, A., and Wiles, P. (1996). Crime and policing in a changing social context. In W. Saulsbury, J.T. Mott, and T. Newburn (Eds.), *Themes in contemporary policing*. London: Independent Committee of Inquiry into the Roles and Responsibilities of the Police.

Bottoms, A.E. (1977). Reflections on the renaissance of dangerousness. *Howard Journal of Criminal Justice*, 16, 70–96.

Bottoms, A.E. (1980). An introduction to the coming crisis. In A.E. Bottoms and R.H. Preston (Eds.), *The coming penal crisis: A criminological and theological exploration*. Edinburgh: Scottish Academic Press.

Bouquet, T. (1997). I am the law. *Reader's Digest* (May), 52–58.

Bowling, B., and Saulsbury, W.E. (1992). *A multi-agency approach to racial harassment*. London: Home Office.

Box, S. (1971). *Deviance, reality and society*. London: Holt, Rinehart and Winston.

Brake, M., and Hale, C. (1992). *Public order and private lives: The politics of law and order*. London: Routledge.

Bresler, F. (1993). *Interpol: A history and examination of 70 years of crime solving*. London: Mandarin Paperbacks.

Bright, J. (1991). Crime prevention: The British experience. In K. Stenson and D. Cowell (Eds.), *The politics of crime control*. London: Sage.

Brody, S.R. (1976). *The effectiveness of sentencing* (Home Office Research Study No. 35). London: HMSO.

Brown, B. (1995). *CCTV in town centres: Three case studies* (Crime Detection and Prevention Series 68). London: Home Office, Police Research Group.

Brownlee, I. (1994). Pre-trial reviews, court efficiency and justice. *Howard Journal of Criminal Justice*, 33, 109–120.

Bruce, S. (1994). Northern Ireland: Reappraising loyalist violence. *Conflict Studies*, 249.

Bruggeman, W. (1987). Cross-border observation. In C. Fijnaut and R. Hermans (Eds.), *International symposium on surveillance techniques*. Lochem: van den Brink.

Bunyan, T. (1992). *Statewatching the new Europe: A handbook on the European state*. London: Statewatch.

Butler, A.J.P. (1996). Managing the future: A chief constable's view. In F. Leishman, B. Loveday, and S. Savage (Eds.), *Core issues in policing*. Harlow: Longman.

Butt, P.A. (1991). European border controls: Who needs them? *Public Policy and Administration*, 6(2), 35–54.

Cameron-Waller, S. (1993a). *Interpol's Point of View*. Paper delivered at European Institute of Public Administration (Schengen: A First Assessment After the Opening of Frontiers), 14–15 October, Luxembourg, unpublished.

Cameron-Waller, S. (1993b). *Organized crime—criminal intelligence: The future role of Interpol in Europe*. Paper presented to the Tenth European Policing Executive Conference International Association of Chiefs of Police, Basel, Switzerland, 10–12 May.

Campbell, A. (1981). *Girl delinquents*. Oxford: Basil Blackwell.

Cannings, D. (1990). *Policing in Europe: Towards 1992*. Exeter: Devon and Cornwall Constabulary.

Carlen, P. (1983). *Women's imprisonment*. Milton Keynes: Open University.

Carlen, P. (1985). *Criminal women*. Cambridge: Polity Press.

Carr, G. (1975). *The angry brigade: The cause and the case*. London: Gollancz.

Carson, W.G., and Wiles, P. (Eds.) (1971). *Crime and delinquency in Britain: Sociological readings*. London: Martin Robertson.

Cavadino, M., and Dignan, J. (1997). *The penal system: An introduction* (2nd ed.). London: Sage.

Chambliss, W.J., and Seidman, R.T. (1971). *Law, order and power*. Reading, MA: Addison-Wesley.

Chatterton, M.R. (1992). *Controlling police work: Strategies and tactics of the lower ranks—Their past and future relevance*. Paper presented at the Conference on Social Order in Post-Classical Sociology, University of Bristol.

Chaudhary, V., and Walker, M. (1996). The petty crime war. *The Guardian*, 21 November.

Chenery, S., Ellingworth, D., Tseloni, A., and Pease, K. (1995). Crimes which repeat: Undigested evidence from the British Crime Survey 1992. *International Journal of Risk, Security and Crime Prevention*, 1,207–1,216.

Chu, Yiu Kong. (1996). *Hong Kong triads: An economic analysis of organised crime*. Unpublished Ph.D. Thesis, University of Exeter.

Clarke, R., and Mayhew, P. (Eds.) (1980). *Designing out crime*. London: HMSO.

Cleede, W., and Parsons, K. (1987). *Police non-lethal force manual: Your choice this side of deadly*. Harrisburg, PA: Stackpole Books.

Cloward, R.A., and Ohlin, L.E. (1960). *Delinquency and opportunity: A theory of delinquent gangs*. New York: Free Press.

Cohen, A.K. (1955). *Delinquent boys: The culture of the gang*. New York: Free Press.

Cohen, S. (1972). *Folk devils and moral panics: The creation of the mods and rockers*. London: MacGibbon and Kee.

Cohen, S. (1979). The punitive city: Notes on the dispersal of social control. *Contemporary Crises*, 3, 339–363.

Cohen, S. (1981). Footprints in the sand: A further report on criminology and the sociology of deviance in Britain. In M. Fitzgerald, G. McLennan, and J. Pawson (Eds.), *Crime and society: Readings in history and theory*. London: Routledge and Kegan Paul in association with The Open University Press.

Cohen, S. (1985). *Visions of social control*. Cambridge: Polity Press.

Cohen, S. (1988). *Against criminology*. New Brunswick, NJ: Transaction.

Cohen, S. (1994). Social control and the politics of reconstruction. In D. Nelken (Ed.), *The futures of criminology*. London: Sage.

Cohen, S. (Ed.) (1971). *Images of deviance*. Harmondsworth: Penguin.

Cohen, S., and Taylor, L. (1972). *Psychological survival: The experience of long term imprisonment*. Harmondsworth: Penguin.

Collins, E. (1997). *Killing rage*. London: Granta.

Coogan, T.P. (1987). *The IRA*. London: Fontana.

Coogan, T.P. (1993). *De Valera: Long fellow, long shadow*. London: Hutchinson.

Council of Europe. (1994). *Crime and Economy* (Criminological Research, Vol. 32). Strasburg: Council of Europe.

Council of the EU. (1995a). *Joint action of 10 March 1995 adopted by the Council on the basis of Article K.3 of the Treaty on European Union concerning the Europol Drugs Unit* (95/73/JA) (OJ, L 62/1–3), 20 March 1995.

Council of the EU. (1995b). *Council Act of 26 July 1995 drawing up the Convention based upon Article K.3 of the Treaty on European Union, on the Establishment of a European Police Office (Europol Convention)* (OJ, C 316/1–32), 27 November 1995.

Council of the EU. (1996a). *Joint Action of 14 October 1996 adopted by the Council on the basis of Article K.3 of the TEU providing for a common framework for the initiatives of the EU Member States concerning liaison officers* (OJ, L 268/2–4), 19 October 1996.

Council of the EU. (1996b). *Joint Action of 16 December 1996 adopted by the Council on the basis of Article K.3 of the Treaty on European Union extending the mandate given to the Europol Drugs Unit* (96/748/JA) (OJ, L 342/4), 31 December 1996.

Council of the European Communities/Commission of the European Communities. (1992). *Treaty on European Union*. Luxembourg: OPEC.

Council of Ministers. (1995). *Report of the Council of Ministers on the Functioning of the Treaty on European Union, 10 April 1995* (Cm. 2866, May). London: HMSO.

Cowell, D., Jones, T., and Young, J. (Eds.) (1982). *Policing the riots*. London: Junction Books.

Crawford, A., Jones, T., Woodhouse, T., and Young, J. (1990). *Second Islington crime survey*. London: Middlesex Polytechnic.

Currie, E. (1985). *Confronting crime*. New York: Pantheon.

Dahrendorf, R. (1959). *Class and class conflict in an industrial society*. Stanford, CA: Stanford University Press.

Davies, A. (1984). *Where did the forties go?: A popular history*. London: Pluto Press.

Dean, J. (1997a). Combined tactics. *Police Review*, 18 April: 22–23.

Dean, J. (1997b). Mallon's law. *Police Review*, 21 March: 16–18.

Degenhardt, H.W. (1983). *Political Dissent*. London: Longman.

Dennis, N., and Erdos, G. (1992). *Families without fatherhood*. London: IEA Health and Welfare Unit.

Dobson, C., and Payne, R. (1977). *The Carlos complex*. London: Hodder and Stoughton.

Doherty, M., and East, R. (1985). Bail decisions in magistrates' courts. *British Journal of Criminology*, 25, 251–266.

Donald, J. (1985). Anxious moments: The Sweeney in 1975. In M. Alvarado and J. Stewart (Eds.), *Made for television: Euston Films Limited*. London: BFI.

Donziger, S.R. (Ed.) (1996). *The real war on crime*. New York: Harper.

Dorn, N. (1993). Subsidiarity, police cooperation and drug enforcement. *European Journal of Criminal Policy and Research*, 1(2), 30–47.

Downes, D., and Morgan, R. (1994). Hostages to fortune? The politics of law and order in post-war Britain. In M. Maguire, R. Morgan, and R. Reiner (Eds.), *The Oxford handbook of criminology*. Oxford: Clarendon Press.

Downes, D.M. (1966). *The delinquent solution: A study in sub-cultural theory*. London: Routledge and Kegan Paul.

Dunbar, I. (1985). *A sense of direction*. London: Home Office.

EDU. (1995a). *Europol Drugs Unit—Working Programme: July 1995–December 1995*. Report to the Council on Justice and Home Affairs, Ref: 10002/95.

EDU. (1995b). *Report on the activities of the Europol Drugs Unit 1 January and 30 June 1995: Six month Progress Report*, Report to the Council on Justice and Home Affairs, Ref: 10001/95.

Edwards, S. (1984). *Women on trial*. Manchester: Manchester University Press.

Erikson, K. (1966). *Wayward puritans*. New York: John Wiley and Sons.

EU-USA. (1995). *New transatlantic agenda and joint action plan*. In General Secretariat of the Council of the European Union, Press Release 12296/95 (Presse 356), 3 December 1995.

Farrell, G. (1995). Predicting and preventing re-victimisation. In M. Tonry and D.P. Farrington (Eds.), *Building a safer society*. Chicago: University of Chicago Press.

Feeley, M. (1979). *The process is the punishment*. New York: Sage.

Felson, M. (1986). Linking criminal choices, routine activities, informal control and criminal outcomes. In D.B. Cornish and R.V. Clarke (Eds.), *The reasoning criminal: Rational choice perspectives on offending*. London: Springer-Verlag.

Fijnaut, C. (1994). International policing in Europe: Present and future. *European Law Review*, 19(6), 599–619.

Fode, H. (1993). Cooperation on law enforcement, criminal justice and legislation in Europe. In H.G. Schermers (Ed.), *Free movement of persons in Europe: Legal problems and experiences*. London: Martinus Nijhoff.

Foucault, M. (1977). *Discipline and punish: The birth of the prison*. London: Allen Lane.

Fyfe, J. (1989). The split second syndrome and other determinants of police violence. In R. Dunham and G. Alpert (Eds.), *Critical issues in policing: Contemporary readings*. Prospect Heights, IL: Waveland Press.

Gamble, A. (1988). *The free economy and the strong state*. London: Macmillan.

Garland, D. (1985). *Punishment and welfare: A history of penal strategies*. Aldershot: Gower.

Garland, D. (1988). British criminology before 1935. *British Journal of Criminology*, 28(2).

Garland, D. (1994). Of crimes and criminals: The development of criminology in Britain. In M. Maguire, R. Morgan, and R. Reiner (Eds.), *The Oxford handbook of criminology*. Oxford: Clarendon Press.

Garland, D. (1996). The limits of the sovereign state: strategies of crime control in contemporary society. *British Journal of Criminology*, 36(4), 445–471.

Gelsthorpe, L., and Morris, A. (1988). Feminism and criminology in Britain. *British Journal of Criminology*, 28(2): 215–223.

Gelsthorpe, L., and Morris, A. (Eds.) (1990). *Feminist perspectives in criminology*. Buckingham: Open University Press.

Gelsthorpe, L., and Morris, A. (1994). Juvenile justice 1945–1992. In M. Maguire, R. Morgan, and R. Reiner (Eds.), *The Oxford handbook of criminology*. Oxford: Clarendon Press.

Gendreau, P. (1996). Offender rehabilitation: What we know and what needs to be done. *Criminal Justice and Behaviour*, 23, 144–161.

Gendreau, P., Little, T., and Goggin, C. (1995). *A meta-analysis of the predictors of adult offender recidivism: Assessment guidelines for classification and treatment*. Department of Psychology, University of New Brunswick. (User report submitted to the Corrections Branch, Ministry Secretariat, Solicitor General of Canada.)

Gibbons, S. (1996). Reclaiming the streets. *Police Review*, 13 September, 18–21.

Giddens, A. (1979). *Central problems in social theory*. London: Macmillan.

Giddens, A. (1990). *The consequences of modernity*. Cambridge: Polity.

Gilroy, P. (1987). *There ain't no black in the Union Jack*. London: Hutchinson.

Gilroy, P. (1992). The end of antiracism. In J. Donald and A. Rattansi (Eds.), *Race, culture and difference*. London: Sage.

Goldner, A. (1968). The sociologist as partisan: Sociology and the welfare state. *American Sociologist* (May): 103–116.

Goldstein, H. (1977). *Policing a free society*. Cambridge, MA: Harvard University Press.

Graham, J., and Bowling, B. (1996). *Young people and crime* (Home Office Research Study No. 145). London: Home Office.

Greaves, G. (1986). The police and the public. In J. Benyon and C. Bourne (Eds.), *The police: Powers, procedures and proprieties*. Oxford: Pergamon.

Green, D. (1987). *The new right*. Brighton: Harvester Wheatsheaf.

Greene, J.R. (1993). Civic accountability and the police: Lessons learned from police and community relations. In R.G. Dunham and G.P. Alpert (Eds.), *Critical issues in policing: Contemporary readings*. Prospect Heights, IL: Waveland Press.

Gregory, F. (1991). Border control systems and border controllers: A case study of the British police response to proposals for a Europe sans frontieres. *Public Policy and Administration*, 6(1), 39–50.

Gregory, F., and Collier, A. (1992). Cross-frontier crime and international crime—Problems, achievements and prospects with reference to European police cooperation.

In M. Anderson and M. den Boer (Eds.), *European police cooperation: Proceedings of a seminar*. Edinburgh: University of Edinburgh.

Gregory, J., and Lees, S. (1996). Attrition in rape and sexual assault cases. *British Journal of Criminology*, 36(1), 235–245.

Guardian. (1994). EU accord on phonetapping. 2 December, 16.

Gusfield, J. (1963). *Symbolic crusade: Status politics and the American temperance movement*. Urbana: University of Illinois.

Hall, S., Critcher, C., Clarke, J., Jefferson, A., and Roberts, B. (1978). *Policing the crisis: Mugging, the state and law and order*. London: MacMillan.

Hall, S., and Jefferson, T. (Eds.) (1976). *Resistance through rituals: Youth subcultures in post-war Britain*. London: Hutchinson.

Hamai, K., Ville, R., Harris, R., Hough, M., and Zvekic, U. (Eds.) (1995). *Probation around the world: A comparative study*. London: Routledge.

Hanmar, J. (1978). Violence and the social control of women. In G. Littlejohn (Ed.), *Power and the state*. London: Croom Helm.

Hanmar, J., and Saunders, S. (1984). *Well founded fear*. London: Hutchinson.

Hansard (1997). *Parliamentary debates*. London: HMSO.

Harrington, M. (1963). *The other America: Poverty in the United States*. Baltimore: Penguin.

Hauber, A., Hofstra, B., Toornvliet, L., and Zandbergen, A. (1996). Some new forms of functional social control in the Netherlands and their effects. *British Journal of Criminology*, 36(2), 199–219.

Hay, D., Linebaugh, J., and Thompson, E.P. (1975). *Albion's fatal tree*. London: Allen Lane.

Hebenton, B., and Thomas, T. (1995). *Policing Europe: Cooperation, conflict and control*. London: St. Martin's Press.

Heidensohn, F.M. (1968). The deviance of women: A critique and an enquiry. *British Journal of Sociology*, 19, 160–173.

Heidensohn, F.M. (1987). Women and crime: Questions for criminology. In P. Carlen and A. Worrall (Eds.), *Gender, crime and justice*. Milton Keynes: Open University Press.

Her Majesty's Inspectorate of Constabulary. (1992). *Equal opportunities in the police service*. London: Home Office.

Hirschel, J.D., and Wakefield, W. (1995). *Criminal justice in England and the United States*. Westport, CT: Praeger.

Hirst, P.Q. (1975). Radical deviancy theory and Marxism: A reply to Taylor and Walton. In I. Taylor, P. Walton, and J. Young (Eds.), *Critical criminology*. London: Routledge and Kegan Paul.

HMG. (1994). *The Intelligence Services Act 1994*. London: HMSO.

HMG. (1996). *The Security Service Act 1996*. London: HMSO.

HMG. (1997). *The Police Act 1997*. London: HMSO.

HMSO. (1986). *The sentence of the court*. London: HMSO.

HMSO. (1988). *Punishment, custody and the community* (Cm. 424). London: HMSO.

HMSO. (1990). *Crime, justice and protecting the public* (green paper). London: HMSO.

HMSO. (1990). *Crime, justice and protecting the public* (white paper). London. HMSO.

HMSO. (1991). *Safer communities: The local delivery of crime prevention through the partnership approach* (The Morgan Report). London: HMSO.

HMSO. (1993). *Social trends, 23*. London: HMSO.

HMSO. (1994). *Criminal statistics England and Wales 1994* (Cm. 3010). London: HMSO.

Hoffman, A. (1971). *Steal this book*. New York: Pirate Editions Grove Press.

Holdaway, S. (1979). Police-black relations: The professional solution. *The British Police*. London: Edward Arnold.

Holdaway, S. (1983). *Inside the British police: A force at work*. Oxford: Blackwell.

Holdaway, S. (1991). *Recruiting a multi-racial police force*. London: HMSO.

Holdaway, S. (1996). *The racialisation of British policing*. Basingstoke: Macmillan.

Holdaway, S. (1997a). Constructing and sustaining race within the police workforce. *British Journal of Sociology*, 48(1), 19–34.

Holdaway, S. (1997b). Some recent approaches to the study of race in criminological research. *British journal of criminology*, Summer: 214–225.

Holdaway, S., and Barron, A.M. (1997). *Resignation? The experience of Black and Asian police officers*. Basingstoke: Macmillan.

Home Affairs Committee. (1989). *Drug trafficking and related serious crime*. 7th Report, House of Commons, Session 1988–89, HC 370. London: HMSO.

Home Affairs Committee. (1990). *Practical police cooperation in the European community*. 7th Report, House of Commons, Session 1989–90, HC 363-I and II, Vol. I and Vol. II, 20 July, London: HMSO.

Home Affairs Committee. (1992). *Migration control at the external border of the European community*. Minutes of evidence, House of Commons, Session 1991–92, HC 215-i, ii and iii, 5, 12 and 26 February, London: HMSO.

Home Affairs Committee. (1994). *Organised crime*. Minutes of evidence and memoranda, House of Commons, Session 1994–95, HC 18-II, 16 November, London: HMSO.

Home Office. (1973). *Report on the work of the Prison Department 1972*. (Cm. 5375). London: HMSO.

Home Office. (1984). *Probation in England and Wales: Statement of national objectives and priorities*. London: HMSO.

Home Office. (1988). *Punishment, custody and the community* (Cm. 424). London: HMSO.

Home Office. (1990). *Crime, justice and protecting the public* (Cm. 965). London: HMSO.

Home Office. (1991). *Custody, care and justice: The way ahead for the prison service in England and Wales* (Cm. 1647). London: HMSO.

Home Office. (1992). *Report of Her Majesty's Chief Inspector of Prisons April 1991–March 1992* (Cm. 203). London: HMSO.

Home Office. (1995). *Review of probation officer recruitment and qualifying training*. London: Home Office.

Home Office. (1996a). *Press Release 114/96*. London: HMSO.

Home Office. (1996b). *The Security Service Act 1996*. London: Home Office.

Home Office. (1996c). *Victims charter* (2nd ed.). London: HMSO.

Home Office. (1996d). *The prison population in 1995*. (Statistical Bulletin). London: The Home Office.

Hood, R. (1992). *Race and sentencing*. Oxford: Oxford University Press.

Hope, T.J. (1994). Unpacking the crime rate. Paper delivered at American Society of Criminology Annual Meeting, Miami, November 1994.

Hough, M. (1995). *Anxiety about crime: Findings from the 1994 British Crime Survey* (Home Office Research Study 147). London: Home Office.
Hough, M., and Mayhew, P. (Eds.) (1982). *Crime and public housing*. London: HMSO.
Hucklesby, J. (1996). Bail or jail. *Journal of Law and Society*, 23, 213–225.
Hudson, B. (1987). *Justice through punishment*. London: Macmillan.
Hudson, B. (1993). *Penal policy and social change*. London: Macmillan.
Hudson, B. (1996). *Understanding justice*. Buckingham: Open University Press.
Ianni, F., and Ianni, A.J. (1994). *Black Mafia*. New York: Simon and Schuster.
I'Anson, J., and Wiles, P. (1995). *The Sedgefield Community Force: The results of a survey of the public's response to the introduction of the force*. Sheffield: Centre for Criminological and Legal Research, University of Sheffield.
ICVS. (1997). *Criminal victimisation in eleven industralised countries: Key findings from the 1996 International Victimisation Survey*. Noordwijk, Netherlands: ICVS.
Interpol. (1989). Resolution AGN/57/RES 10. *International Criminal Law Review*, 417, 10–11.
Interpol. (1991). European Continental Meeting. *International Criminal Police Review*, 433, 30–31.
Interpol. (1992). *ICPO-Interpol: General Information*. Lyon, France: ICPO.
International Criminal Police Review. (1987). 409, 34.
International Criminal Police Review. (1989). 421, 2, 37.
Interpol. General Secretariat. (1990). The European Secretariat. *International Criminal Police Review* (424) (May–June), 12.
Jarvis, F.J. (1972). *Advise, assist and befriend: A history of the probation and after-care service*. London: NAPO.
Jefferson, T. (1993). The racism of criminalization: Policing and the reproduction of the criminal other. In L. Gelsthorpe (Ed.), *Minority ethnic groups in the criminal justice system*. Cambridge: Cambridge University, Institute of Criminology.
Johnson, S.D., Bowers, K., and Hirschfield, A. (1997). New insights into the spatial and temporal distribution of repeat victimisation. *British Journal of Criminology*, 37, 224–241.
Johnson, T.A., Misner, G.E., and Brown, L.P. (1981). *The police and society: An environment for collaboration and cooperation*. Englewood Cliffs, NJ: Prentice-Hall.
Johnston, L. (1993). Privatization and protection: Spatial and sectoral ideologies in British policing and crime prevention. *Modern Law Review*, 56(6), 771–792.
Johnston, L. (1996). Policing diversity: The impact of the public–private complex in policing. In F. Leishman, B. Loveday, and S.P. Savage (Eds.), *Core issues in policing*. London: Longman.
Johnston, L. (1997). New Labour and the usual suspects. *Chartist* (March–April), 14–15.
Jones, H. (1956). *Crime and the penal system*. London: University Tutorial Press.
Jones, T., Maclean, B., and Young, J. (1986). *The Islington crime survey: Crime victimisation and policing in inner London*. Aldershot: Gower.
Jones, T., and Newburn, T. (forthcoming). *Private security and public policing*. Oxford: Oxford University Press.
Jones, T., Newburn, T., and Smith, D.J. (1994). *Democracy and policing*. London: Policy Studies Institute.
Joubert, C. (1995). National and international aspects of undercover policing. *The Police Journal*, LXVIII(4), 305–318.

Keith, M. (1993a). *Race, riots and policing: Lore and disorder in a multi-racist society.* London: UCL Press.

Keith, M. (1993b). Review of S. Scheingold, *The politics of street crime. British Journal of Criminology*, 33(2), 278–279.

King, R.D., and Morgan, R. (1980). *The future of the prison system.* London: Gower.

Kingsley, H. (1994). *The Bill: The first ten years.* London: Boxtree.

Kinsey, R. (1984). *The Merseyside crime survey: First report.* Liverpool: Merseyside County Council.

Kinsey, R., Lea, J., and Young, J. (1986). *Losing the fight against crime.* Oxford: Blackwell.

Kraska, P.B., and Kappeler, V.E. (1997). Militarizing American police: The rise and normalization of paramilitary units. *Social Problems*, 44(1), 1–17.

Lambert, J. (1970). *Crime, police and race relations.* London: Oxford University Press.

Lea, J., and Young, J. (1982). Race and crime. *Marxism Today*, 29–30.

Lea, J., and Young, J. (1984). *What is to be done about law and order?* Harmondsworth: Penguin.

Learmont, J. (1995). *Review of prison service security in England and Wales and the escape from Parkhurst Prison on Tuesday 3 January 1995* (Cm. 3020). London: HMSO.

Leishman, F., and Savage, S. (1993). The police service. In D. Farnham and S. Horton (Eds.), *Managing the new public services.* London: Macmillan.

Lemert, E. (1951). *Social pathology: A systematic approach to the study of sociopathic behaviour.* New York: McGraw-Hill.

Leonard, E. (1982). *Women, crime and society: A critique of criminological theory.* London: Longman.

Leppard, D. (1994). Police set to use machine guns to fight UK crime. *Sunday Times*, 15 May.

Levi, M. (1993). The extent of cross-border crime in Europe: The view from Britain. *European Journal of Criminal Policy and Research*, 1(3), 57–76.

Levi, M., and Maguire, M. (1992). Crime and cross-border policing in Europe. In J. Bailey (Ed.), *Social Europe.* London: Longman.

Liazos, A. (1972). The poverty of the sociology of deviance: Nuts, sluts and perverts. *Social Problems*, 20, 102–120.

Loader, I. (1997). Private security and the demand for protection in contemporary Britain. *Policing and Society*, 7, 143–162.

Lombroso, C. (1976). *L'Uomo delinquente.* Milan: Hoepli.

Loveday, B. (1992). Right agendas: Law and order in England and Wales. *International Journal of the Sociology of Law*, 20, 297–319.

Loveday, B. (1996a). Auditing the new police authorities. *County News*, 89(8), 18–19.

Loveday, B. (1996b). *Crime and policing: An analysis of victimisation and the provision of police service* (Occasional Paper No. 3). Portsmouth: Institute of Police and Criminological Studies.

Lustgarten, L. (1986). *The governance of police.* London: Sweet and Maxwell.

Lygo, Sir Raymond. (1991). *Management of the prison service: A report.* London: Home Office.

Maguire, M. (1993). Crime statistics, patterns and trends. In M. Maguire, R. Morgan, and R. Reiner (Eds.), *The Oxford handbook of criminology*. Oxford: Clarendon Press.

Maguire, M., Morgan, R., and Reiner, R. (Eds.) (1994). *The Oxford handbook of criminology*. Oxford: Oxford University Press.

Mair, G., and Lloyd, C. (1996). Policy and progress in the development of bail schemes in England and Wales. In F. Paterson (Ed.), *Understanding bail in Britain*. Scottish Office: HMSO.

Mair, G., Lloyd, C., and Sibbitt, R. (1994). *Intensive probation in England and Wales: An evaluation* (Home Office Research Study No. 133). London: HMSO.

Mannheim, H., and Wilkins, L. (1955). *Prediction methods in borstal training*. London: HMSO.

Manning, P. (1977). *Police work*. Cambridge, MA: M.I.T. Press.

Marks, H. (1996). *Mr. Nice*. London: Secker and Warburg.

Martin, J.P. (1988). The development of criminology in Britain 1948–60. *British Journal of Criminology*, 28(2), 157–164.

Martinson, R. (1974). What works?—Questions and answers about prison reform. *The Public Interest*, 35, 22–54.

Mason, D. (1994). On the dangers of disconnecting race and racism. *Sociology*, 28(4), 845–858.

Mason, P. (1995). Prime time punishment: The British prison and television. In D. Kidd-Hewitt and R. Osborne (Eds.), *Crime and the media: The post-modern spectacle*. London: Pluto Press.

Matthews, R., and Francis, P. (Eds.) (1996). *Prisons 2000: An international perspective on the current state and future of imprisonment*. Basingstoke: Macmillan.

Matthews, R., and Young, J. (1992). Reflections on realism. In J. Young and R. Matthews (Eds.), *Rethinking criminology: The realist debate*. London: Sage.

Matza, D. (1964). *Delinquency and drift*. New York: John Wiley and Sons.

Mawby, R.I., and Walklate, S. (1994). *Critical victimology: The victim in international perspectives*. London: Sage.

Mawby, R.I., and Walklate, S. (1997). The impact of burglary: A tale of two cities. *International Review of Victimology*, 4, 267–295.

Maxfield, M.G. (1984). *Fear of crime in England and Wales* (Home Office Research Study No. 78). London: HMSO.

May, J. (1979). *Committee of inquiry into the United Kingdom Prison services: Report* (Cm. 7673). London: HMSO.

May, T. (1991). *Probation: Politics, policy and practice*. Buckingham: Open University Press.

May, T. (1994). Probation and community sanctions. In M. Maguire, R. Morgan, and R. Reiner (Eds.), *The Oxford handbook of criminology*. Oxford: Oxford University Press.

Mayhew, P.M., Clarke, R.V.G., Sturman, A., and Hough, J.M. (1976). *Crime as opportunity* (Home Office Research Study No. 34). London: HMSO.

McBarnet, D. (1981). *Conviction*. London: Macmillan.

McConville, M., and Mirsky, C. (1994). Re-defining and structuring guilt in systemic terms. In M. McConville and L. Bridges (Eds.), *Criminal justice in crisis*. Aldershot: Edward Elgar.

McConville, M., Sanders, A., Bridges, L., and Leng, R. (1994). *Standing accused*. Oxford: Oxford University Press.

McConville, M., Sanders, A., and Leng, R. (1991). *The case for the prosecution*. London: Routledge.

McKenzie, I.K. (1996). Crossing the Atlantic: Interview with Gina Haynes. *Police Review*, 27 September, 22–24.

McKenzie, I.K., and Gallagher, G.P. (1989). *Behind the uniform: The police of England and America*. Hemel Hempstead: Harvester Wheatsheaf.

McLaughlin, E., and Muncie, J. (Eds.) (1996). *Controlling crime*. London: Sage.

McMahon, B. (1994). Police leader: We are cannon fodder. *Evening News*, 17 May.

McWilliams, W. (1983). The mission to the English police courts: 1876–1936. *Howard Journal of Criminal Justice*, 22, 129–147.

McWilliams, W. (1985). The mission transformed: Professionalisation of probation between the wars. *Howard Journal of Criminal Justice*, 22(4), 257–274.

McWilliams, W. (1986). The English probation system and the diagnostic ideal. *Howard Journal of Criminal Justice*, 25(4), 241–260.

Melossi, D., and Pavarini, M. (1981). *The prison and the factory: Origins and the penitentiary system*. London: Macmillan.

Metropolitan Police Act, 1829. London: HMSO.

Metropolitan Police Instruction Book. (1985). London: Metropolitan Police (Restricted).

Miles, R. (1989). *Racism*. London: Routledge.

Miller, W.B. (1958). Lower class culture as a generalising milieu of gang delinquency. *Journal of Social Issues*, 14, 5.

Mirrlees-Black, C., Mayhew, P., and Percy, A. (1996). *The 1996 British Crime Survey: England and Wales*. London: Home Office.

Morgan, P. (1996). Bail in England and Wales: Understanding the operation of bail. In F. Paterson (Ed.), *Understanding bail in Britain*. Scottish Office: HMSO.

Morgan, R. (1994). Imprisonment. In M. Maguire, R. Morgan, and R. Reiner (Eds.), *The Oxford handbook of criminology*. Oxford: Oxford University Press.

Morgan, R., and Jones, S. (1992). Bail or jail? In S. Casale and E. Stockdale (Eds.), *Criminal justice under stress*. London: Blackstone.

Morison, J., and Leith, P. (1992). *The barrister's world*. Oxford: Oxford University Press.

Morris, T. (1957). *The criminal area: A study in social ecology*. London: Routledge and Kegan Paul.

Morris, T. (1988). British criminology: 1935–48. *British Journal of Criminology*, 28, 2.

Morrison, S., and O'Donnell, I. (1994). *Armed robbery: A study in London* (Occasional Paper No. 15). Oxford: Centre for Criminological Research.

Moss, R. (1972). *Urban guerillas*. London: Temple Smith.

Moxey, M., and McKenzie, I.K. (1993). Assaults on police. *Policing*, 9, 172–186.

Mulcahy, A. (1994). The justifications of justice. *British Journal of Criminology* 34, 411.

Muncie, J., and Sparks, R. (Eds.) (1991). *Imprisonment: European perspectives*. Hemel Hempstead: Harvester Wheatsheaf.

Munday, R. (1993). Jury trial, continental style. *Legal Studies*, 13, 204.

Mungham, G., and Bankowski, Z. (1976). The jury in the legal system. In P. Carlen (Ed.), *Sociology of law*. Keele: University of Keele.

Mungham, G., and Pearson, G. (Eds.) (1976). *Working class youth culture*. London: Routledge and Kegan Paul.

National Advisory Commission on Civil Disorders. (1968). *Report* (The Kerner Report). Washington, DC: GPO.

National Deviancy Conference. (1980). *Permissiveness and control: The fate of the sixties legislation*. London: MacMillan.

Netherlands Presidency. (1991). *Press release TREVI*. Meeting of Ministers, December 1991.

NCIS. (1994). Personal Communication, 25 January.

NCIS. (1995a). *National Criminal Intelligence Service: Annual Report 1994/95*. London: NCIS.

NCIS. (1995b). Press release 14/95, 20 November.

NCIS. (1996a). *National Criminal Intelligence Service: Annual Report 1995/1996*. London: NCIS.

NCIS. (1996b). *Nexus*: The National Criminal Intelligence Service bi-yearly Bulletin No. 1. London: NCIS.

Nelken, D. (Ed.) (1994). *The futures of criminology*. London: Sage.

Newburn, T. (1995). *Crime and criminal justice policy*. Harlow: Longman.

Newing, J., and Crump, R.R. (1974). *Footpad crime and its community effect in Lambeth*. London: A7 Division, New Scotland Yard.

Newman, K. (1984). *Report of the Commissioner of Police of the Metropolis for 1983*. London: HMSO.

Newman, O. (1972). *Defensible space: Crime prevention through environmental design*. New York: Macmillan.

Norman, P. (1995). *The terrorist finance unit and the joint action group on organised crime: Models of policing to combat transnational organised crime*. Paper delivered at Policing the Peace: An International Conference, University College, Galway, Ireland.

Norman, P. (1996). *European police cooperation: Police accountability and the policing of internationally-mobile offending in England and Wales*. Unpublished Ph.D. Thesis, University of Sussex.

Norman, P. (1997). Interpol v. Europol. *International Police Review*, 1(1), 28–33.

Norris, C., Fielding, N., Kemp, C., and Fielding, J. (1992). Black and blue: An analysis of the influence of race on being stopped by the police. *British Journal of Sociology*, 43, 207–218.

Northam, G. (1988). *Shooting in the dark*. London: Faber and Faber.

O'Mahony, P. (1997). Zero tolerance policy could waste Garda time. *The Irish Times*, 11 March.

Opinion: FF and Crime. (1997). *The Irish Times*, 7 March.

Orr, J. (1997). Strathclyde's spotlight initiative. In N. Dennis (Ed.), *Zero tolerance: Policing a free society*. London: IEA Health and Welfare Unit.

Pacey, A. (1995). Tackling money laundering: The case for a financial intelligence task force. Opening address at the NCIS/OICJ Second International Conference, London, May 1995.

Packer, H. (1968). *The limits of criminal sanction*. Stanford, CA: Stanford University Press.

Patterson, F., and Whitaker, C. (1994). *Operating bail*. Edinburgh: HMSO.

Patterson F., and Whitaker, C. (1995). Criminal justice cultures: Negotiating bail and remand. In L. Noaks (Ed.), *Contemporary issues in criminology*. Cardiff: University of Wales Press.

Pearson, G. (1983). *Hooligan: A history of respectable fears*. London: Macmillan.

Pease, K. (1994). Crime prevention. In M. Maguire, R. Morgan, and R. Reiner (Eds.), *Oxford handbook of criminology*. Oxford: Oxford University Press.

Phillipson, M. (1971). *Sociological aspects of crime and delinquency*. London: Routledge and Kegan Paul.

Player, E., and Jenkins, M. (1994). *Prisons after Woolf: Reform through riot*. London: Routledge.

Plummer, K. (1979). Misunderstanding labelling perspectives. In D. Downes and P. Rock (Eds.), *Deviant interpretations*. London: Macmillan.

Pollard, C. (1997). Zero tolerance: Short-term fix, long-term liability? In N. Dennis (Ed.), *Zero tolerance: Policing a free society*. London: IEA Health and Welfare Unit.

Police Federation. (1995). *Survey of members*. Surbiton: Police Federation.

Potter, K. (1996a). More baton training urged by coroner at inquest hearing. *Police Review*, 16 August.

Potter, K. (1996b). Spotlight on Strathclyde. *Police Review*, 25 October.

Potter, K. (1996c). Zero tolerance. *Police Review*, 19 July.

Pryce, K. (1979). *Endless pressure*. Harmondsworth: Penguin.

PSI. (1983). *Police and people in London* (Vol. IV). London Policy Studies Institute.

Quinney, R. (1969). *Criminal justice in American society*. Boston: Little, Brown.

Quinney, R. (1970a). *The social reality of crime*. Boston: Little, Brown.

Quinney, R. (Ed.) (1970b). *The problem of crime*. New York: Dodd, Mead.

RCP. (1962). *Royal Commission on the police: Final report*. London: HMSO.

Read, S. (1997). Below zero. *Police Review*, 17 January.

Reiner, R. (1985). *The politics of the police*. Brighton: Harvester Wheatsheaf.

Reiner, R. (1986). The modern bobby: Development of the British police. *Policing*, 2(4), 258–275.

Reiner, R. (1991). *Chief constables*. Oxford: Oxford University Press.

Reiner, R. (1992). *The politics of the police* (2nd ed.). Hemel Hempstead: Harvester Wheatsheaf.

Reiner, R. (1993). Race, crime and justice: Models of interpretation. In L. Gelsthorpe (Ed.), *Minority ethnic groups in the criminal justice system*. Cambridge: Cambridge University Press.

Reiner, R. (1994). The dialectics of Dixon: The changing image of the TV cop. In M. Stephens and S. Becker (Eds.), *Police force, police service*. London: Macmillan.

Reiss, A. (1971). *The police and the public*. New Haven, CT: Yale University Press.

Rex, J. (1982). West Indian and Asian youth. In B. Troyna (Ed.), *Black youth in crisis*. London: George Allen and Unwin.

Richman, J. (1995). What happened to the sociology of the street? In S. Edgell, S. Walklate, and G. Williams (Eds.), *Debating the future of the public sphere*. Aldershot: Avebury, 221–234.

Rock, P. (1988a). *A history of British criminology*. Oxford: Oxford University Press.

Rock, P. (1988b). The present state of criminology in Britain. *British Journal of Criminology*, 28(2), 105–120.

Rock, P. (1994). The social organisation of British criminology. In M. Maguire, R. Morgan, and R. Reiner (Eds.), *The Oxford handbook of criminology*. Oxford: Oxford University Press.

Rock, P., and McIntosh, M. (Eds.) (1974). *Deviance and social control*. Harmondsworth: Penguin.

Romeanes, T.J. (1996). *Problem oriented policing: The Cleveland approach*. Cleveland: Cleveland Constabulary.

Rose, N. (1996). The death of the social? Re-figuring the territory of government. *Economy and Society*, 25(3), 327–356.

Royal Commission on Criminal Justice. (1993). *Report*. London: HMSO.

Royal Commission on Criminal Procedure. (1981). *Report*. London: HMSO.

Runciman, W.G. (1966). *Relative deprivation and social justice*. London: Routledge and Kegan Paul.

Rutherford, A. (1996). *Transforming criminal policy*. Winchester: Waterside Press.

Sanders, A. (1985). Class bias in prosecutions. *Howard Journal of Criminal Justice*, 24, 176–199.

Sanders, A. (1996a). Access to justice in the police station. In R. Young and D. Wall (Eds.), *Access to criminal justice*. London: Blackstone.

Sanders, A. (Ed.) (1996b). *Prosecutions in common law jurisdictions*. Aldershot: Dartmouth.

Sanders, A. (1997). From suspect to trial. In M. Maguire, R. Morgan, and R. Reiner (Eds.), *Oxford handbook of criminology*. Oxford: Oxford University Press.

Sanders, A., Bird, S., Weber, L., and Creaton, J. (1997). *Victims with learning disabilities: Negotiating the criminal justice system*. Oxford: Centre for Criminological Research.

Sanders, A., and Young, R. (1994a). *Criminal justice*. London: Butterworths.

Sanders, A., and Young, R. (1994b). The rule of law, due process and pre-trial criminal justice. *Current Legal Problems*, 47, 125–130.

Sargent, S., Brown, J., and Gourlay, R. (1995). Who wants to carry a gun? *Policing*, 10(4), 242–252.

Savage, S.P. (1990). A war on crime? Law and order policies in the 1980s. In S. Savage and L. Robins (Eds.), *Public policy under Thatcher*. London: Macmillan.

Savage, S.P., Atkinson, R., and Robins, L. (1994). *Public policy in Britain*. London: Macmillan.

Savage, S.P., Charman, S., and Cope, S. (1997). ACPO: A force to be reckoned with? *Criminal Lawyer* (April), 15–23.

Savage, S.P., and Nash, M. (1994). Yet another agenda for law and order: British criminal justice policy and the Conservatives. *International Criminal Justice Review*, 4, 37–51.

Savage, S.P., and Robins, L. (Eds.) (1990). *Public policy under Thatcher*. London: Macmillan.

Scarman, L. (1981). *The Brixton disorders: 10–12 April 1981* (Cm. 8427). London: HMSO.

Scarman, L. (1986). *The Scarman Report: The Brixton Disorders 10–12 April 1981*. Harmondsworth: Penguin.

Schermers, H.G. (Ed.) (1969). *Free movement of persons in Europe: Legal problems and experiences*. London: Martinus Nijhoff.

Schutz, A. (1967). *Collected papers 1: The problem of social reality*. The Hague: Martinus Nijhoff.

Scraton, P. (Ed.) (1987). *Law, order and the authoritarian state*. Milton Keynes: Open University Press.

Scraton, P., and Chadwick, K. (1991). The theoretical and practical priorities of critical criminology. In K. Stenson and D. Cowell (Eds.), *The politics of crime control*. London: Sage.

Searchlight. (1986). London: British Anti-facist Movement.

Searchlight. (1988). London: British Anti-facist Movement.

Select Committee. (1971–1972). *Select Committee on Race Relations and Immigration: Police/immigrant relations*. London: HMSO.

Select Committee. (1976–1977). *Select Committee on Race Relations and Immigration: The West Indian community*. London: HMSO.

Shaw, R. (1996). Supervising the dangerous in the community. In N. Walker (Ed.), *Dangerous people*. London: Blackstone Press.

Shearing, C.D., and Stenning, P.C. (1983). Private security—Implications for social control. *Social Problems*, 30(5), 493–506.

Shipley, P. (1976). *Revolutionaries in modern Britain*. London: Bodley Head.

Shover, N. (1996). *Great pretenders: Pursuits and careers of persistent thieves*. New York: Westview.

SI. (1964). *Prison rules*. Made under the Prison Act 1952. Statutory Instrument 388. London: HMSO.

Simon, F., and Weatheritt, M. (1984). *The use of bail and custody by London magistrates' courts*. London: HMSO.

Skogan, W. (1990). *The police and public in England and Wales* (Home Office Research Study No. 117). London: Home Office.

Smart, C. (1977). *Women, crime and criminology: A feminist critique*. London: Routledge and Kegan Paul.

Smith, B. (1960). *Police systems in the United States* (3rd ed.). New York: Harper and Brothers.

Smith, D.J. (1997). Ethnic origins, crime and criminal justice in England and Wales. *Crime and Justice*, 21, 101–182.

Smith, D.J., and Gray, J. (1983). *Police and people in London*. London: Policy Studies Institute.

Smith, D.J., and Gray, J. (1986). *Police and people in London*. Aldershot: Gower.

Smith, J.C. (1996). *Smith and Hogan: Criminal law* (8th ed.). London: Butterworths.

Sparks, R.F. (1981). Surveys of victimisation. In M. Tonry and N. Morris (Eds.), *Crime and Justice 3*. Chicago: University of Chicago Press.

Sparks, R.F. (1996a). Penal austerity: The doctrine of less eligibility reborn? In R. Matthews and P. Francis (Eds.), *Prisons 2000: An international perspective on the current and future state of imprisonment*. London: Macmillan.

Sparks, R.F. (1996b). Prisons, punishment and penalty. In E. McLaughlin and J. Muncie (Eds.), *Controlling crime*. London: Sage.

Spillius, A. (1995). In America, mall rats have teeth. *Independent on Sunday*, 29 October, 4.

Statewatch. (1996). EDU to exchange data with US. *Statewatch Bulletin*, 6(1), 1–2.

Statewatch. (1997). UN-UK-Canada: Fighting terrorism. *Statewatch Bulletin*, 7(1), 4–5.

Storbeck, J. (1995). Speech delivered to a conference on Europol, hosted by the Green Group of the European Parliament, 3 July 1995, Brussels. *Statewatch Bulletin*, 5(4), 2.

Straw, J. (1995). Straw and order. *New Statesman and Society*, 15 September.
Stenson, K., and Cowell, D. (Eds.) (1991). *The politics of crime control*. London: Sage.
Sudnow, D. (1965). Normal crimes. *Social problems*, 12, 255.
Sunday Times Insight Team. (1997). Ulster. *Sunday Times*.
Swart, A.H.J. (1992). Police and security in the Schengen agreement and Schengen convention. In H. Meijers (Ed.), *Schengen: Internationalisation of the central chapters of the law on aliens, refugees, privacy and the police* (2nd rev. ed.). Leiden, Netherlands: Stitching NJCM.
Sykes, G.M., and Matza, D. (1957). Techniques of neutralisation. *American Sociological Review*, 22, 225–229.
Sykes, G.W. (1993). The functional nature of police reform: The myth of controlling the police. In R.G. Dunham and G.P. Alpert (Eds.), *Critical issues in policing: Contemporary readings*. Prospect Heights, IL: Waveland Press.
Tabarelli, W. (1987). Baltica 86, an international exercise on controlled deliveries. In C. Fijnaut and R. Hermans (Eds.), *International symposium on surveillance techniques*. Lochem, Netherlands: Van den Brink.
Tame, C.R. (1991). Freedom, responsibility and justice: The criminology of the new right. In K. Stenson and D. Cowell (Eds.), *The politics of crime control*. London: Sage.
Taylor, I. (1981). *Law and order: Arguments for socialism*. London: Macmillan.
Taylor, I. (1995). Private homes and public others: An analysis of talk about crime in suburban South Manchester in the mid-1990s. *British Journal of Criminology*, 35(2), 263–285.
Taylor, I., and Taylor., L. (Eds.) (1973). *Politics and deviance: Papers from the national deviancy conference*. Harmondsworth: Penguin.
Taylor, I., and Walton, P. (1975). Radical deviancy theory and Marxism: A reply to Paul Q. Hirst's *Marx and Engels on law crime and morality*. In I. Taylor, P. Walton, and J. Young (Eds.), *Critical criminology*. London: Routledge and Kegan Paul.
Taylor, I., Walton, P., and Young, J. (1973). *The new criminology: For a social theory of deviance*. London: Routledge and Kegan Paul.
Taylor, I., Walton, P., and Young, J. (Eds.) (1975). *Critical criminology*. London: Routledge and Kegan Paul.
Thio, A. (1973). Class bias in the sociology of deviance. *American Sociologist*, 8 (February), 1–12.
Thompson, E.P. (1975). *Whigs and hunters*. London: Allen Lane.
Thrasher, G.E. (1927). *The gang*. Chicago: University of Chicago Press.
Tierney, J. (1996). *Criminology: Theory and context*. London: Prentice-Hall.
Travis, A. (1997). Petty crime brings big payoff. *The Guardian*, 21 April, 8.
Trevi (1990). *Trevi programme of action: Relating to the reinforcement of borders*, June, Dublin. Reprinted in *Practical police co-operation in the European Community*. London: HMSO.
Trevi Ministers. (1993). Ministerial agreement on the establishment of the Europol Drugs Unit, 2 June, Copenhagen, unpub.
Trickett, A., Osborn, D., Seymour, J., and Pease, K. (1992). What is different about high crime areas? *British Journal of Criminology*, 32, 81–89.
Tupman, W.A. (1987a). *Beyond terrorism: Towards a theory of scenarios of political violence* (Brookfield Paper No. 1). Exeter: University of Exeter, Centre for Police and Criminal Justice Studies.

Tupman, W.A. (1987b). *Towards a typology of terrorism: Criticisms and definitions in the field of political violence* (Brookfield Paper No. 4). Exeter: University of Exeter, Centre for Police and Criminal Justice Studies.

Turk, A. (1969). *Criminality and the social order*. Chicago: Rand McNally.

Van Duyne, P. (1993). Organised crime markets in a turbulent Europe. *European Journal on Criminal Policy and Research*, 1(3), 10–30.

Veness, D. (1994). The crime without borders: A British view. In L.P. Raine and F.J. Cilluffo (Eds.), *Global organized crime: The new empire of evil*. Washington, DC: Center for Strategic and International Studies.

Vold, G.B. (1958). *Theoretical criminology*. New York: Oxford University Press.

Waddington, D. (1992). *Contemporary issues in public disorder*. London: Routledge.

Waddington, P.A.J. (1986). Mugging as a moral panic. *British Journal of Sociology*, 37 (2), 245–259.

Waddington, P.A.J. (1996). Stop and search. *Police Review*, 19 April, 16–17.

Waddington, P.A.J. (1997). Policing with the gloves off. *Police Review*, 25 April, 26–27.

Walker, M. (1987). Interpreting race and crime statistics. *Journal of the Royal Statistical Society*, A150 (Part 1), 39–56.

Wall, D. (1996). *Policing (Unit 1): The historical development of policing, University of Leeds*. http://www.leeds.ac.uk/law/teaching/lawdw/cyberpolice/po10.htm.

Wardlaw, G. (1989). *Political terrorism*. Cambridge: Cambridge University Press.

Weber Brooks, L. (1993). Police discretionary behaviour: A study of style. In R.G. Dunham and G.P. Alpert (Eds.), *Critical issues in policing: Contemporary readings*. Prospect Heights, IL: Waveland Press.

White, R. (1994). Street life: Police practices and youth behaviour. In R. White and C. Alder (Eds.), *The police and young people in Australia*. Cambridge: Cambridge University Press.

Wiles, P. (Ed.) (1976). *The sociology of crime and delinquency in Britain: Vol. 2. The new criminolgies*. London: Martin Robertson.

Wilkins, L.T. (1964). *Social deviance*. London: Tavistock.

Wilkinson, P. (1981). *The new fascists*. London: Grant McIntyre.

Willis, C. (1983). *The use, effectiveness and impact of police stop and search powers* (Home Office Research Paper No. 15). London: Home Office.

Willis, C., and Stevens, P. (1979). *Race, crime and arrests* (Home Office Research Study No. 58). London: HMSO.

Willmott, P. (1966). *Adolescent boys in east London*. London: Routledge and Kegan Paul.

Willmott, P., and Young, M. (1957). *Family and kinship in east London*. London: Routledge and Kegan Paul.

Wilson, D., and Holdaway, S. (1984). Black police in the United Kingdom. *Policing*, 1(1), 20–30.

Wilson, J.Q. (1968). *Varieties of police behaviour*. Cambridge, MA: Harvard University Press.

Wilson, J.Q. (1975). *Thinking about crime*. New York: Basic Books.

Wilson, J.Q. (1983). *Thinking about crime* (2nd ed.). New York: Basic Books.

Wilson, J.Q. (1991). *On character: Essays by James Q. Wilson*. Washington, DC: American Enterprise Institute.

Wilson, J.Q., and Herrnstein, R. (1985). *Crime and human nature*. New York: Simon and Schuster.

Wilson, J.Q., and Kelling, G.L. (1982). Broken windows: The police and neighbourhood safety. *The Atlantic Monthly* (March), 29–38.

Woolf, Lord Justice. (1991). *Prison disturbances April 1990: Report of an inquiry* (Cm. 1456). London: HMSO.

Wootton, B. (1959). *Social science and social pathology*. London: Allen and Unwin.

Young, J. (1971). *The drugtakers: The social meaning of drug use*. London: Paladin.

Young, J. (1975). Working-class criminology. In I. Taylor, P. Walton, and J. Young (Eds.), *Critical criminology*. London: Routledge and Kegan Paul.

Young, J. (1986). The failure of criminology: The need for a radical realism. In R. Matthews and J. Young (Eds.), *Confronting crime*. London: Sage.

Young, J. (1988). Radical criminology in Britain: The emergence of a competing paradigm. *British Journal of Criminology*, 28(2), 100–121.

Young, J. (1991). Left realism and the priorities of crime control. In K. Stenson and D. Cowell (Eds.), *The politics of crime control*. London: Sage.

Young, J. (1994). Incessant chatter: Recent paradigms in criminology. In M. Maguire, R. Morgan, and R. Reiner (Eds.), *The Oxford handbook of criminology*. Oxford: Oxford University Press.

Zander, M., and Henderson, J. (1993). *Crown Court study, Royal Commission on Criminal Justice* (Home Office Research Study No. 19). London: HMSO.

Zedner, L. (1994). Victims. In M. Maguire, R. Morgan, and R. Reiner (Eds.), *The Oxford handbook of criminology*. Oxford: Oxford University Press.

Zedner, L. (1997). Victims. In M. Maguire, R. Morgan, and R. Reiner (Eds.), *The Oxford handbook of criminology* (2nd ed.). Oxford: Oxford University Press.

Index

About the Contributors

NIGEL BREARLEY is Senior Lecturer at the Institute of Police and Criminological Studies (IPCS) of the University of Portsmouth. He is the co-author (with Mike King) of *Public Order Policing: Contemporary Perspectives on Strategy and Tactics* (1996). Current research interests include the history and functions of criminal investigation and developments in criminological theory.

SIMON HOLDAWAY is Professor of Sociology in the Department of Sociological Studies of the University of Sheffield. He has published widely in the fields of deviance and policing. He is the author of the seminal text, *Inside the British Police: A Force at Work* (1983). He is currently examining the role of groups representing black police officers in the UK.

LES JOHNSTON is Professor of Sociology at the University of Teesside. He has published widely in the sociological field, and his papers have included examinations of police accountability and of the police complaints system in the UK. He is the author of a number of key texts in the area of policing and social control. His book, *The Rebirth of Private Policing* (1994), has been critically acclaimed.

FRANK LEISHMAN, a criminologist, is a former Scottish police officer who served as a detective and specialised in dealing with drug-related crime. Formerly a senior lecturer at the University of Portsmouth, he is now a Principal Lecturer at Southampton Institute, Southampton, England. He is a fluent Japanese speaker and has written extensively on Japanese policing and criminal justice systems and on media representations of the police.

IAN K. McKENZIE is a former senior police officer of the London Metropolitan Police and holds a Ph.D. from the University of Bath. He is the Director of the Institute of Police and Criminological Studies (IPCS) of the University of Portsmouth. He is the principal author of *Behind the Uniform: The Police of Britain and America* (1989).

MIKE NASH is a Senior Lecturer in the School of Social and Historical Studies of the University of Portsmouth. He is a former probation officer and is the author of a number of papers on criminal justice, danger and the role of the probation service.

PAUL NORMAN is a Lecturer at the Institute of Police and Criminological Studies (IPCS) of the University of Portsmouth. He was recently awarded the degree of Doctor of Philosophy (D.Phil.) by the University of Sussex. His thesis examined and discussed the nature of transnational and international crime in Europe.

KEN PEASE is Professor of Criminology at Huddersfield University. He formerly held a similar post at Manchester University. He is currently on the board of the government's Crime Prevention Agency. He has been an adviser to the United Nations and the Council of Europe on crime control matters and has published widely on criminal statistics and crime prevention. He is the holder of the OBE (Order of the British Empire).

ANDREW SANDERS is Professor of Criminology and Criminal Justice at the University of Bristol. He has published many articles, books and book chapters on aspects of criminal law in the UK. He was formerly the Deputy Director of the Institute of Criminology at the University of Oxford.

STEPHEN P. SAVAGE is the former Director and founder of the Institute of Police and Criminological Studies of the University of Portsmouth. He is the author of a number of texts including *Criminology and Criminal Justice* (forthcoming) and is co-editor of *Core Issues in Policing* (1995). He is Professor of Criminology at the IPCS and is just completing research into aspects of the work of the Association of Chief Police Officers.

W.A. TUPMAN was formerly the director of the Centre for Police and Criminal Justice Studies at the University of Exeter. He has written extensively about terrorism and terrorist activity and has lectured to audiences across the globe on such matters.

ISBN 0-275-95881-7
90000>
EAN
9 780275 958817
HARDCOVER BAR CODE